Microsoft® Access®
Projects for Windows 95

Marianne Fox
Lawrence C. Metzelaar
Butler University

The Benjamin/Cummings Publishing Company, Inc.

Menlo Park, California • Reading, Massachusetts
New York • Don Mills, Ontario • Harlow, U.K. • Amsterdam
Bonn • Paris • Milan • Madrid • Sydney • Singapore • Tokyo
Seoul • Taipei • Mexico City • San Juan, Puerto Rico

Sponsoring Editor: *Maureen A. Allaire*

Project Editor: *Nancy E. Davis, Kathy G. Yankton*

Editorial Assistant: *Heide Chavez*

Executive Editor: *Michael Payne*

Project Manager: *Adam Ray*

Associate Production Editor: *Jennifer Englander*

Marketing Manager: *Melissa Baumwald*

Custom Publishing Operations Manager: *Michael Smith*

Manufacturing Supervisor: *Janet Weaver*

Composition and Film Buyer: *Vivian McDougal*

Copy Editor: *Barbara Conway*

Technical Editor: *Lynda Fox Fields*

Proofreader: *Holly McLean Aldis, Roseann Viano*

Indexer: *Mark Kmetzko*

Ordering from the SELECT System

For more information on ordering and pricing policies for the SELECT System of microcomputer applications texts and their supplements, please contact your Addison-Wesley • Benjamin/Cummings sales representative or call our SELECT Hotline at 800/854-2595.

The Benjamin/Cummings Publishing Company, Inc.
2725 Sand Hill Road
Menlo Park, CA 94025
http://www.aw.com/bc/is
bc.is@aw.com

Getting Started

Welcome to the *SELECT Lab Series.* We invite you to explore how you can take advantage of the newest Windows 95 features of the most popular software applications using this up-to-date learning package.

Greater access to ideas and information is changing the way people work. With Windows 95 applications you have greater integration capabilities and access to Internet resources than ever before. The *SELECT Lab Series* helps you take advantage of these valuable resources with special assignments devoted to the Internet and additional connectivity resources which can be accessed through our web site, **http://www.aw.com/bc/is.**

The key to using software is making the software work for you. The *SELECT Lab Series* will help you learn to use software as a productivity tool by guiding you step-by-step through case-based projects similar to those you will encounter at school, work, or home. When you are finished with this learning package, you will be fully prepared to use the resources this software offers. Your success is our success.

A GUIDED TOUR

To facilitate the learning process, we have developed a consistent organizational structure for each module in the *SELECT Lab Series.*

You begin using the software almost immediately. A brief **Overview** introduces the software package and the basic application functions. **Getting Help** covers the on-line Help feature in each package. **A Note to the Student** explains any special conventions or system configurations observed in a particular module.

Each module contains six to eight **Projects,** an **Operations Reference** of all the operations covered in each module, an extensive **Glossary** of **key terms,** and an **Index.**

The following figures introduce the elements you will encounter as you use each SELECT module.

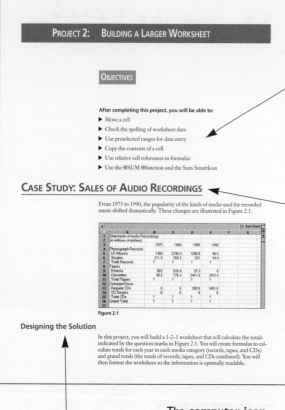

PROJECT 2: BUILDING A LARGER WORKSHEET

OBJECTIVES

After completing this project, you will be able to:

▶ Move a cell
▶ Check the spelling of worksheet data
▶ Use preselected ranges for data entry
▶ Copy the contents of a cell
▶ Use relative cell references in formulas
▶ Use the @SUM @function and the Sum SmartIcon

CASE STUDY: SALES OF AUDIO RECORDINGS

From 1975 to 1990, the popularity of the kinds of media used for recorded music shifted dramatically. These changes are illustrated in Figure 2.1.

Figure 2.1

Designing the Solution

In this project, you will build a 1-2-3 worksheet that will calculate the totals indicated by the question marks in Figure 2.1. You will create formulas to calculate totals for each year in each media category (records, tapes, and CDs) and grand totals (the totals of records, tapes, and CDs combined). You will then format the worksheet so the information is optimally readable.

Each project begins with **Learning Objectives** that describe the skills and commands you will master.

Projects revolve around **Case Studies**, which provide real-world scenarios so you can learn an application in a broader context.

Each topic begins with a brief explanation of concepts you will learn and the operations you will perform.

Designing the Solution introduces you to important problem-solving techniques. You will see how to analyze the case study and design a solution before you sit down at the computer.

The **computer icon** provides a cue that you should begin working at the computer, and **Numbered steps** guide you step-by-step through each project, providing detailed instructions on how to perform operations.

Visual cues such as **screen shots** provide examples of what you will see on your own computer screen, reinforce key concepts, and help you check your work.

Exit points identify good places in each project to take a break.

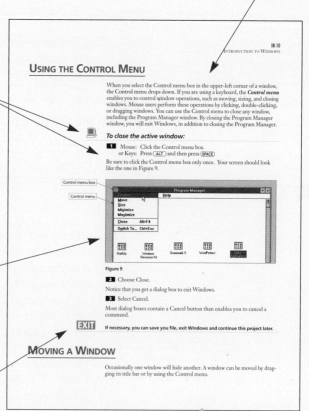

USING THE CONTROL MENU

When you select the Control menu box in the upper-left corner of a window, the Control menu drops down. If you are using a keyboard, the **Control menu** enables you to control window operations, such as moving, sizing, and closing windows. Mouse users perform these operations by clicking, double-clicking, or dragging windows. You can use the Control menu to close any window, including the Program Manager window. By closing the Program Manager window, you will exit Windows, in addition to closing the Program Manager.

To close the active window:

1 Mouse: Click the Control menu box.
or Keys: Press (ALT) and then press (SPACE)

Be sure to click the Control menu box only once. Your screen should look like the one in Figure 9.

Control menu box

Control menu

Figure 9

2 Choose Close.

Notice that you get a dialog box to exit Windows.

3 Select Cancel.

Most dialog boxes contain a Cancel button than enables you to cancel a command.

EXIT If necessary, you can save you file, exit Windows and continue this project later.

MOVING A WINDOW

Occasionally one window will hide another. A window can be moved by dragging its title bar or by using the Control menu.

Key Terms are boldfaced and italicized and appear throughout each project.

Margin figures show on-screen tools that are often convenient alternatives to menu commands presented in the numbered steps.

Tips, Reminders, Cautions, and **Quick Fixes** appear throughout each project to highlight important, helpful, or pertinent information about each application.

Study Questions (Multiple Choice, Short Answer, and For Discussion) may be used as self-tests or homework assignments.

Review Exercises present hands-on tasks to help you build on skills acquired in the projects.

Assignments require critical thinking and encourage synthesis and integration of project skills.

Each project ends with **The Next Step** which discusses the concepts from the project and proposes other uses and applications for the skills you have learned, a **Summary,** and a list of **Key Terms and Operations**.

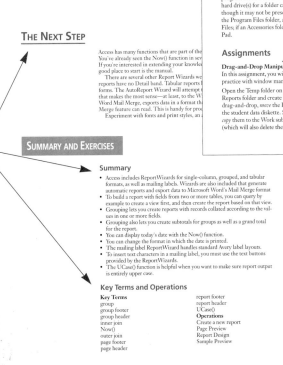

FOLLOWING THE NUMBERED STEPS

To make the application modules easy to use in a lab setting, we have standardized the presentation of hands-on computer instructions as much as possible. The numbered step sections provide detailed, step-by-step instructions to guide you through the practical application of the conceptual material presented. Both keystroke and mouse instructions are used according to which one is more appropriate to complete a task. The instructions in the module assume that you know how to operate the keyboard, monitor, and printer.

Tip When you are using a mouse, unless indicated otherwise, you should assume that you are clicking the left button on the mouse. Several modules provide instructions for both mouse and keyboard users. When separate mouse and keyboard steps are given, be sure to follow one method or the other, but not both.

Each topic begins with a brief explanation of concepts. A computer icon or the ▶ symbol and a description of the task you will perform appear each time you are to begin working on the computer.

For Example:

To enter the address:

1 Type `123 Elm Street` and press `(ENTER)`

Notice that the keys you are to press and the text you are to type stand out. The text you will type appears in a special typeface to distinguish it from regular text. The key that you are to press mimics the labels of the keys on your keyboard.

When you are to press two keys or a key and a character simultaneously, the steps show the keys connected either with a plus sign or a bar.

For Example: $(SHFT)+(TAB)$
$(CTRL)+C$

When you are to press keys sequentially, the keys are not connected and a space separates them.

For Example: $(CTRL)$ $(PGDN)$
$(HOME)$ $(HOME)$ $(\uparrow)$

Be sure to press each key firmly, but quickly, one after the other. Keys begin repeating if you hold them down too long.

In some instances margin figures of single icons or buttons will appear next to the numbered steps. Margin figures provide visual cues to important tools that you can select as an alternative to the menu command in the numbered step.

For typographical conventions and other information unique to the application, please see *A Note to the Student* in the Overview of each module.

THE *SELECT* LAB SERIES—A CONNECTED LEARNING RESOURCE

The *SELECT Lab Series* is a complete learning resource for success in the Information Age. Our application modules are designed to help you learn fast and effectively. Based around projects that reflect your world, each module helps you master key concepts and problem-solving techniques for using the software application you are learning. Through our web site you can access dynamic and current information resources that will help you get up to speed on the Information Highway and keep up with the ever changing world of technology.

Explore our web site **http://www.aw.com/bc/is** to discover:

- **B/C Link Online:** Our on-line newsletter which features the latest news and information on current computer technology and applications.

- **Student Opportunities and Activities:** Benjamin/Cummings' web site connects you to important job opportunities and internships.

- **What's New:** Access the latest news and information topics.

- **Links:** We provide relevant links to other interesting resources and educational sites.

THE TECHSUITE

This module may be part of our new custom bundled system—the **Benjamin/Cummings TechSuite.** Your instructor can choose any combination of concepts texts, applications modules, and software to meet the exact needs of your course. The TechSuite meets your needs by offering you one convenient package at a discount price.

SUPPLEMENTS

Each module has a corresponding Instructor's Manual with a Test Bank and Transparency Masters. For each project in the student text, the Instructor's Manual includes Expanded Student Objectives, Answers to Study Questions, and Additional Assessment Techniques. The Test Bank contains two separate tests (with answers) consisting of multiple choice, true/false, and fill-in questions that are referenced to pages in the student's text. Transparency Masters illustrate 25 to 30 key concepts and screen captures from the text.

The Instructor's Data Disk contains student data files, answers to selected Review Exercises, answers to selected Assignments, and the test files from the Instructor's Manual in ASCII format.

ACKNOWLEDGMENTS

The Benjamin/Cummings Publishing Company would like to thank the following reviewers for their valuable contributions to the *SELECT Lab Series*.

Joseph Aieta
Babson College

Tom Ashby
Oklahoma CC

Bob Barber
Lane CC

Robert Caruso
Santa Rosa Junior College

Robert Chi
California State
Long Beach

Jill Davis
State University of New
York at Stony Brook

Fredia Dillard
Samford University

Peter Drexel
Plymouth State College

Ralph Duffy
North Seattle CC

David Egle
University of Texas,
Pan American

Jonathan Frank
Suffolk University

Patrick Gilbert
University of Hawaii

Maureen Greenbaum
Union County College

Sally Ann Hanson
Mercer County CC

Sunil Hazari
East Carolina University

Bruce Herniter
University of Hartford

Lisa Jackson
Henderson CC

Cynthia Kachik
Santa Fe CC

Bennett Kramer
Massasoit CC

Charles Lake
Faulkner State
Junior College

Ron Leake
Johnson County CC

Randy Marak
Hill College

Charles Mattox, Jr.
St. Mary's University

Jim McCullough
Porter and Chester
Institute

Gail Miles
Lenoir-Rhyne College

Steve Moore
University of
South Florida

Anthony Nowakowski
Buffalo State College

Gloria Oman
Portland State University

John Passafiume
Clemson University

Leonard Presby
William Paterson
College

Louis Pryor
Garland County CC

Michael Reilly
University of Denver

Dick Ricketts
Lane CC

Dennis Santomauro
Kean College of
New Jersey

Pamela Schmidt
Oakton CC

Gary Schubert
Alderson-Broaddus College

T. Michael Smith
Austin CC

Cynthia Thompson
Carl Sandburg College

Marion Tucker
Northern Oklahoma
College

JoAnn Weatherwax
Saddleback College

David Whitney
San Francisco State
University

James Wood
Tri-County
Technical College

Minnie Yen
University of Alaska,
Anchorage

Allen Zilbert
Long Island University

*To everyone at Benjamin/Cummings who helped
make this book possible.*

Contents

OVERVIEW   1

Objectives   1
Using Database Management Software   1
Using Access for Windows 95   2
A Note to the Student   4
Starting Access   5
Using Toolbars, Menus, and Dialog Boxes   7
Getting On-Screen Help   9
    Using Contents to Get Help   9
    Using Index to Get Help   11
    Using Find to Get Help   12
    Using Answer Wizard to Get Help   13
    Using the Help Button   14
Exiting Access   15
The Next Step   16
Summary and Exercises   16
Summary   16
Key Terms and Operations   16
Study Questions   17
    Multiple Choice   17
    Short Answer   17
    For Discussion   17

PROJECT 1: PREVIEWING THE POWER OF ACCESS   18

Objectives   18
Case Study: Managing Your Music Collection   18
    Designing the Solution   18
Stepping Through the Database Wizard   18
    Selecting and Saving a Predefined Database   20
    Adding Optional Fields and Sample Data   23
    Selecting a Style for Screen Displays   25
    Selecting a Style for Printed Reports   26
    Selecting a Title and Picture   27
Entering and Editing Data in Tables   29
    Using a Form to Add Records   29
    Using a Form to Edit Records   31
Previewing and Printing a Report   33
The Next Step   36
Summary and Exercises   37
Summary   37
Key Terms and Operations   37
Study Questions   37
    Multiple Choice   37
    Short Answer   37
    For Discussion   38

Review Exercises   39
    Creating a Personal Address Book   39
    Creating an Inventory of Personal Property   39
Assignments   39
    Using Contents in On-Screen Help   39
    Using Index in On-Screen Help   39
    Cataloging Your Video Tape Collection   39
    Tracking Your Workout   39

PROJECT 2: DESIGNING AND CREATING A DATABASE   40

Objectives   40
Case Study: Coordinating Volunteer Activities   40
    Designing the Solution   40
Determining Objectives and Outputs   41
    Creating a Data Dictionary   43
    Organizing Data in Tables   45
    Deciding on Primary Keys   46
    Planning Links between Tables   46
    Assigning an Appropriate Data Type   46
    Estimating Field Size   47
    Adding Comments   47
Creating the Organizations Table Using Table Wizard   48
    Renaming a Field   51
    Specifying a Primary Key   53
Creating the Volunteers Table Using Table Wizard   56
    Adding Fields   59
    Using Lookup Wizard   61
Creating the Time Cards Table   64
The Next Step   66
Summary and Exercises   66
Summary   66
Key Terms and Operations   67
Study Questions   67
    Multiple Choice   67
    Short Answer   68
    For Discussion   69
Review Exercises   69
    Creating the Companies Table   70
    Creating the Applications Table   70
    Creating the Interviews Table   71
Assignments   71
    Viewing On-Screen Help on Table Wizard   71
    Using Help's Answer Wizard to Learn More about Other Data Types   71
    Using Help's Answer Wizard to Learn about Changing Field Sizes   71
    Putting on a Fund-Raiser   71

PROJECT 3: ENTERING AND EDITING DATA 72

Objectives 72
Case Study: Coordinating Volunteer Activities II 72
    Designing the Solution 72
Setting Field Properties 74
    Designating Fields as Required 77
    Specifying Formats and Input Masks 78
    Setting Default Values 83
    Assigning Validation Rules and Text 84
Defining Relationships among Tables 85
Entering and Editing Data in Datasheet View 90
Entering and Editing Data in a Form 93
    Creating a Form with Form Wizard 93
    Modifying a Form 98
Completing Data Entry 101
The Next Step 104
Summary and Exercises 105
Summary 105
Key Terms and Operations 105
Study Questions 106
    Multiple Choice 106
    Short Answer 107
    For Discussion 107
Review Exercises 108
    Modifying Field Properties 108
    Setting Relationships 108
    Creating Forms 109
    Using Forms to Enter Data 109
Assignments 110
    Writing Validation Rules 110
    Viewing On-Screen Help on Relationships 111
    Viewing On-Screen Help on Forms 111
    Putting on a Fund-Raiser (Part Two) 111

PROJECT 4: CONVERTING DATA INTO INFORMATION 112

Objectives 112
Case Study: Coordinating Volunteer Activities III 112
    Designing the Solution 112
Finding a Match 114
Using Filters to Select Records 117
    Filtering by Selection 118
    Filtering by Form 120
Using Queries to Select and Organize Data 125
    Using Simple Query Wizard 128
    Resizing and Hiding Columns 130
    Sorting on One or More Fields 131
    Printing Results 134
Creating Reports with Report Wizard 136
    Creating a List 138
    Summarizing Information 140
    Using Subgroups in a Report 144
The Next Step 147
Summary and Exercises 147
Summary 147
Key Terms and Operations 148
Study Questions 148
    Multiple Choice 148
    Short Answer 149
    For Discussion 150

Review Exercises 150
    Finding Matches 150
    Filtering by Selection 150
    Filtering by Form 151
    Creating a Query 151
    Creating a Report 151
Assignments 151
    Exploring Other Wizards 151
    Comparing Select Queries and Filters 152
    Learning about Action Queries 152
    Putting on a Fund-Raiser (Part Three) 152

PROJECT 5: REVISITING QUERIES 153

Objectives 153
Case Study: Tracking Sales 153
    Designing the Solution 153
Specifying Multiple Criteria 154
Creating Calculated Fields 162
    Using Arithmetic Operators 163
    Using a String Operator 167
    Working with Functions 172
Using Predefined Calculations 177
Analyzing Data with Crosstab Queries 181
The Next Step 184
Summary and Exercises 185
Summary 185
Key Terms and Operations 185
Study Questions 185
    Multiple Choice 185
    Short Answer 187
    For Discussion 187
Review Exercises 187
    Using And and Or Criteria in a Query 187
    Creating a Calculated Field 188
    Selecting a Predefined Calculation 188
    Creating a Crosstab Query 188
Assignments 189
    Learning about the Between/And Operator 189
    Learning about the Like Operator 189
    Finding Top Values 189
    Putting on a Fund Raiser (Part Four) 190

PROJECT 6: REVISITING REPORTS 191

Objectives 191
Case Study: Tracking Sales II 191
    Designing the Solution 191
Working in Report Design View 198
    Using the Toolbox 199
    Editing, Sizing, and Moving a Control 201
    Adding and Aligning a Control 204
    Specifying a Sort 206
    Changing Number Format 208
    Changing Font Size 209
    Adding Lines and Special Effects 211
Creating Labels 214
The Next Step 217
Summary and Exercises 217
Summary 217
Key Terms and Operations 218

Study Questions 218
  Multiple Choice 218
  Short Answer 219
  For Discussion 220
Review Exercises 220
  Modifying an Existing Query 221
  Creating a Report with Report Wizard 221
  Making Changes in Report Design View 222
Assignments 222
  Changing Report Format 222
  Revising a Fund-Raiser Report in Report Design View 223
  Creating Fund-Raiser Mailing Labels 223

Study Questions 251
  Multiple Choice 251
  Short Answer 253
  For Discussion 253
Review Exercises 253
  Appending Records 253
  Creating a Forms Switchboard 254
  Changing a Sales Commission with an Update Query 255
  Creating a Merge Application 256
Assignments 256
  Learning About Delete Queries 256
  Applying Skills to the Fund-Raising Database 256
  Learning about Macros 256

PROJECT 7: MAKING MAINTENANCE EASY 224

Objectives 224
Case Study: Tracking Sales III 224
  Designing the Solution 224
Using Action Queries to Maintain Data 225
  Editing Records with an Update Query 225
  Archiving Records with a Make Table Query 228
  Adding Records with an Append Query 229
Entering Data in a Subform 231
Creating Form Letters 235
Viewing Objects with a Switchboard 243
The Next Step 250
Summary and Exercises 251
Summary 251
Key Terms and Operations 251

APPENDIX A 257

OPERATIONS REFERENCE 259

GLOSSARY 267

INDEX 269

Overview

Objectives

After completing this Overview, you should be able to:

▶ Start Access

▶ Describe the components of the Access screen

▶ Execute commands using menus and toolbars

▶ Navigate dialog boxes

▶ Access on-screen Help

▶ Exit Access

Imagine processing 12,000 enrollments for continuing education classes during a two-week period at a local university. Picture yourself managing registration and recording performance for 800 individuals competing in 25 track and field events. Or suppose you coordinate volunteer work on a college campus, finding students whose interests and schedules fit with an organization's needs. How do you make important decisions based on the data collected and still have time to handle all of the other responsibilities of your position? Database management software can provide the answer.

USING DATABASE MANAGEMENT SOFTWARE

A *database* is a collection of related data. A *database management system (DBMS)* is a system that stores data in a database and permits retrieval of selected information. For example, the entries in the yellow pages published by a phone company constitute a manual database. In that database you retrieve information by finding the category of interest, such as pizza, and viewing an alphabetized list of providers along with associated phone numbers. Folders in a file cabinet form a database, such as folders containing patient information in a physician's office. If the folders are arranged alphabetically by last name, you can easily locate and review information on one patient.

Database management software is a tool you use to manage data electronically. The essential functions of a database program are the abilities to create a database structure; add, edit, and delete data; arrange data into meaningful orders; and display or print selected information. Using a DBMS program, you can set up forms to enter and display data, queries to select and organize your data, and professional-looking reports to communicate information.

A *relational database management system (RDBMS)* is a system that stores data by subject and retrieves information based on predefined relationships among subjects. For example, a dealership maintains data on several subjects including vehicles available to sell and vehicles sold. The first subject includes data on make, model, features, and list price. The second subject includes data on the buyer's name, address, and phone number, the price paid, and the salesperson. Using an RDBMS, you can display or print information from several subjects, such as a daily sales report showing make, model, price paid, and salesperson. The vehicle identification number defines the relationship between the two subjects.

USING ACCESS FOR WINDOWS 95

Microsoft Access is among the best-selling relational database management systems in the world. Each database consists of one or more tables; a *table* is a collection of data about a particular subject organized in a row-and-column format. Figure 0.1 shows the Products table, one of several tables in the Northwind database (a sample application provided by Access). This database serves the information needs of a mail-order company, Northwind Traders, that distributes 77 food products in eight categories.

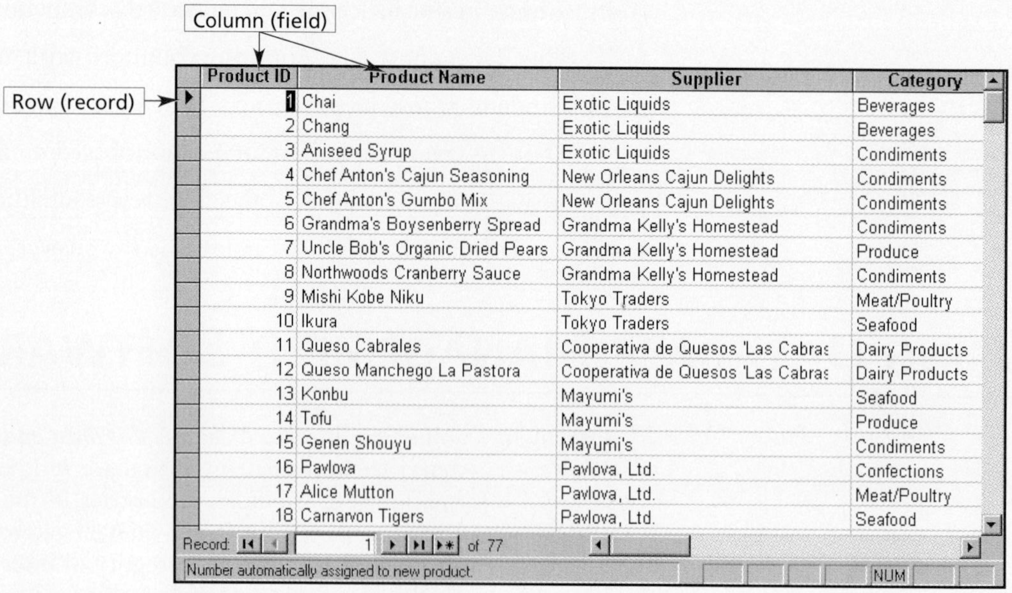

	Product ID	Product Name	Supplier	Category
	1	Chai	Exotic Liquids	Beverages
	2	Chang	Exotic Liquids	Beverages
	3	Aniseed Syrup	Exotic Liquids	Condiments
	4	Chef Anton's Cajun Seasoning	New Orleans Cajun Delights	Condiments
	5	Chef Anton's Gumbo Mix	New Orleans Cajun Delights	Condiments
	6	Grandma's Boysenberry Spread	Grandma Kelly's Homestead	Condiments
	7	Uncle Bob's Organic Dried Pears	Grandma Kelly's Homestead	Produce
	8	Northwoods Cranberry Sauce	Grandma Kelly's Homestead	Condiments
	9	Mishi Kobe Niku	Tokyo Traders	Meat/Poultry
	10	Ikura	Tokyo Traders	Seafood
	11	Queso Cabrales	Cooperativa de Quesos 'Las Cabras	Dairy Products
	12	Queso Manchego La Pastora	Cooperativa de Quesos 'Las Cabras	Dairy Products
	13	Konbu	Mayumi's	Seafood
	14	Tofu	Mayumi's	Produce
	15	Genen Shouyu	Mayumi's	Condiments
	16	Pavlova	Pavlova, Ltd.	Confections
	17	Alice Mutton	Pavlova, Ltd.	Meat/Poultry
	18	Carnarvon Tigers	Pavlova, Ltd.	Seafood

Column (field)

Row (record)

Record: 1 of 77

Number automatically assigned to new product.

Figure 0.1

In a table, a *field* is a category of information, such as Product ID or Product Name in Figure 0.1. A *record* is a collection of related fields, such as product 1 named Chai, a beverage supplied by Exotic Liquids, or product 10 named Ikura, a seafood item supplied by Tokyo Traders.

Using Access, you can quickly view only those records meeting your search criteria and limit display to selected fields. Figure 0.2 shows the results of a query to find the ten most expensive products. You see only the product name and unit price fields, and the records appear in descending order, with the most expensive item first.

Ten Most Expensive Products	Unit Price
Côte de Blaye	$263.50
Thüringer Rostbratwurst	$123.79
Mishi Kobe Niku	$97.00
Sir Rodney's Marmalade	$81.00
Carnarvon Tigers	$62.50
Raclette Courdavault	$55.00
Manjimup Dried Apples	$53.00
Tarte au sucre	$49.30
Ipoh Coffee	$46.00
Rössle Sauerkraut	$45.60

Figure 0.2

On-screen forms provide a convenient layout for viewing and editing data. Figure 0.3 shows the Categories form in the Northwind database. You could use this form to view the name, description, and picture representing each of the eight food categories. You could also use the scroll bar in the lower portion of the form to view or edit product data in each category.

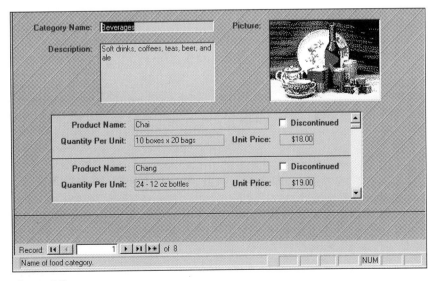

Figure 0.3

Access also provides the tools to create complex, professional-looking reports. Figure 0.4 illustrates the top portion of a report grouping employee sales by country, and then by salesperson within each country. The report includes percentage calculations and also notes if actual sales exceeded an individual's goal.

Employee Sales by Country
Sales from 1/1/95 to 12/31/95

Country: UK

Salesperson:	Buchanan, Steven		*Exceeded Goal!*	
	Order ID:	**Sale Amount:**	**Percent of Salesperson's Total:**	**Percent of Country Total:**
	10812	$1,693	8.60%	1.40%
	10823	$2,826	14.35%	2.33%
	10841	$4,581	23.26%	3.78%
	10851	$2,603	13.22%	2.15%

Figure 0.4

If you're thinking that such a powerful program must be difficult to learn, you'll find that numerous *wizards* make it possible for you to create and use a sophisticated database system with little knowledge. A *wizard* asks you questions and builds an object such as a database, table, query, form, or report based on your answers. For example, **Database Wizard** builds a complete application including tables, forms, and reports. You can choose among 22 personal and business applications, including asset tracking, donations, event management, inventory, membership, and the music collection database you will create in Project 1.

A NOTE TO THE STUDENT

The projects in this module assume that your system is equipped with a mouse or trackball and that you are comfortable working in a Windows 95 environment.

Because Access allows you to customize the work area, the screen displays on your system may vary slightly from the figures in this module. For example, you can display file names with or without details such as the file size and the date and time saved.

The projects in this module present popular applications for database management. We suggest that you first read this Overview to learn about basic Access screens and the powerful Help feature. In Project 1 you will preview the power of Access by using Database Wizard to create a complete application. Your database will include tables, forms, queries, and reports concerning a music collection. As you work through Projects 2, 3, and 4 in sequence, you will develop a campus volunteer center DBMS without using Database Wizard. After you design the database, you will create tables, set field properties that control and validate data, and enter and edit data. You can then turn your attention to creating custom data entry forms, queries to retrieve data, and custom reports with help from other wizards. Let's begin!

STARTING ACCESS

An *icon* is an on-screen symbol that represents a program file, data file, or some other function. A *toolbar* contains buttons, each of which represents a command that you can execute by positioning the mouse pointer over the button and then clicking it. You can start Access by clicking its icon on the Windows 95 desktop or the Microsoft Office toolbar, as shown in Figure 0.5.

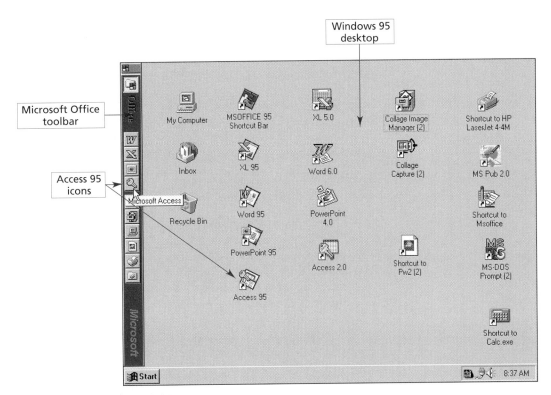

Figure 0.5

Reminder Your screen displays may vary from those shown in this module. Some of the icons on your Windows 95 desktop are likely to be different than those shown in Figure 0.5.

You can also load Access by clicking Start in the lower-left corner of the desktop, choosing Programs, and then selecting Microsoft Access. After starting Access you will see a screen similar to the one shown in Figure 0.6.

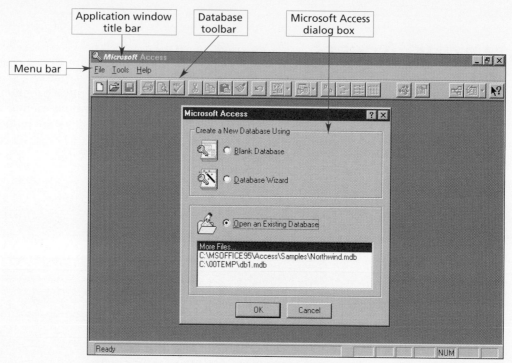

Figure 0.6

The application window title bar indicates that you are using Microsoft Access. The ***menu bar,*** located just below the title bar, is a horizontal listing of Access commands currently available. Only three commands are available if all databases are closed; seven commands are available if a database is open. Selecting an option on the menu bar causes related commands to appear in a ***pull-down menu,*** in which each new option is listed below the previous one.

In Figure 0.6, the Database toolbar appears below the menu bar. As you work, buttons that are not available will appear dim.

Tip The name of a button appears each time the mouse pointer rests on a button. If this feature is not active, you can choose Toolbars from the View menu and select Show ToolTips.

The Microsoft Access dialog box occupies most of the remainder of the screen. A ***dialog box*** appears whenever additional information is needed to complete a task. Why don't you take a look at this screen for yourself? In the steps that follow, you will start the Access relational database program.

To start Access:

1 Double-click the Access icon on your Windows 95 desktop.
After a brief display showing copyright information, the Microsoft Access
dialog box shown in Figure 0.6 appears.

2 Select Cancel to close the dialog box.

USING TOOLBARS, MENUS, AND DIALOG BOXES

Tip If you are already familiar with using toolbars, menus, and dialog
boxes in another Windows product, you might want to skip this section
and continue with the section called "Getting On-screen Help."

Access automatically displays a toolbar supporting the current operation.
For example, if you are creating or changing a table design, the Table
Design toolbar will appear near the top of the screen. Clicking a button on
a toolbar executes the associated Access command.

When a database is open, Access includes a powerful set of commands
grouped within the seven options on the menu bar, as shown in Figure 0.7.
One letter of every menu option, called a mnemonic letter, is underlined.
You can choose a menu bar option by using a mouse to click the option
name or by pressing (ALT) in combination with the mnemonic letter.
Options on a pull-down menu that appear dim, such as Save in Figure 0.7,
are not currently available. Choosing an option that is followed by an
arrowhead, such as Get External Data, opens a submenu. Choosing an
option that is followed by an ellipsis (. . .), such as Page Setup or Print,
opens a dialog box.

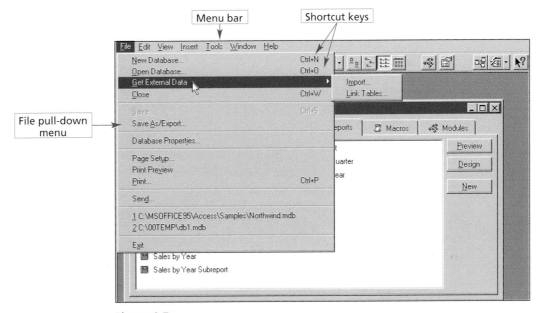

Figure 0.7

For some common command sequences, Access has assigned a key or key combination called a shortcut. Using these *shortcut keys* (sometimes called accelerator keys), you can bypass several menu selections. For example, five shortcut keys are available for file management tasks, such as (CTRL)+**O** to open a database and (CTRL)+**P** to print. If a shortcut key is available, it appears to the right of its associated command on a pull-down menu.

Tip If you start to choose from a menu and do not wish to continue, you can press the left mouse button after positioning the mouse pointer anywhere outside the menu, or you can press (ESC) one or more times.

You can select an option within a dialog box by positioning the mouse pointer and pressing the left mouse button, or by pressing (TAB) until the desired option is highlighted and then pressing (ENTER) Some options within a dialog box appear in sets called *radio buttons.* These options are so named because, as on a radio, you can specify only one choice from a set of items. In Figure 0.6, Open an Existing Database is selected.

Most dialog boxes contain one or more *command buttons,* which you can select to execute the named operations. Buttons may change as you make selections within a dialog box. If an ellipsis (. . .) appears after the name in a command button, selecting that button opens another dialog box. The Print dialog box shown in Figure 0.8 contains OK, Cancel, Setup, and Properties.

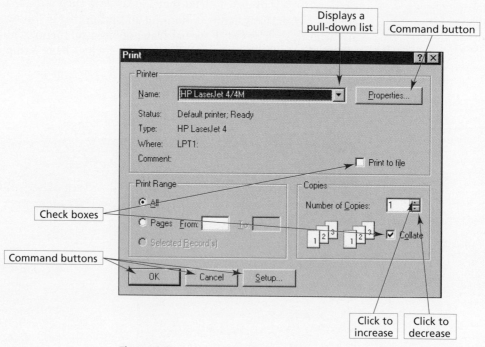

Figure 0.8

A down arrow at the right end of a box indicates the existence of a ***pull-down list,*** which shows related options. If you were to select the arrow at the right end of the Name box shown in Figure 0.8, you would see a display of printers.

You can use a ***check box*** to turn an option on or off. A checkmark ($\checkmark$) within the box indicates an option is on. The absence of a checkmark indicates the option is off. In Figure 0.8, for example, the Print to file option is not selected, and the Collate option is selected.

At this point you know how to specify most settings within dialog boxes and choose from toolbars and menus. For more information, you can use the powerful on-screen Help feature.

GETTING ON-SCREEN HELP

Access provides information about the program on the screen. This information can either be ***context-sensitive Help,*** which provides information about the operation in progress, or information of a more general nature. Help is available through options on the Help menu and a Help button, as described in the following sections.

Using Contents to Get Help

The Access Help Topics dialog box appears if you choose Help in the menu bar and then choose Microsoft Access Help Topics. You can choose among four tabs in the dialog box: Contents, Index, Find, and Answer Wizard. Instructions appear below each tab. When Contents is the current folder, as shown in Figure 0.9, you can select a topic by clicking a closed-book icon or the associated text.

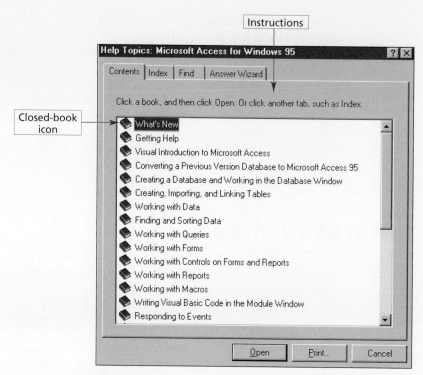

Figure 0.9

In the following steps you will view several screens accessed through the Access Help Topics dialog box. By exploring other topics on your own, you will have a better idea of the help available on-screen.

To use the Contents feature of on-screen Help:

1 Choose Help from the menu bar, and then choose Microsoft Access Help Topics.

2 Select the Contents tab, if Contents is not already the current folder. The Access Help Topics dialog box shown in Figure 0.9 appears.

3 Select *Finding and Sorting Data*, and then click Open.
The icon in front of *Finding and Sorting Data* changes to an open book, and a sublist of four topics preceded by closed-book icons appears.

Tip You can also select a topic by double-clicking its description or associated icon.

4 Select *Finding Data Using Filters*, and then click Open.
A long list of related topics appears, part of which is shown in Figure 0.10. A question mark icon indicating Help precedes each topic.

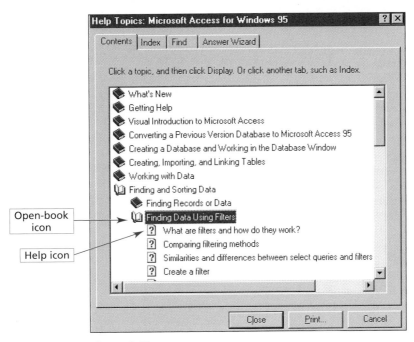

Figure 0.10

5 Select *What are filters and how do they work?*, and then select Display. Information about the selected topic appears.

6 Click each radio button at the left to view information about filters.

7 Select Close.

Using Index to Get Help

If you know the exact name of the feature about which you need help, you can look up information about the topic by selecting Index from the Help Topics dialog box. The two-part instructions to use the box appear near the top, as shown in Figure 0.11.

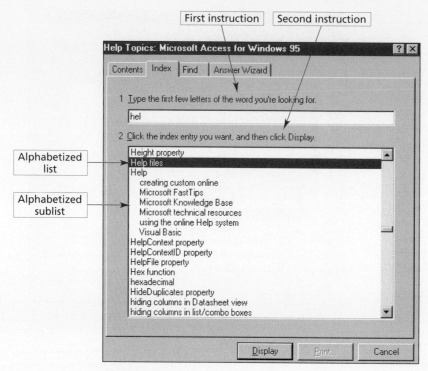

Figure 0.11

As you start to type your search word or phrase, Access displays an alphabetized list of topics that start with the same letters. Some topics, such as *Help* in Figure 0.11, display a sublist of topics. In the following steps you will use this feature to display information on using the online Help system.

To use the Index feature of on-screen Help:

1 Choose Microsoft Access Help Topics from the Help menu.

2 Select the Index tab in the Help Topics dialog box.

3 Type **hel** in the top box, as shown in Figure 0.11.

4 Select *using the online Help system*, and then select Display.
The Getting Assistance while you work screen appears.

> **Tip** Clicking the color bar in front of a named topic, such as *Screen Tips* or *Step-by-step Answers,* displays additional information about the associated topic.

5 View other information as desired, and then select Close.

Using Find to Get Help

You can search the Help database for any mention of a specified word or phrase by selecting Find from the Help Topics dialog box. This box contains three instructions to help you use it, as shown in Figure 0.12.

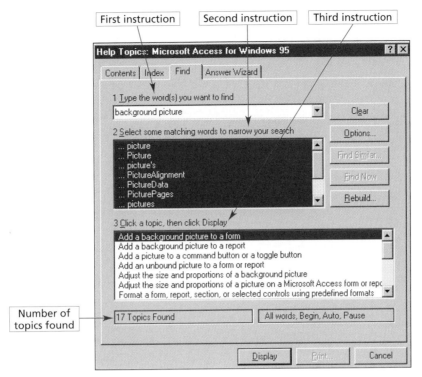

Figure 0.12

If the list of found topics is longer than the current screen display, you can use the scroll bar to view the complete list of topics. In the following steps you will use this feature to display information about shortcut keys.

To use the Find feature of on-screen Help:

1 Choose Microsoft Access Help Topics from the Help menu.

2 Select the Find tab.
The message "Loading Word List" appears briefly.

3 Type **background picture** in the box under the first instruction, as shown in Figure 0.12.

4 Select *Add a background picture to a report* from the list that appears under the third instruction, and then select Display.

> **Tip** You can select the Options button and then select Print Topic to print the information in the current Help Topics dialog box.

5 After viewing the information, select Help Topics to restore display of the Find folder.

Using Answer Wizard to Get Help

Access also provides **Answer Wizard** that will display a list of topics related to a search you define in your own words. There are two instructions to use the Answer Wizard dialog box, as shown in Figure 0.13.

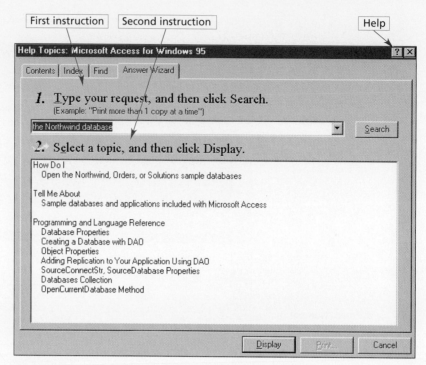

Figure 0.13

Answer Wizard will show you step-by-step instructions on how to complete a specific task if you select a topic in the *How Do I* section. Selecting a *Tell Me About* topic displays a general explanation. The *Programming and Language Reference* topics help users set up advanced applications.

In the following steps you will use Answer Wizard to learn about the Northwind sample database provided by Access.

To use the Answer Wizard feature of on-screen Help:

1 Select the Answer Wizard tab from the Help Topics dialog box.

2 Type **the Northwind database** as your request, and then select Search.

The list of related topics appears as shown in Figure 0.13.

3 Select *Sample databases and applications included with Microsoft Access* in the *Tell Me About* section, and then select Display.

4 Select Help Topics to restore display of the Answer Wizard folder.

5 Explore viewing other Help topics of your choice.

6 Click the Close icon in the upper-right corner of the Help Topics dialog box, or select the Cancel command button in the lower-right corner.

Using the Help Button

If you are using a mouse, you can take advantage of PowerPoint's Help button, which allows you to view information about a command or window item on the screen. You must first click the Help button on a toolbar, as shown in Figure 0.14, or the Help button within a dialog box, as shown in Figure 0.13. The pointer changes to an arrow with a question mark. You then position the pointer on the item you would like to know more about and click again. In the following steps you will use the Help button to view information about the Undo button.

To use the Help button:

1 Click the Help button at the right end of the Database toolbar. The mouse pointer changes to an arrow with a question mark.

2 Move the pointer until it rests on the Undo button (left of center on the Database toolbar).

3 Press the left mouse button.
Information about undoing an action appears as shown in Figure 0.14.

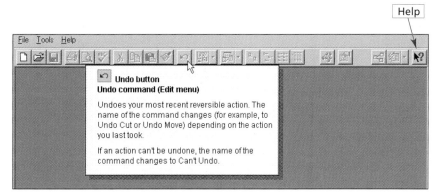

Figure 0.14

4 Click outside the information box to exit Help.

EXITING ACCESS

When you finish working on a database, you can save or discard your changes and then continue developing another database or exit Access. You will start the process to leave the current database editing session by choosing from options (or the corresponding shortcut keys) on the File menu shown in Figure 0.7.

The Close option appears only if a database is in use. You will choose Close if you want to close the current database but continue working in Access. You will choose Exit if you want to quit working in Access. Whichever option you select, you will be prompted to save the current database if it contains any unsaved changes (saving a database is discussed in Project 1).

To exit Access:

1 Choose Exit from the File menu.

Reminder   You can also exit an application by clicking the Close button in the upper-right corner of the screen.

THE NEXT STEP

At this point you have a lot of information about the Access work environment. As you complete subsequent projects, you will have many opportunities to choose from menus, select buttons, and indicate your preferences in dialog boxes. However, these step-by-step instructions do not include using on-screen Help. Starting now, get in the habit of viewing on-screen Help about each new topic you encounter.

This concludes the Overview. You can either exit Access, go on to work the Study Questions, or proceed to Project 1.

SUMMARY AND EXERCISES

Summary

- Access is a powerful database management system (DBMS) that allows you to enter, edit, and display data using forms; select and organize your data; and create professional-looking reports to communicate information.
- Access is a relational DBMS that stores data by subject and retrieves information based on predefined relationships among subjects.
- A database consists of one or more tables that store data in a row-and-column format. In a table, a field (column) is a category of information and a record (row) is a collection of related fields.
- Numerous wizards are available. A wizard builds an object such as a database, table, query, form, or report based on your answers to questions.
- You can execute commands using menu bars, pull-down menus, and toolbar buttons. Quite often you must also specify settings in a dialog box to complete an operation.
- Whenever you want information about some feature of Access, you can use the extensive on-screen Help feature.

Key Terms and Operations

Key Terms
Answer Wizard
check box
command button
context-sensitive Help
database
database management software
database management system
 (DBMS)
Database Wizard
dialog box
field
icon
menu bar
pull-down list

pull-down menu
radio button
record
relational database management
 system (RDBMS)
shortcut key
table
toolbar
wizard

Operations
Start Access
Get on-screen help
Exit Access

Study Questions

Multiple Choice

1. Which of the following is a method to choose a menu bar option?
   a. Use a mouse to click the name of the option.
   b. Press [CTRL] in combination with the mnemonic letter.
   c. Both a and b.
   d. None of the above.

2. Which of the following is not one of the folders in the Microsoft Access Help Topics dialog box?
   a. Find
   b. Search for Help On
   c. Index
   d. Answer Wizard

3. Which of the following is a database term for category of information?
   a. field
   b. record
   c. table
   d. database

4. Which option would you choose from the File pull-down menu to quit Access?
   a. Close
   b. Exit
   c. Quit
   d. Stop

5. Which folder in the Microsoft Access Help Topics dialog box would you select to search the Help database for any mention of a specified word or phrase?
   a. Find
   b. Contents
   c. Help button
   d. Answer Wizard

Short Answer

1. On-screen help can be general in nature or provide information about the operation in progress. What is the term used to describe help related to the operation in progress?

2. If an option on a pull-down menu is not currently available, how does that option appear relative to options that are available?

3. If you make a mistake while choosing from menus, what key can you press one or more times to restore the appropriate screen for restarting the sequence?

4. Which Access wizard creates a complete business or personal application?

5. What term describes a database management system that stores data by subject and retrieves information based on predefined relationships among subjects?

For Discussion

1. Describe the essential functions of a database program.

2. You frequently have to issue commands to perform various database management functions. Explain the various ways you can issue a command using Access. Include a description of the menu structure, toolbars, and shortcut keys in your discussion.

3. Think of a database that you might use. Give an example of a field and a record for that database.

Objectives

After completing this project, you should be able to:

► Select a database application

► Step through Database Wizard

► Enter and edit data using a form

► Preview and print a report

CASE STUDY: MANAGING YOUR MUSIC COLLECTION

Imagine that you own and manage a small business that provides DJs (disc jockeys) for special events. Your music collection—more than 1000 compact discs, tapes, and records—continues to grow, and you spend hours making selections for each booking.

Recently you purchased a computer system for the business that includes Windows 95 and Access. You plan to set up an electronic database management system that reduces the preparation time for each job and allows you to compile a variety of music lists for prospective clients.

Designing the Solution

In this situation there is very little design work to do. Using the Database Wizard, you can select a predefined Music Collection application. Access will set up the objects you need—tables, forms, and reports—and provide sample data on request. After modifying the objects as necessary, you can quickly focus your attention on using the information system.

STEPPING THROUGH THE DATABASE WIZARD

The Microsoft Access dialog box shown in Figure 1.1 appears after you load Access. At this point you can create a new database or open an existing one.

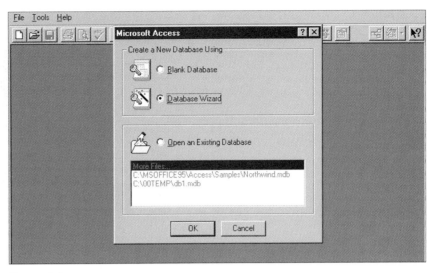

Figure 1.1

The first two options in the Microsoft Access dialog box apply to creating a new database. Database Wizard allows you to select among 22 personal and business databases listed in the Databases folder of the New dialog box, as shown in Figure 1.2.

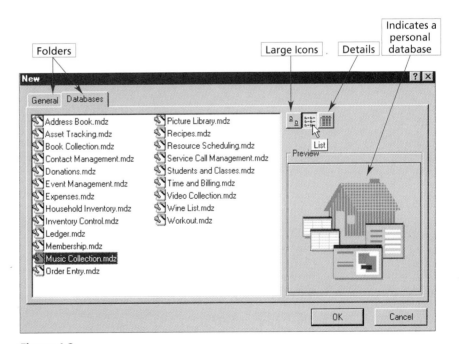

Figure 1.2

Tip If you find that Access does not provide a predefined application similar to the one you need, you can select Blank Database and create your own tables, forms, queries, and reports with the help of other wizards. You can select Blank Database from the Microsoft Access dialog box or the General folder of the New dialog box.

The three buttons above the Preview area vary the display of listed items. Selecting the List button results in a two-column display of all predefined database options.

Selecting a predefined database from the alphabetized list displays an image representing a personal or business database in the Preview area on the right. A house in the background indicates a personal database, as shown for Music Collection in Figure 1.2.

After you select, name, and save a predefined database, Access displays a series of Database Wizard dialog boxes. First you will view suggested tables, which you can modify to meet your specific needs. You'll also be able to select background color and design for screens, and add a title and print style for reports.

Tip If you tell Database Wizard to include sample data, you can immediately use the predefined forms and reports. You can then decide if revisions are necessary before entering your own data.

In the following sections you will select the predefined application Music Collection, save the database, and complete all Database Wizard dialog boxes.

Selecting and Saving a Predefined Database

Selecting a predefined database or Blank Database opens the File New Database dialog box. The entries you make in this box determine the name, type, and location of your new database. If you selected a predefined database, Access suggests a name, such as Music Collection1. You can accept that name or type a new name, as shown in Figure 1.3.

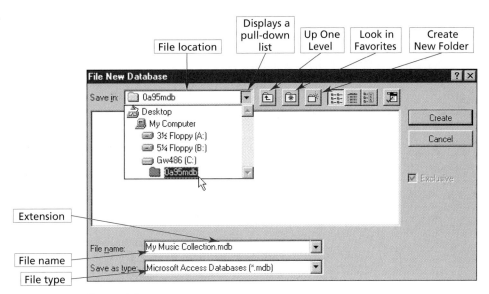

Figure 1.3

Windows 95 file names can contain up to 256 characters, including spaces. Access assigns the three-character extension .mdb, indicating a master database. It is this extension that Windows 95 uses to associate a file with the application that created it.

Tip The file name extension may be hidden. To display extensions, use My Computer or Windows Explorer to open the folder you want to look at. After choosing Options from the View menu, select the View tab and make sure the Hide MS-DOS File Extensions box is not checked.

In addition to a file name, you will specify a file location. Clicking the down arrow at the right end of the Save In box displays drives and folders for your system. You will select the drive and then select an existing folder or create a new one. In Figure 1.3 the folder 0a95mdb on drive C is selected.

Caution The predefined Music Collection database with sample data requires over 1.2 million characters of storage space, nearly the capacity of a 3-½-inch high-density disk. If you are working in a school lab environment, your instructor will tell you where to store your files.

In the following steps you will select and save the predefined Music Collection database.

To select an application:

1 Load Access.
The Microsoft Access dialog box shown in Figure 1.1 appears.

2 Select Database Wizard, and then select OK.
The New dialog box appears with two folders, General and Databases.

3 Select Databases, if that is not the current folder.

4 Select the List button to view the names of all predefined databases.

5 Select Music Collection, as shown in Figure 1.2, and then select OK.
The File New Database dialog box appears.

To save the database:

1 Type or point to the name of the folder where you want to store your database.

Tip Use the Up One Level button and Look in Favorites button to help navigate the storage areas on your system.

2 Edit the suggested file name to read `My Music Collection.mdb`
3 Select Create.
The initial Database Wizard dialog box shown in Figure 1.4 appears.

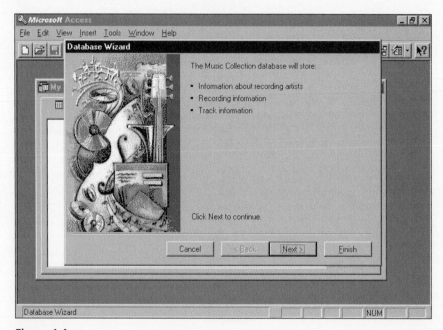

Figure 1.4

4 Select Next>.
The Database Wizard dialog box shown in Figure 1.5 appears.

Selected table | Selected fields | Optional fields | More fields

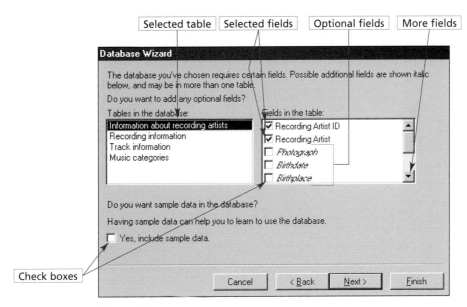

Figure 1.5

Adding Optional Fields and Sample Data

Database Wizard creates the four Music Collection tables listed at the left side of the dialog box shown in Figure 1.5. The fields in the selected table appear on the right side of the dialog box. Field names that appear in a normal typeface are required, while those in italics are optional. A checkmark indicates a selected field.

The Information about recording artists table has three required fields—Recording Artist ID, Recording Artist, and Notes. You can also add one or more of the optional fields *Photograph*, *Birthdate*, *Birthplace*, and *Date of Death*.

In the following steps you will add an optional field to two of the four tables and specify that you want sample data included for each table.

Tip You can delete sample data and add your own after you learn how to use an application.

To add an optional field to a predefined table:

1 Select the Information about recording artists table, if that table is not already highlighted.

2 Select *Birthplace* in the Fields list.

A checkmark appears in the box preceding *Birthplace*, as shown in Figure 1.6.

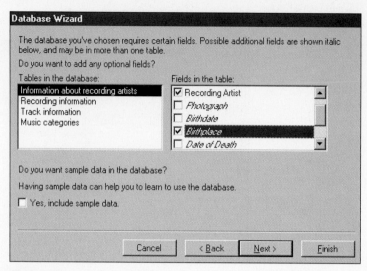

Figure 1.6

3 Select the Recording information table.

4 Scroll down the Fields in the Table list and select *Purchase Price.*
A checkmark appears in the box preceding *Purchase Price.*

5 In the lower-left corner of the dialog box, select the Yes, include
sample data button.
A checkmark appears in the check box, as shown in Figure 1.7.

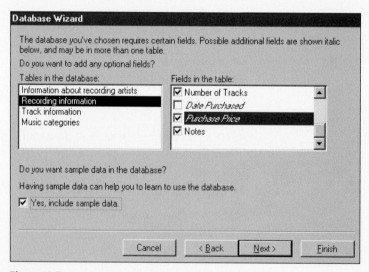

Figure 1.7

6 Select Next>.
The Database Wizard dialog box shown in Figure 1.8 appears.

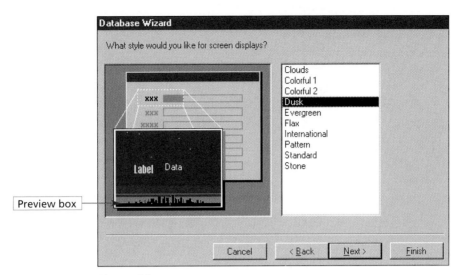

Figure 1.8

Selecting a Style for Screen Displays

Using the Database Wizard dialog box shown in Figure 1.8, you can preview and select one of ten styles to add background scenery and color to your screen displays. You will select a style from the list on the right side of the dialog box. The preview box on the left displays a sample of the selected style. In the following steps you will view several styles and then select one.

To select a style for screen displays:

1 Select *Clouds.*
The preview box displays a color background that includes clouds.

2 Select *International.*
The preview box displays a globe in the background.

3 Select your choice of other styles.

4 Select *Dusk.*
The style shown in Figure 1.8 appears.

5 Select Next>.
The Database Wizard dialog box shown in Figure 1.9 appears.

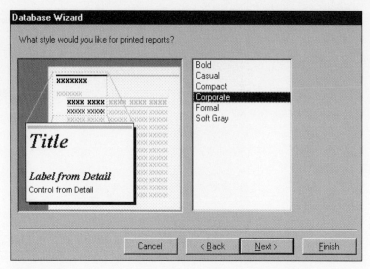

Figure 1.9

Selecting a Style for Printed Reports

Database Wizard offers six predefined combinations of type fonts and sizes that you can apply to your printed reports. You will select a style from the list on the right side of the dialog box. The preview box on the left displays a sample of the selected style.

Figure 1.9 shows a sample of the Corporate print style. In the following steps you will view several print styles and then select one.

To select a print style:

1 Select *Casual.*
The preview box displays a sample of the Casual style.

2 Select *Soft Gray.*
The display in the preview box changes to show a sample of the Soft Gray style.

3 Select your choice of other print styles.

4 Select *Corporate,* and then select Next>.
The Database Wizard dialog box shown in Figure 1.10 appears.

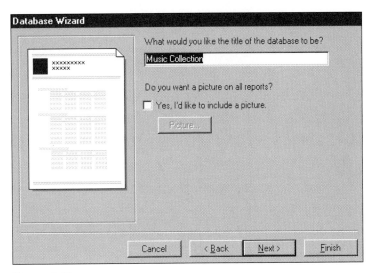

Figure 1.10

Selecting a Title and Picture

You can specify a title to appear on screen displays and printouts. Database Wizard will suggest a name, such as *Music Collection* shown in Figure 1.10. This name does not have to be the same as the one you used to save the database on disk.

You can also add a picture to reports by selecting the check box below the title. A picture is an image that has been converted (digitized) to a disk file. There are many techniques used to digitize images. Access prefers pictures created using the bitmap technique. These files end with the extension .bmp or display the file type Bitmap Image in detail view.

If you select Yes, I'd like to include a picture, the Picture command button becomes active. If you know where bitmap pictures are stored on your computer system, you can select Picture to access the Insert Picture dialog box and choose an image.

At this point you will have provided all the information needed to build your database. After Database Wizard creates the tables, forms, and reports in the Music Collection database, you will see the Main Switchboard dialog box shown in Figure 1.11.

Main menu of the
switchboard

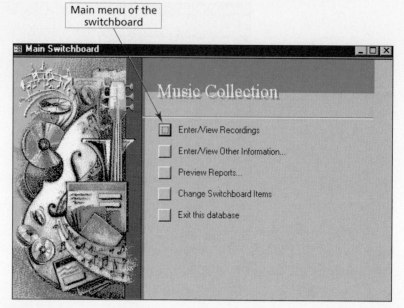

Figure 1.11

A *switchboard* is a menu system that helps users navigate through a database. Using the switchboard, you can update tables, view data stored in the tables, and display or print reports.

To accept the current title and picture settings and complete Database Wizard screens:

1 Select Next>.

The wizard accepts the name Music Collection and displays the final Database Wizard dialog box.

2 Check that your settings match those shown in Figure 1.12.

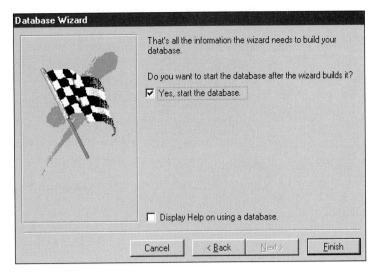

Figure 1.12

3 Select Finish.
After a brief delay while Database Wizard creates tables, forms, and reports, you will see the Music Collection switchboard shown in Figure 1.11.

EXIT If necessary, you can select the last option on the switchboard now to exit the database. You can then exit Access and continue this project later.

ENTERING AND EDITING DATA IN TABLES

Data stored in a database has value only if it is relevant, timely, and accurate. When you design a database, you determine what data is relevant to the objectives of the database. The frequency with which you enter and edit data determines its timeliness. Two factors affect accuracy: the quality of the data collected and the precision of data entry.

To keep a database current, you will add records to tables, change data in existing records, and delete unwanted records. In the following sections you will add and edit records in your new Music Collection database.

Using a Form to Add Records

During the process to create a database system, Database Wizard sets up one or more forms on which to add, edit, and view data. Figure 1.13 shows one of the forms created for use with the Music Collection database.

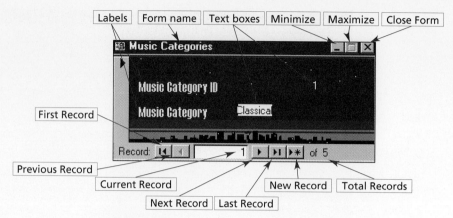

Figure 1.13

The form name and the Minimize, Maximize, and Close Form buttons appear at the top of the form. Several buttons at the bottom of the form help you navigate through the table. By clicking the appropriate button, you can display the first or last record, the previous or next record, or a blank new record. You can also see the number of the current record and the total number of records.

A form can display data from one or more tables. The form shown in Figure 1.13 is a simple one, containing only two *text boxes* and the corresponding *labels.* A text box generally displays data from a table. A *label* describes its associated control or some other portion of the form.

In the following steps you will use the Music Categories form to add a new record to the categories table.

To add a new record using a form:

1 If necessary, load Access and open the My Music Collection database.

2 Select Enter/View Other Information, the second option on the Music Collection Main Switchboard (see Figure 1.11).
The Forms Switchboard shown in Figure 1.14 appears.

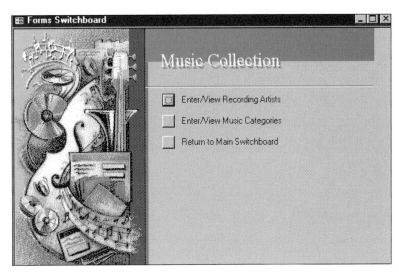

Figure 1.14

3 Select Enter/View Music Categories, the second option on the Forms Switchboard.
The form shown in Figure 1.13 appears.

 4 Click New Record, the last of the buttons at the bottom of the form.
A blank record 6 appears.

5 Type **Blues** in the Music Category text box and press (ENTER)
A blank record 7 appears.

 6 Close the form by clicking the Close Form button in the upper-right corner of the Music Categories form.

7 Select Return to Main Switchboard.

Using a Form to Edit Records

When data in a record is no longer valid, it must be changed. The editing process involves accessing the invalid record and changing the data field or fields that are inaccurate.

You can edit a record on a form by selecting (highlighting) the contents of a field and then typing the new data. You can also make another selection in a *combo box*, as shown in Figure 1.15. A **combo box** displays a list of allowable entries.

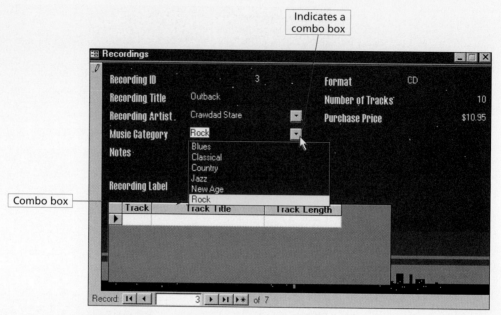

Figure 1.15

In the following steps you will display the form and record shown in Figure 1.15, type a change in purchase price, and select a different music category from choices in a combo box.

To change an existing record:

1 Select Enter/View Recordings, the first option on the Main Switchboard.

2 Display record 3.

Reminder Use the buttons at the bottom of the form to move to a different record.

3 Select 12.98 in the Purchase Price field.

4 Type **10.95**

5 Click the down arrow at the right end of the Music Category text box.
The combo box shown in Figure 1.15 appears.

6 Select Country.

7 Close the form.
The Main Switchboard appears on the screen.

EXIT If necessary, you can exit this database now. You can then exit Access and continue this project later.

PREVIEWING AND PRINTING A REPORT

The rows (records) and columns (fields) of a table contain data, as shown in Figure 1.16 for the Recordings table in the Music Collection database.

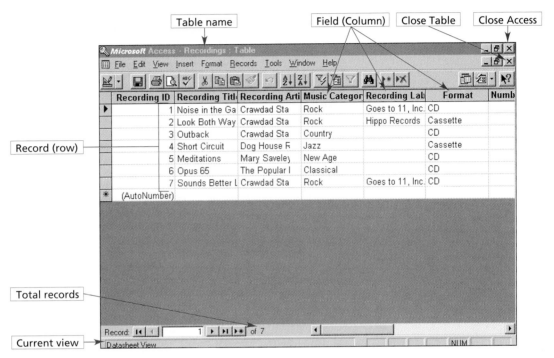

Figure 1.16

A field is a type of information, such as *Music Category, Recording Label,* or *Format.* A record is a collection of related fields, such as the record for Look Both Ways, a recording classified as rock, performed by Crawdad Stare, and distributed on cassette by Hippo Records.

Compare the datasheet (table) view in Figure 1.16 to the report shown in Figure 1.17.

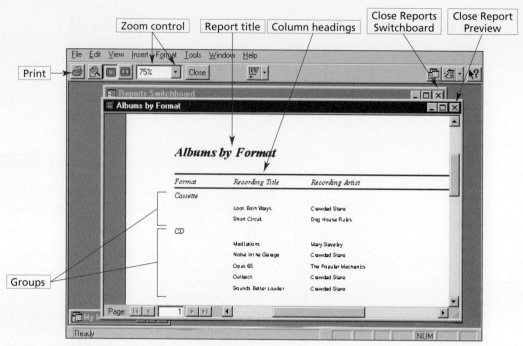

Figure 1.17

In the table, records display in the order in which they were entered, and you see only as many fields as can fit across the screen. The report groups similar records according to format (cassette or CD), limiting display to three fields. Within each group, records appear in alphabetical order by recording title. The report title, column headings, and horizontal lines add the finishing touches to professional-looking output.

> **Tip** If you want to see more or less of a report on the screen, you can vary the magnification by changing the zoom setting. When you are satisfied with the content and format of the report, you can produce a printed report by selecting Print at the left end of the toolbar.

During the process to create a database system, Database Wizard sets up one or more reports. You can view the names of reports on the Reports Switchboard, as shown in Figure 1.18 for the Music Collection database.

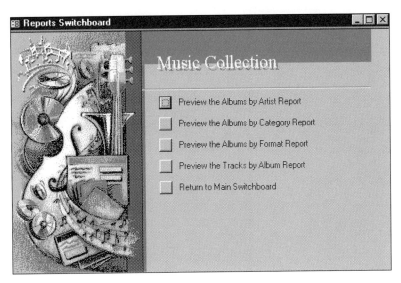

Figure 1.18

In the following steps you will view several reports created by Database Wizard for the Music Collection database. You will also print one of the reports.

To preview and print a report:

1 If necessary, load Access and open the My Music Collection database.

2 Select Preview Reports, the third option on the Music Collection Main Switchboard (see Figure 1.11).
The Reports Switchboard shown in Figure 1.18 appears.

3 Select Preview the Albums by Format Report.

4 Set zoom to 75%, and use the scroll bar to view all of the data, as shown in Figure 1.17.

5 Close the Albums by Format preview.

6 Select Preview the Albums by Artist Report, and set zoom to 50%.
Your screen displays the report shown in Figure 1.19.

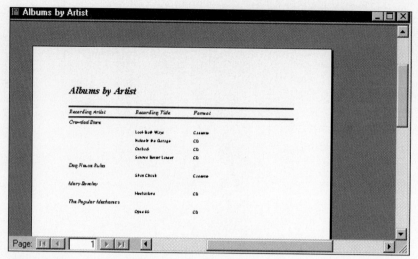

Figure 1.19

7 Select Print, the first button in the toolbar.
Your printout matches the screen display shown in Figure 1.19.

To close the switchboards and the database:

1 Close the Albums by Artist preview.
The Reports Switchboard appears.

2 Select Return to Main Switchboard.

3 Select Exit this database.

THE NEXT STEP

In this project you had a brief exposure to the power of Access. You selected
a predefined Music Collection database, which put Database Wizard to
work creating the required tables, forms, and reports. You performed basic
data management tasks such as modifying the suggested design, entering
and editing data using a form, and communicating information through
reports sent to the screen or printer. On your own you might select one of
the other predefined personal or business databases, include sample data,
and repeat activities until you are comfortable using and closing the
switchboards, forms, and reports.

This concludes Project 1. You can either exit Access or go on to work
the Study Questions, Review Exercises, and Assignments.

SUMMARY AND EXERCISES

Summary

- Selecting a predefined database application causes Database Wizard to create the required tables, forms, and reports for one of 22 personal or business databases.
- The tables, forms, and reports that constitute a database are stored in a single file with an .mdb extension.
- You can modify a table suggested by Database Wizard by adding optional fields.
- Requesting sample data allows you to work with forms and reports before entering your own data.
- Database Wizard dialog boxes allow you to select a style for screen displays, a style for printed reports, and a title and picture to appear on screen displays and printouts.
- Database Wizard creates a menu system called the switchboard, which you can use to update tables, view data stored in tables, and display or print reports.
- A form displays data from one or more tables on the screen. You can add, edit, and view data using a form.
- A report sends information to the screen or printer in a professional-looking format. Report options include limiting the number of fields, grouping similar records, and presenting records in a meaningful order.

Key Terms and Operations

Key Terms	Operations
combo box	Create an application using Database Wizard
label	
switchboard	Enter and edit data using a form
text box	Preview and print reports

Study Questions

Multiple Choice

1. Database Wizard sets up a predefined database application, automatically creating some features but making others optional. Which of the following is optional when Database Wizard creates the database?
   a. switchboard
   b. sample data
   c. both a and b
   d. none of the above

2. What is the three-character file name extension that indicates an Access database?
   a. .dbm
   b. .dbf
   c. .mdb
   d. none of the above

3. Using Database Wizard, you can add optional fields to a predefined table. The names of these optional fields appear
   a. italicized.
   b. in boldface.
   c. underlined.
   d. in a normal typeface.

4. Selecting a style for screen displays
   a. adds sample data to your database.
   b. adds background scenery and color to your screen displays.
   c. adds type fonts and sizes to your printed reports.
   d. All of the above.

5. How many predefined databases are available using Database Wizard?
   a. 15
   b. 20
   c. 25
   d. none of the above

Short Answer

1. Data stored in a database has value only if it is _____, _____, and _____.

2. Database Wizard provides two categories of predefined databases. What are the two categories?

3. You can add a picture to reports. What file type does Access prefer for this picture?

4. What is the name of the menu system that helps users navigate through a database?

5. On a form, a(n) _____ displays a list of allowable entries.

For Discussion

1. What is Database Wizard? What determines whether or not you would use this feature of the Access program?

2. Database Wizard creates one or more forms for a predefined database application. Describe the purpose and layout (text boxes and labels) of a form.

3. Database Wizard creates one or more reports for a predefined database application. Describe the enhancements you can view in a report that are not available when viewing the same data in a table.

Review Exercises

Creating a Personal Address Book

1. Load Access and select Database Wizard.

2. Select and save the Address Book database.

3. Add fields for nicknames and mobile phone numbers (do not add sample data).

4. Select a style for screen displays and printed reports.

5. Provide an appropriate title to appear on screen displays and printouts (do not include a picture).

6. Use a form(s) to enter ten records.

7. View predefined reports (also print if instructed to do so).

8. Close the database.

Creating an Inventory of Personal Property

1. Load Access and select Database Wizard.

2. Select and save the Household Inventory database.

3. Add fields for manufacturer's name and photograph, and add sample data.

4. Select a style for screen displays and printed reports.

5. Provide an appropriate title to appear on screen displays and printouts (do not include a picture).

6. Use a form(s) to edit two records.

7. View predefined reports (also print if instructed to do so).

8. Close the database.

Assignments

Using Contents in On-Screen Help

Using Contents in on-screen Help, view the Visual Introduction to Microsoft Access. Read the three sections titled *What is a database, Tables: What they are and how they work*, and *Customizing a table*. Write a brief summary of what you learned about databases, tables, and how they are related.

Using Index in On-Screen Help

Use Index to learn about creating a database using Database Wizard. Write a brief summary explaining the steps necessary to create a database using Database Wizard.

Cataloging Your Video Tape Collection

Use Database Wizard to create a database that will track your collection of video tapes. Use a form(s) to add data. Print one or more reports providing information about your collection.

Tracking Your Workout

Use Database Wizard to create a database that will track your exercise program. Use a form(s) to add data. Print one or more reports providing information about your workouts and performance.

PROJECT 2: DESIGNING AND CREATING A DATABASE

Objectives

After completing this project, you should be able to:

▶ Design a database management system

▶ Create a table with Table Wizard

▶ Create a table on your own

CASE STUDY: COORDINATING VOLUNTEER ACTIVITIES

Assume that you are a summer intern at your campus volunteer center. Recently the center acquired Access for Windows 95 software, and the director has asked you to create an Access database management system to provide information about student volunteers and agencies in need of help.

Designing the Solution

No formal design process is necessary when you create and maintain a small information system for your own use, such as the music collection database you created with Database Wizard in Project 1. When you design a larger system for use by others, however, there is a lot of work to do! You must first talk with users of the new system so that you understand the database objectives and desired outputs. With that information you are prepared to develop a *data dictionary,* which shows the tables, fields, and relationships you feel are needed to accomplish the goals of the database. After users review and approve your design as detailed in the data dictionary, you can load Access and use a variety of wizards to set up the tables, queries, forms, and reports that constitute the information system.

> **Tip** Working through such a formal process to design a multiuser database can be tedious and time-consuming, often taking weeks before output is available. Taking time to interact with users at the design stage, however, makes it far less likely that you'll have major revisions to table structures, queries, forms, and reports later on.

This project focuses on the initial steps in the database design process: understanding the database objectives and desired outputs, developing a data dictionary, and creating the necessary tables. In subsequent projects you will enter and edit data as well as output information.

DETERMINING OBJECTIVES AND OUTPUTS

Setting up interviews with users is an excellent way to start the database design process. You will use these meetings to gain a clear understanding of problems with the current information system and users' expectations concerning the new database. As soon as possible after each interview, you should write down your conclusions regarding objectives and desired outputs.

> **Tip** You may need to interview an individual more than once to have the necessary depth of information. Do not rely on recall of verbal comments as the basis for your written analysis. If the person being interviewed agrees, tape the conversation. You might also prepare a list of questions, with space for comments on the responses you receive.

To give you a glimpse of the interview process, imagine that you are the intern in the following dialogue with the director of the campus volunteer center.

Intern	*You told me earlier that your current system provides information in two areas: students interested in volunteering and organizations that have volunteer opportunities. Let's focus on students for a moment. How do you collect and store data on those individuals interested in volunteering?*
Director	The campus newspaper and radio station donate space and time for us to promote opportunities for volunteer service. We also post flyers in every building. Any student interested in volunteering is invited to phone or stop by the center. One of my two assistants writes the student's name, local address, and local phone number on an index card, and also notes whether the student can provide transportation. Preferences for type of volunteer activity are written on the back of the card, as are days and times available to work. The cards are filed in alphabetical order by last name.
Intern	*Does this system provide the information you need in a timely manner?*

Director   The card system meets my objectives of knowing which students are interested in volunteering and being able to contact a specific student. However, using the card file to find students for a specific volunteer opportunity just doesn't work. For example, this morning I had a phone call from an organization looking for two students to work with teens at a gym on Saturday mornings. To process that request using our current system, a staff member has to read the notes on the backs of the student cards, and then phone potential volunteers. All too often we find out that a student's interests and availability have changed, and the search for a match starts again. I'm in favor of dropping data on interests and availability, which is so hard to keep current, and collecting e-mail (electronic mail) names instead. Hours of staff time could be saved by sending a single e-mail message about a volunteer opportunity and inviting interested parties to respond.

Intern   *I've noted your desire to exclude data on student interests and availability but retain local phone numbers and add e-mail names. Do you want to include local addresses?*

Director   Not for students. However, we do need to communicate by mail and fax with organizations needing volunteers.

Intern   *I'm confident that I understand what's needed to contact students interested in volunteering. With a computerized database, however, you can output information in ways that weren't possible with a manual system. What student-related information would you like to have that's not available now?*

Director   Let me toss a couple of ideas your way, and we can both be thinking about the details before meeting again tomorrow at noon. My top priority is to provide some recognition for outstanding service each month, but until now I've not had the resources to record volunteer hours, much less total them. The dean of students would like a summary of student volunteer activity by college or major each term. Once in awhile an organization will request a report showing all volunteer activity provided to that organization by our students within a specified time frame. I'd like to send a similar report to each organization every month. Students often ask me to write letters of recommendation. It would be very helpful if I could refer to a list showing volunteer activity of a single student, with information clustered by term or agency. How's that for a preliminary "wish list?"

Intern   *Using Access, those wishes can come true! If you will make sketches of the reports you'd like to have, we should be able to finish the student part of our design discussion over lunch tomorrow. Afterward I'll meet with your assistant who works directly with the volunteer organizations.*

As soon as possible after each interview, you should write your conclusions regarding database objectives and desired outputs. You should refer to these notes when you compose a ***database objective statement,*** which is one-paragraph explanation of the goal of the complete system, and develop a list of desired outputs.

Tip You may also find it helpful to mention your perceptions of information that won't be available with the new system. For example, users should clearly understand they will not be able to search the volunteer center database for the names of students whose interests and availability fit the needs of an organization needing volunteers.

Be sure to circulate among users the database objective statement, a list of desired outputs, and sketches of suggested reports. After users review, revise, and approve these preliminary design documents, you can start work on a data dictionary.

CREATING A DATA DICTIONARY

Once users clearly specify what they want for output, it's time to think about the data needed to produce the output. A good first step is looking over the sketches of desired reports and listing the data items that appear in each report. The next steps in the design process, considered by many to be the most difficult, involve separating the data items into some logical arrangement and planning enough tables to avoid entering data more than once.

Tip The formal procedure by which data items are grouped into tables and tables are grouped into databases is called *normalization*. In-depth information about the normalizing process can be found in texts on database design.

The data dictionary serves as a worksheet that defines the tables and field specifications in a database. You will use this worksheet when you actually create the database on the computer. Later the data dictionary can be used as a reference document to keep near the computer.

Figure 2.1 illustrates a data dictionary for the Volunteer Center database, with field names listed in the fourth column. Although you can specify up to 64 characters in a field name, including spaces, each name should be just long enough to describe the field.

Tip If you type an uppercase letter within a field name, Access automatically inserts a space before that letter whenever the field name appears on-screen or in printed output. For example, ContactFirstName will display as Contact First Name.

Table/Data Cross Reference			Field Specifications - Volunteer Center Database			
Organizations Table	Volunteers Table	Time Cards Table	Field Name	Field Size	Data Type	Comments
x		x	OrganizationID		Text	User supplied. Contains letter code such as HH (Habitat for Humanity) or MOW (Meals on Wheels). Primary key in organizations table: required in both tables
x			OrganizationName	30	Text	Full name of the organization such as Meals on Wheels
x			ContactFirstName	12	Text	Full name of contact such as Michelle
x			ContactLastName	15	Text	Last name of contact such as Fox, Smith-Jones, or Van Horn
x			Address	35	Text	Street address or post office box
x			City	20	Text	City such as Greenwood or Indianapolis
x			State	2	Text	2-digit state code; default value IN (for Indiana) may be edited
x			ZipCode	10	Text	Zip code such as 46299 or 46299-9999; controlled by an input mask
x			WorkPhone	14	Text	Phone number such as (317)111-1111; controlled by an input mask
x			FaxNumber	14	Text	Fax number such as (317)111-1112; controlled by an input mask
	x	x	Volunteer ID	12	Text	Social security number. Primary key in Volunteers table; required in both tables
	x		FirstName	12	Text	First name of student volunteer such as Eric
	x		LastName	15	Text	Last name of student volunteer such as Fox or Smith-Jones
	x		College	18	Text	Chose one:Arts & Sciences, Business, Education, Fine Arts, Pharmacy
	x		Major	30	Text	Major such as Marketing, Secondary Education, or Biology
	x		EmailName	20	Text	E-mail name/address in the form name@school.edu
	x		LocalPhone	9	Text	Phone while at school; controlled by an input mask
	x		Birthdate		Date/Time	Date of birth; controlled by input mask mm/dd/yy
	x		HasCar		Yes/No	√ = can provide transportation
		x	DateWorked		Date/Time	Date of volunteer service; controlled by input mask mm/dd/yy
		x	HoursWorked		Number	Total hours to nearest quarter hour such as 1.5, 3.25, 6, or 4.75

Figure 2.1

The three columns on the left constitute a table/data cross-reference that shows the planned distribution of fields among three tables named Organizations, Volunteers, and Time Cards. Each *x* represents a field in the associated table. For example, the four fields named OrganizationID, VolunteerID, DateWorked, and HoursWorked make up the Time Cards table. The remaining columns in the data dictionary provide information about field specifications.

> *Tip* You can create an electronic data dictionary using spreadsheet or word processing software. The data dictionary shown in Figure 2.1 was developed using the table feature in Microsoft Word for Windows 95.

In this project the critical task of developing the data dictionary has been done for you. However, before you create the tables identified in the data dictionary, let's look at the thought processes underlying table selection and field specifications suggested for the Volunteer Center database.

Caution Avoid skipping over or merely skimming through the next six sections so that you can "get to the good part" of working with the Access software. If you do not thoroughly understand the terms and design concepts involved, you will find it very hard to design a relational database on your own.

Organizing Data in Tables

Opinions may vary on the number of tables to set up for a given database. You should, however, follow some general guidelines to organize data in tables. To start with, look for data items that relate to the same subject and separate them from data items dealing with another subject. For example, analyzing interview notes and sketches of desired outputs from volunteer center staff reveals that some data items relate to organizations, while others describe students and their volunteer efforts. In this situation you should plan for at least one table for organization-specific data and at least one table for student-specific data.

You should then check that the tables you have in mind eliminate unnecessary duplication of data, sometimes referred to as ***redundant data.*** Setting up *organization*-related items in one table will not result in duplicate data. The name, contact person, address, phone number, and fax number for each organization will only be entered once. However, putting all *student*-related data items in one table would result in duplicate data. Some sample records illustrate the problem.

Imagine that a pharmacy student named Anna Weist volunteered 4 hours every other Friday during November for Meals on Wheels and 10 hours the Saturday before Thanksgiving on a Habitat for Humanity project. Consider how a table might look if you mix data describing a student (first name, last name, e-mail name, and college) with data describing that student's volunteer efforts (the volunteer organization, the date worked, and the hours involved).

First Name	Last Name	E-mail Name	College	Organization	Date Worked	Hours Worked
Anna	Weist	AWEIST	Pharmacy	Meals on Wheels	11/1/96	4
Anna	Weist	AWEIST	Pharmacy	Meals on Wheels	11/15/96	4
Anna	Weist	AWEIST	Pharmacy	Habitat for Humanity	11/23/96	10
Anna	Weist	AWEIST	Pharmacy	Meals on Wheels	11/29/96	4

The First Name, Last Name, E-mail Name, and College fields in the sample table contain redundant data. These details about a specific student should appear only once in the database. However, repeating the identity of an organization such as Meals on Wheels is necessary because this student or any other student can work for one organization many times.

Creating two student-related tables instead of one in the Volunteer Center database will eliminate unnecessary duplication of data. Look again at Figure 2.1. The fields in the Volunteers table will store data describing students, one record only for each student interested in volunteer work. A separate Time Cards table will store details of actual volunteer efforts, with one record per activity and multiple records possible for one volunteer.

Tip Plan to use coded data where possible. For example, being able to enter a code such as MOW instead of the full name Meals on Wheels would speed data entry in the Time Cards table where multiple entries are possible. Accuracy would likely improve as well because there are fewer characters to type.

Deciding on Primary Keys

A table's *primary key,* which can be one field or a combination of fields, makes each record unique. When you add new records to a table that has a primary key, Access checks for duplicate data and won't let you repeat data in the primary key field(s). Access won't let you leave a primary key field blank either, which helps ensure that you'll have only valid records in your table.

In the Volunteer Center database, you will designate OrganizationID (containing a unique code such as MOW for Meals on Wheels) as the primary key in the Organizations table, and VolunteerID (containing a student's social security number) as the primary key in the Volunteers table. You will not designate any field as a primary key in the Time Cards table because the same organization code, student ID, date worked, or hours worked can appear more than once.

Planning Links between Tables

What if the director of the volunteer center were to ask for a list of volunteer activity in the last month showing student names, the dates and number of hours worked, and the organizations receiving help? Generating this information requires first and last name data from the Volunteers table, date and number of hours data from the Time Cards table, and name data from the Organizations table.

You can output data from more than one table at a time if a common field provides a link between tables. According to the data dictionary in Figure 2.1, the Organizations and Time Cards tables have the OrganizationID field in common. The VolunteerID field provides the link between the Volunteers and Time Cards tables.

Tip When linking tables, you should link the primary key field from one table to a field in the other table that has the same data type (see the next section) and field size. However, the name of the common field does not have to be the same in both tables.

Assigning an Appropriate Data Type

As part of the data dictionary, you must decide which type of data each field will hold. Access data types include Currency, Date/Time, Number, Text, and Yes/No as well as several others that will not be specified in the Volunteer Center database. Figure 2.1 shows that the data type for most of the fields will be Text, which can store letters, numbers, spaces, or special characters. You will select Currency as the field type to display monetary data and Number as the field type to display most other numeric values. The Volunteer Center database will contain only one number field, the one storing hours worked in the Time Cards table.

Tip   You should specify Text as the field type if a field will contain only numbers that will never be used in calculations, such as social security numbers, zip codes, and phone numbers.

You should specify Yes/No as the data type if the entry in the field indicates Yes, No, True, or False. For example, Yes/No is the appropriate field type for the HasCar field in the Volunteers table, because the contents will indicate Yes, the student can provide transportation or No, the student cannot provide transportation.

If you will store dates or times in a table, you should select Date/Time as the data type. Doing so will allow you to vary display of the data. For example, you could display the 12th day of January in 1997 several ways including 1/12/97, 12-Jan-97, or January 12, 1997. As shown in Figure 2.1, you will assign this field type to the Birthdate field in the Volunteers table and the DateWorked field in the Time Cards table.

Estimating Field Size

Field size refers to the maximum space Access reserves for data. For all field types except Text and Number, Access determines a maximum size automatically according to the data type. For example, the size of a Yes/No field is 1. If the data type is Text, you can specify a field size from 1 to 255 or let Access assign the default size, initially set at 50.

Tip   You should assign a realistic field size but one that is as small as possible. For example, a maximum field size of 20 for a City field is more realistic than the default size of 50. Smaller field sizes require less memory and can result in faster processing.

If you specify Number as the data type, you will choose among predefined settings such as Integer or Single instead of specifying a maximum field size. The setting you select defines the smallest and largest numbers the field can hold as well as the maximum number of decimal places.

Adding Comments

A data dictionary should serve as a planning document, a worksheet guiding the creation of a database, and a reference for those who use the database. Therefore, remarks concerning field setup and contents should be an integral part of a data dictionary, as shown for the Volunteer Center database in Figure 2.1.

The time and effort you spend to organize data in tables, decide on primary keys, plan links between tables, assign appropriate data types, estimate field sizes, and provide comments will give you a clear picture of the database that you can present to users for approval. After users approve the data dictionary, you can see how much help Access wizards provide in converting design to reality.

CREATING THE ORGANIZATIONS TABLE USING TABLE WIZARD

Before you start to set up tables and fields, you should check to see if Database Wizard includes a predefined application that closely resembles the overall database design reflected in the data dictionary. Recall that you can make your selection from the 22 personal and business databases shown in Figure 1.2. A good match exists if the application you choose provides the tables you want and requires only a few field modifications.

If using Database Wizard to create a predefined application would produce tables, forms, and reports requiring a lot of revision, you can set up each object one at a time yourself, with or without the help of other wizards. Let's focus for the moment on creating a table using *Table Wizard,* which asks you questions and builds a table based on your answers.

You can work with Business or Personal sample tables in the Table Wizard dialog box. When you select Business in the lower-left corner of the dialog box, you will see names of business-related sample tables, as shown in Figure 2.2. You can choose among 25 business tables, including Contacts, Customers, Employees, Payments, Projects, Reservations, and Time Billed. If you select Personal in the lower-left corner of the dialog box, you can choose among 20 personal tables, including Household Inventory, Exercise Log, Rolls of Film, Service Records, and Video Collection.

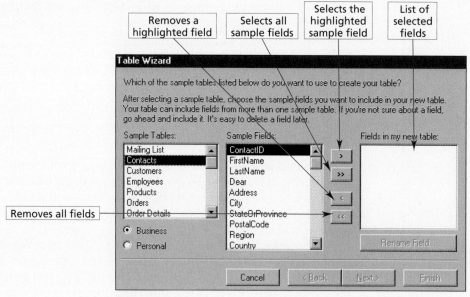

Figure 2.2

In the Table Wizard dialog box, the names of sample tables will appear in the Sample Tables list box on the left, the names of fields available for the selected table will appear in the Sample Fields list box in the middle, and the fields you select for your new table will appear in the list box on the right. General instructions appear above those three boxes. You will be looking for sample tables that resemble those specified in the data dictionary. A good match exists if a sample table you choose provides a number of the fields you need.

You will add or remove fields by double-clicking the name of a field or by using the four buttons between the Sample Fields and Fields in my new table boxes. The arrow on a button indicates the direction of movement. Selecting the button with a single arrow pointing to the right will copy the highlighted sample field name from the middle box to the box on the right. Selecting the button with two arrows pointing to the right will copy all sample fields. You will use the other two buttons to remove previously selected field names, either one at a time (using the button with a single arrow pointing to the left) or all at once (using the button with two arrows pointing to the left).

> **Tip**   If you will need only a few fields from a list of sample fields, select each field one at a time. If you need most of the sample fields, select all of them at once and then remove the ones you don't want to keep.

If you were to browse through the sample tables, you would find that the predefined Contacts table provides all the fields you need for the Organizations table in your Volunteer Center database. In the following sections you will use Table Wizard to create that table.

To create the Volunteer Center database:

1 Start Access.
The Microsoft Access dialog box appears.

> **Tip**   If Access is already active, close all open databases, choose New Database from the File pull-down menu, and select General if that is not the current folder in the New dialog box.

2 Select Blank Database, and then select OK.
The File New Database dialog box opens.

3 Type or point in the Save in list box the name of the folder where you want to store your database.

4 Type **Volunteer Center** in the File name list box, as shown in Figure 2.3 (Access automatically provides the .mdb extension).

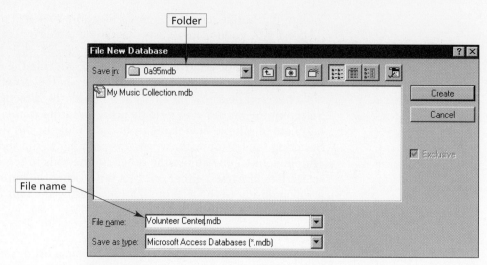

Figure 2.3

5 Select Create.

The Volunteer Center database dialog box appears on the screen with the Tables tab selected, as shown in Figure 2.4.

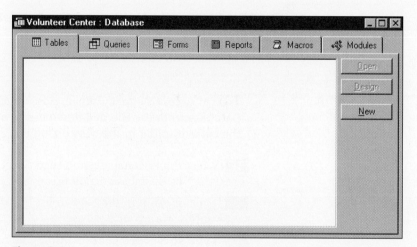

Figure 2.4

To create the Organizations table using Table Wizard:

1 Select New.

The New Table dialog box appears as shown in Figure 2.5.

Figure 2.5

2 Select Table Wizard, and then select OK.
The Table Wizard dialog box appears.

3 Select Business in the lower-left corner, and then select Contacts in the Sample Tables list box.
The three list boxes within the dialog box should match those shown in Figure 2.2.

4 Select the sample field ContactID and press the > button.
Access copies the selected field name from the Sample Fields list box to the Fields in my new table list box.

5 Copy the following field names from the Sample Fields list box to the Fields in My New Table list box in the order given: CompanyName, FirstName, LastName, Address, City, StateOrProvince, PostalCode, WorkPhone, and FaxNumber.

Tip Using a two-step process, you can insert the name of a sample field between two fields already listed for a new table. First select the field in the Fields in my new table list box that you want to precede the inserted field, and then double-click the desired field in the Sample Fields list box. For example, suppose you missed selecting the WorkPhone field in the previous step. To correct this omission, you would select the PostalCode field in the list box on the right and then double-click the WorkPhone field in the middle list box.

At this point you have selected the fields you want in a new table. Do not move to the next screen, however, until you change field names to match those in the data dictionary.

Renaming a Field

You can easily change the name given a sample field by selecting the field you want to rename, selecting the Rename Field command button, and then entering the new name in the Rename Field dialog box shown in Figure 2.6.

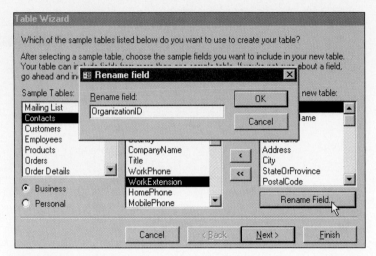

Figure 2.6

In the following steps you will change the names of selected fields to match those listed for the Organizations table in the Volunteer Center data dictionary.

To rename selected fields:

1 Select ContactID in the Fields in my new table list box.

2 Select Rename Field.

3 Type `OrganizationID` in the Rename Field dialog box, as shown in Figure 2.6.

4 Select OK.

5 Repeat steps 1 through 4 five times, renaming as follows:
Change CompanyName to `OrganizationName`
Change FirstName to `ContactFirstName`
Change LastName to `ContactLastName`
Change StateOrProvince to `State`
Change PostalCode to `ZipCode`

6 Scroll to the top of the list of selected field names and check that your renamed fields match those shown in Figure 2.7. Make corrections as necessary.

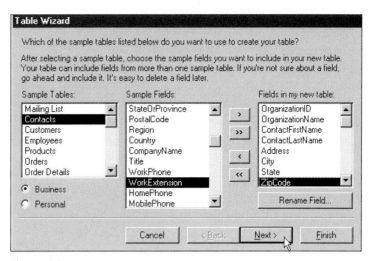

Figure 2.7

Now that you have selected fields for a table and renamed fields to match those shown in the data dictionary, Table Wizard wants to know the table's name and whether or not you will set a primary key.

Specifying a Primary Key

Recall that a primary key, which can be one field or a combination of fields, makes each record in a table unique. Table Wizard will set the key for you or you can specify your own. In the following steps you will name the new table and specify that the unique part of each record will be an organization code.

To name the table, set the primary key, and view the design:

1 Select Next>.

2 Type **Organizations** in the What do you want to name your table? box.

3 Select No, I'll set the primary key.
The settings in your Table Wizard dialog box should match those shown in Figure 2.8. Make corrections as necessary.

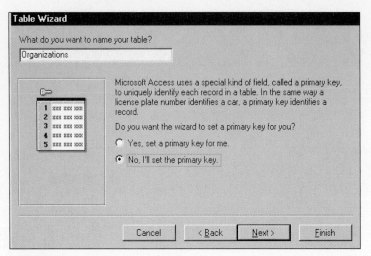

Figure 2.8

4 Select Next>.

5 Enter the specifications for field and type of data shown in Figure 2.9.

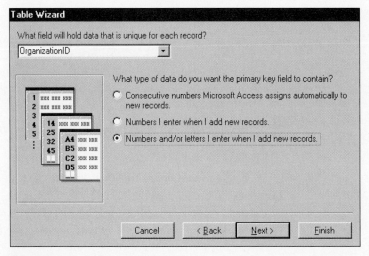

Figure 2.9

6 Select Next>.

Table Wizard indicates that you have supplied all the information necessary to create the Organizations table and asks you what you want to do.

7 Select Modify the table design, as shown in Figure 2.10.

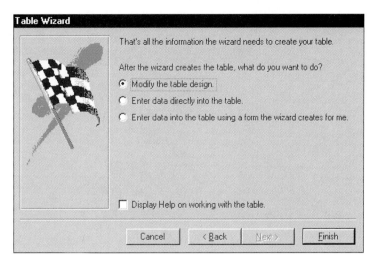

Figure 2.10

8 Select Finish.
Information about the Organizations table appears as shown in Figure 2.11.
The key symbol to the left of the first field name indicates that
OrganizationID is the primary key. You will work with field properties and
enter data in Project 3.

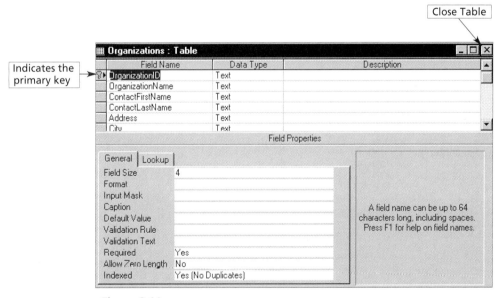

Figure 2.11

9 Close the table.
The Database dialog box appears as shown in Figure 2.12. At this time, the
Organizations table is the only object in the Volunteer Center database.

Close Database

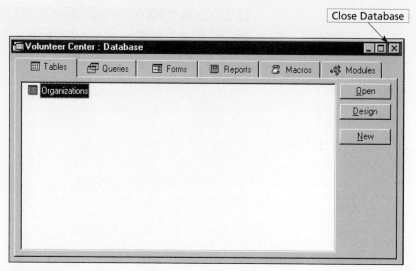

Figure 2.12

EXIT If necessary, you can close the database now. You can then exit Access and continue this project later.

CREATING THE VOLUNTEERS TABLE USING TABLE WIZARD

The Volunteers table will contain personal data about each volunteer. Table Wizard's Employees table can provide most of the fields you need. In the following sections you will use Table Wizard to create the Volunteers table and add a few fields on your own.

To select sample fields for the Volunteers table:

1 If necessary, start Access and open the Volunteer Center database.

2 Select New from the Database dialog box shown in Figure 2.12.

3 Select Table Wizard, and then select OK.

4 Check that Business is selected as the type of sample table, and then select Employees.

5 Copy the following field names from the Sample Fields list box to the Fields in my new table list box: SocialSecurityNumber, FirstName, LastName, EmailName, HomePhone, and Birthdate.

6 Change the name of the SocialSecurityNumber field to VolunteerID, and change the name of the HomePhone field to LocalPhone.
The fields in your new table should match those shown in Figure 2.13.

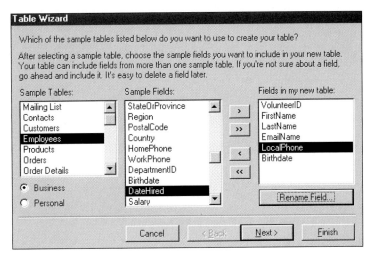

Figure 2.13

 7 Select Next>.

To name the table and specify a primary key:

1 Type **Volunteers** in the What do you want to name your table? box, and then select No, I'll set the primary key.

2 Select Next>.

3 Check that the settings in your dialog box match those shown in Figure 2.14.

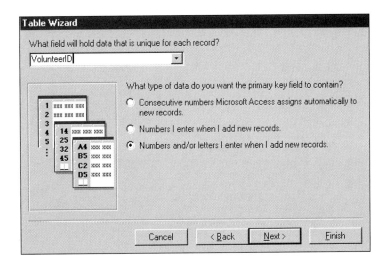

Figure 2.14

4 Select Next>.

A new Table Wizard screen appears, asking if this new table is related to any other table in the database, as shown in Figure 2.15. Access tells you that the new Volunteers table is not related to the Organizations table.

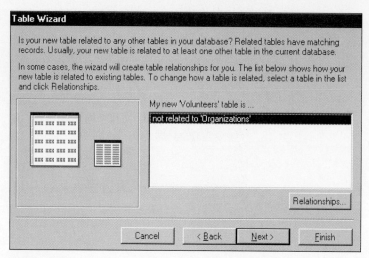

Figure 2.15

5 Select Next> to exit the current Table Wizard dialog box without defining a relationship.
Table Wizard indicates that you have supplied all the information necessary to create the Volunteers table and asks you what you want to do.

6 Select Modify the table design, and then select Finish.
Information about the Volunteers table appears as shown in Figure 2.16. The key symbol to the left of the first field name indicates that VolunteerID is the primary key.

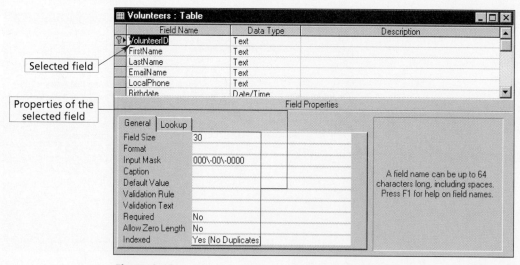

Figure 2.16

The Volunteer Center data dictionary indicates that nine fields are needed in the Volunteers table, as shown in Figure 2.1. You created six of those fields using Table Wizard. In the following sections you will insert the remaining fields.

Adding Fields

Figure 2.16 displays the Table dialog box in ***design view,*** in which you can create and modify the structure of a table. You can also display a table in ***datasheet view,*** in which you can view and modify data. You will switch between the two views to enter data in Project 3.

The design view of a table shows information about fields. Names and associated data types appear in the upper portion of the display, one field per row. Descriptions are not required but may help a user to understand the purpose and content of each field if the data dictionary does not already provide that information. The lower portion of the screen displays settings related to the selected field, such as its size and whether or not an entry is required in the field.

To add a field, you will type the new field name below the last field in the list. To insert a field, you can select Insert Row on the toolbar or choose Field from the Insert menu. Access will create a blank row above the current row. For example, Figure 2.17 shows the results of selecting Insert Row on the toolbar after positioning the pointer in the row containing EmailName.

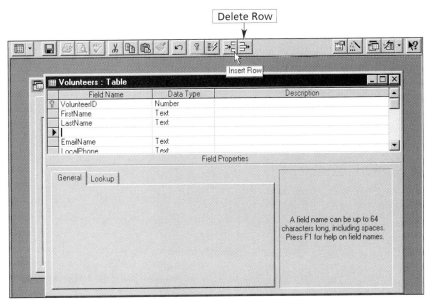

Figure 2.17

In the following steps you will modify the Volunteers table by inserting a text field between existing fields and then adding a Yes/No field.

Quick Fix If you insert a new field in the wrong place, you can eliminate it by positioning the pointer on the row you want to remove and selecting Delete Row in the toolbar.

To insert a field in a table:

1 Click within the field name EmailName.

2 Select Insert Row in the toolbar.

Access creates a blank row, as shown in Figure 2.17.

3 Type **Major** as the field name.

4 Click within the blank Data Type area to the right of the field name Major.

Text appears automatically as the data type.

5 Change Field Size to 30 as shown in Figure 2.18.

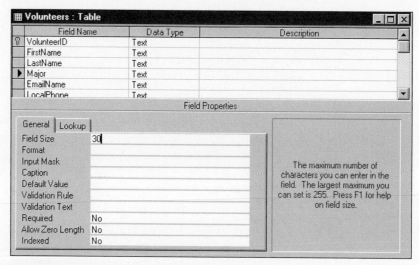

Figure 2.18

To add a field at the end of the table:

1 Scroll to the bottom of the Field Name list.

2 Type **HasCar** as the new field name in the first blank row after Birthdate.

3 Click within the blank Data Type area to the right of the field name HasCar.

4 Click the arrow to display the Data Type list box shown in Figure 2.19.

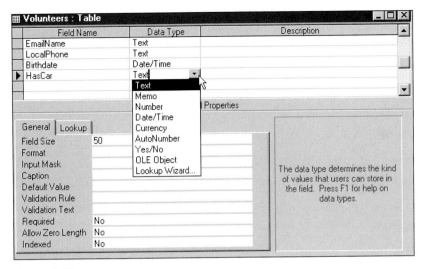

Figure 2.19

5 Select Yes/No as the data type.

6 Scroll to the top of the Field Name list.

Using Lookup Wizard

Access includes Lookup Wizard in the Data Type list box, as shown in Figure 2.20. *Lookup Wizard* creates a lookup column that allows you to choose a value from a list of values. Choosing a value instead of typing it saves time and eliminates typing errors.

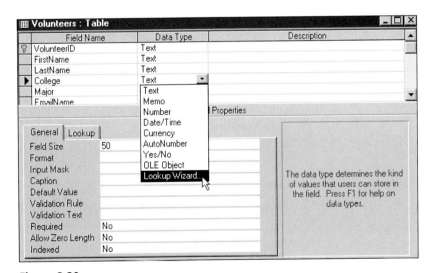

Figure 2.20

You can type the values that you want or tell Access to look up the values in a table. In the following steps you will insert a College field before the Major field in the Volunteers table, select Lookup Wizard, and type the college choices in a single column.

To create a lookup column using Lookup Wizard:

1 Click within the field name Major.

2 Select Insert Row in the toolbar.

3 Type `College` as the field name, move to the next column, and display the list of data types.
Your table dialog box should match the one shown in Figure 2.20.

4 Select Lookup Wizard.
The initial Lookup Wizard dialog box appears, in which you will specify where the lookup column will get its values.

5 Select *I will type in the values that I want*, as shown in Figure 2.21.

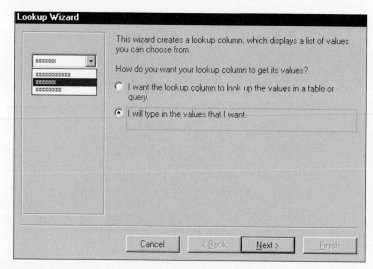

Figure 2.21

6 Select Next>.
Another Lookup Wizard dialog box appears. Instructions to specify the number of columns and change the width of a column appear at the top of the box.

7 Type `Arts & Sciences` for the first value.
Your dialog box should match the one shown in Figure 2.22.

Quick Fix If another dialog box appears requesting a name for the column, you pressed (ENTER) after typing the first value, which caused the next dialog box to appear. Select Back to restore the display shown in Figure 2.22.

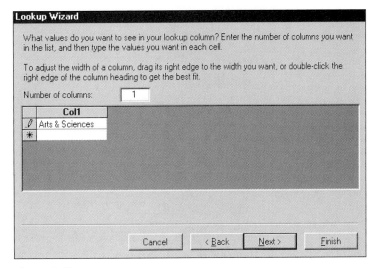

Figure 2.22

8 After clicking in the next blank box, type each of the other values shown in Figure 2.23.

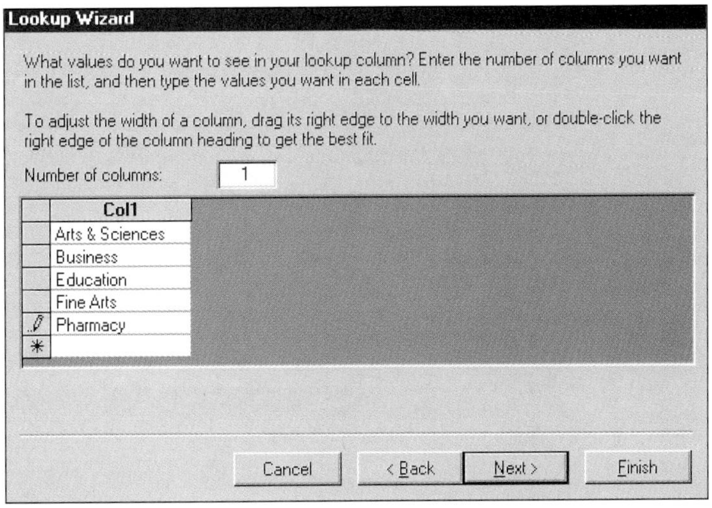

Figure 2.23

9 Select Next>.
The field name College appears automatically as the label for the lookup column.

10 Select Finish to exit Lookup Wizard without changing the suggested label.

11 Close the table, and select Yes when prompted to save the design changes.
Two tables appear in the Tables folder of the Database dialog box, as shown in Figure 2.24.

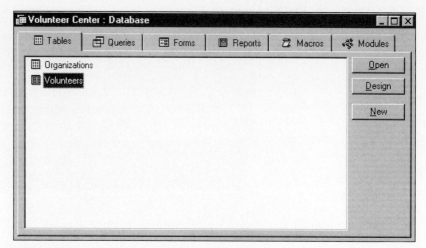

Figure 2.24

CREATING THE TIME CARDS TABLE

According to the data dictionary, the Time Cards table will contain only four fields. In this case you can create a new table on your own in less time than it would take using Table Wizard.

 To specify field names, data types, and field sizes in the Time Cards table:

1 Check that Tables is the active folder in the Volunteer Center Database dialog box, as shown in Figure 2.24.

2 Select New, select Design View, and then select OK.

3 Enter the field name, data type, and field size for the first field, as shown in Figure 2.25.

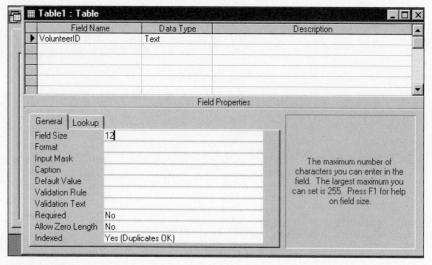

Figure 2.25

4 Type **OrganizationID** as the second field name, select Text as the field type, and change the field size to 5.

5 Type **DateWorked** as the third field name, and select Date/Time as the field type.

6 Type **HoursWorked** as the fourth field name, and select Number as the field type.

7 Select Field Size in the Field Properties area, and then click the arrow to display the predefined options shown in Figure 2.26.

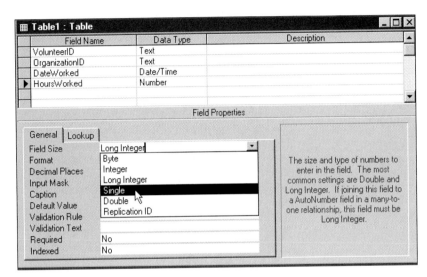

Figure 2.26

8 Select Single.

9 Change Decimal Places to 2.

Your field specifications should match those shown in Figure 2.27. Make corrections as necessary.

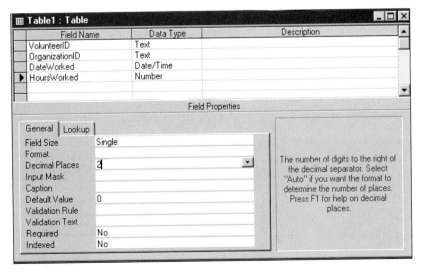

Figure 2.27

To close and save the table and then close the database:

1 Close the table.

2 Select Yes when prompted to save changes to the design of Table 1.

3 Type **Time Cards** in the Save As dialog box, and then select OK.

4 Select No when prompted to create a primary key.

Three tables appear in alphabetical order in the Tables folder of the Database dialog box: Organizations, Time Cards, and Volunteers.

5 Close the database.

THE NEXT STEP

You're beginning to get an idea of just how much work is involved to create a database on your own. In this project you learned that the design work you do before starting Access determines how effective the system will be in meeting your information needs. As a next step, find out all you can about database design. A good reference book on Access, with detailed explanations of design considerations for a sample company, can be a valuable resource.

You also created the basic table structure for the Volunteer Center database by specifying field names, data types, and field sizes. You can expand your knowledge by using on-screen Help to learn about other data types and find out what happens if you change the field size.

This concludes Project 2. You can either exit Access or go on to work the Study Questions, Review Exercises, and Assignments.

SUMMARY AND EXERCISES

Summary

- Designing a multiuser database generally involves stating database objectives, identifying desired outputs, and developing a data dictionary that shows the tables, fields, and relationships needed to accomplish the goals of the database.
- A properly designed database has sufficient tables set up to avoid unnecessary duplication of data, sometimes referred to as redundant data.
- A primary key makes each record in a table unique. Access won't let you repeat data in the primary key field or leave the field blank.
- You can output data from more than one table at a time if a common field provides a link between tables.
- Each field in a table holds a specific type of data. Access data types include Currency, Date/Time, Number, Text, and Yes/No as well as several others.
- Field size refers to the maximum space Access reserves for data. For all field types except Text and Number, Access determines a maximum size automatically, according to the data type.

- Access includes Table Wizard, which asks you questions and builds a business or personal table based on your answers.
- You can create and modify the structure of a table when the Table dialog box appears in design view.
- Lookup Wizard creates a lookup column that allows you to choose a value from a list of values. Choosing a value instead of typing it saves time and eliminates typing errors.

Key Terms and Operations

Key Terms
database objective statement
data dictionary
datasheet view
design view
field size
Lookup Wizard
normalization
primary key

redundant data
Table Wizard

Operations
Add or insert a field
Change field size
Create a table using Table Wizard
Rename a field
Select a data type
Set a primary key

Study Questions

Multiple Choice

1. Which of the following is an excellent way to start designing a multiuser database?
   a. Set up interviews with individuals who will use the system.
   b. Interview the people who designed the previous system.
   c. Design a sample system and see if the user likes it.
   d. Create a data dictionary.

2. Which is not a true statement related to following a formal process to design a multiuser database?
   a. The process can be tedious and time consuming.
   b. Output is generally available within a week.
   c. The process lessens the likelihood of major revisions.
   d. Approval of users should be obtained at several points.

3. Which action should you take with respect to interviewing a user?
   a. Write down your conclusions immediately following an interview.
   b. Tape the interview if the user agrees.
   c. Prepare a list of questions to help guide the interview.
   d. All of the above.

4. Which of the following is a one-paragraph explanation of the goal of a complete system?
   a. data dictionary
   b. database objective statement
   c. mission statement
   d. none of the above

5. What is the term describing a formal process in which data items are grouped into tables and tables are grouped into databases?
   a. data distribution
   b. normalization
   c. rationalization
   d. cross-referencing

6. Which of the following is a guideline for organizing data in tables?
   a. Group items that relate to the same subject.
   b. Group items in such a way as to eliminate unnecessary duplication of data.
   c. Group items so that they appear in alphabetic order.
   d. Both a and b.

7. Which is not a true statement about data types?
   a. Access data types include Currency, Date/Time, Number, Text, and Yes/No.
   b. If you do not specify a data type, Access assigns Number as the data type.
   c. Text fields can store letters, numbers, spaces, and special characters.
   d. If a field will contain only numbers, and the numbers will not be used for calculations, you should specify Text as the data type.

8. Which is not a true statement about the Table Wizard?
   a. Table Wizard asks you questions and builds a table based on your answers.
   b. Table Wizard contains business and personal sample tables.
   c. If you need most, but not all, of the sample fields suggested by Table Wizard, you can select all of them at once and then remove the ones you don't want.
   d. Table Wizard will create the forms necessary to enter data in the new table.

9. If you are entering data in a table, and social security number (SSN) is the primary key in the table, you can
   a. leave the SSN field blank in a record.
   b. enter the same SSN more than once.
   c. both a and b.
   d. None of the above.

10. Which of the following is an advantage of using coded data?
   a. improves data accuracy
   b. speeds data entry
   c. both a and b
   d. None of the above

Short Answer

1. What data type should you select for a field if you want to enter monetary data such as $5.50?

2. What is the next step in a formal design process after determining the objective of the database?

3. Name the design product that contains a list of fields with cross-reference to tables that you will refer to when you create a database.

4. Which wizard provides sample tables you can use to copy data fields into your own table definitions?

5. What field property sets the amount of space for data in a table?

6. Which wizard creates a lookup column that allows you to choose a value from a list of values?

7. If you select a field from a sample table but prefer a different name for the field, what action can you take?

8. Name the setting that makes each record unique in a table.

9. Which view mode shows information about fields?

10. What data type should you select for a field if you want to enter a zip code such as 43250?

For Discussion

1. Describe the major steps in the database design process. Include in your answer an explanation of why the design process focuses on outputs before inputs.

2. Explain the purpose and content of a data dictionary.

3. Discuss the purpose of organizing data into tables within a relational database.

4. Discuss the role of wizards such as Table Wizard. Include in your discussion how wizards can be of benefit even if they do not create the exact result that you need.

5. In this project you created a lookup column for college data in the Volunteer Center database. Explain the advantages of using the lookup feature, and give another example of how this feature might be used in the Volunteer Center database.

Review Exercises

The data dictionary shown in Figure 2.28 describes the design of the Job Search database, a multitable information system tracking job search efforts and results. Complete the following exercises to set up the three tables. In the Project 3 Review Exercises you will make a few more design changes and enter data in these tables.

Table/Data Cross Reference			Field Specifications - Job Search Database			
Companies Table	Applications Table	Interviews Table	Field Name	Field Size	Data Type	Comments
x	x	x	CompanyID	10	Text	User supplied. Contains letter code such as ABTECH. Primary key in Companies table; required in all three tables.
x			CompanyName	30	Text	Full name of the organization such as ABC Technologies, Inc.
	x		FirstName	12	Text	First name of person to contact such as Michelle
	x		LastName	15	Text	Last name of person to contact such as Fox, Smith-Jones, or van Horn
	x		Title	25	Text	Position of person to contact such as Human Resources Director
	x		Note: The applications table would not be complete without Address, City State and Zip Code Fields. However, you will omit these fields in the review exercise to reduce setup and data entry time.			
	x		SendDate		Date/Time	Date sent an application letter with attached resume
	x		OpenPosition	25	Text	Title of the open position such as Staff Accountant
	x		RatePerHour		Currency	Rate per hour up to two decimal places, such as $11.25 or $10.00
	x		InfoSource	20	Text	Lookup column: Placement Office Networking, Newspaper Ad
	x		ResponseDate		Date/Time	Blank field unless response received; enter date on response letter
	x		InterviewInvite		Yes/No	√ = invited to interview
		x	FirstName	12	Text	First name of interviewer
		x	LastName	15	Text	Last name of interviewer
		x	Title	25	Text	Position of interviewer such as Vice President of Marketing
		x	InterviewDate		Date/Time	Date of the interview
		x	StartTime		Date/Time	Start time of the interview
		x	Notes		Memo	Personal comments about the interview

Figure 2.28

Creating the Companies Table

1. Start Access, select Blank Database, specify where you want to store the new database, and name the database Job Search.

2. From the Tables folder of the Job Search Database window, create a new table using Table Wizard. Select Categories from the Business sample tables, and select both sample fields for the new table.

3. Change the name of CategoryID, to CompanyID, and change the name of CategoryName to CompanyName.

4. Type **Companies** as the name of the table, and specify that you want Access to set the primary key.

5. Specify that you want to modify the table design, and then change the data type of CompanyID to Text.

6. Change the size of Text fields to match those shown in the data dictionary.

7. Check your results against Figure 2.28, make changes as necessary, and close the table, saving your changes.

Creating the Applications Table

1. From the Tables folder of the Job Search Database window, create a new table using Design View.

2. Enter the field name, data type, and field size for each of the eleven fields in the Applications table as shown in the data dictionary in Figure 2.28.

Hints Be sure to start with the CompanyID field. Set two decimal places for the currency field RatePerHour. Use Lookup Wizard and type the values for the InfoSource field.

3. Close the table, save it using the name Applications, and select No when prompted to create a primary key.

Creating the Interviews Table

1. From the Tables folder of the Job Search Database window, create a new table using Design View.

2. Enter the field name, data type, and field size for each of the seven fields in the Interviews table as shown in the data dictionary in Figure 2.28.

3. Close the table, save it using the name Interviews, and select No when prompted to create a primary key.

Assignments

Viewing On-Screen Help on Table Wizard

Use Answer Wizard to look up *What is Table Wizard?* When the list of topics appears, read *Create a table*.

Using Help's Answer Wizard to Learn More about Other Data Types

Use Answer Wizard to read about Memo, AutoNumber, Currency, OLE Object, and Lookup Wizard fields. Write a brief description of each data type, including a description of the data type, and give an example of how it might be used.

Using Help's Answer Wizard to Learn about Changing Field Sizes

Use Help to look up information about field sizes. Write a brief description about changing numeric and text field sizes. Include in your discussion how to change the field size and the potential problems that can occur when you change the Field Size property.

Putting on a FundRaiser

Assume that your school, club, dorm, fraternity, or sorority is sponsoring a fund raiser. There will be contests such as darts, pitch and putt golf, and a walk-a-thon. There will be a picnic in the afternoon and a dance in the evening. Sponsors have agreed to contribute money for points earned for each event or mile walked. Naturally a database system will make your job managing the fund raiser easier. Using the skills you learned in this project, design a database system that will track events, sponsors, and participants. After you have completed the design process, use the data dictionary to create the database and its associated tables.

Objectives

After completing this project, you should be able to:

▶ Designate a field as required

▶ Specify an input mask

▶ Set a default value

▶ Assign a validation rule and associated text

▶ Define relationships among tables

▶ Create a form

▶ Enter and edit data in datasheet view and a form

CASE STUDY: COORDINATING VOLUNTEER ACTIVITIES II

Developing and using a database management system generally involves three phases: designing and creating the database, entering and editing data, and converting data into information. In your job as a summer intern for your campus volunteer center, you have nearly finished the first phase, which involved working with end users on design matters and creating three tables. Now you are ready to work on data entry concerns, taking advantage of built-in editing features and on-screen data entry forms.

Designing the Solution

The acronym GIGO (garbage in, garbage out) applies to database management. You cannot rely on information provided in reports if data are wrong or missing. Access allows you to customize fields in a table to help ensure that data are complete, accurate, and presented in a consistent manner. Figure 3.1 shows a Help screen displaying five customizing techniques you can apply to a field.

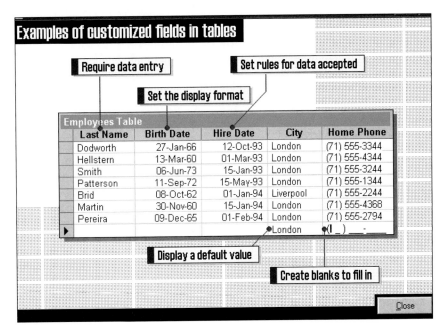

Figure 3.1

Other built-in editing features relate to common fields. For example, you can tell Access that a ***one-to-many relationship*** exists between two tables that share a common field. In a one-to-many relationship, data restricted to one entry in one table can be duplicated in its related table. Figure 3.2 shows the one-to-many relationships you should specify in the Volunteer Center database.

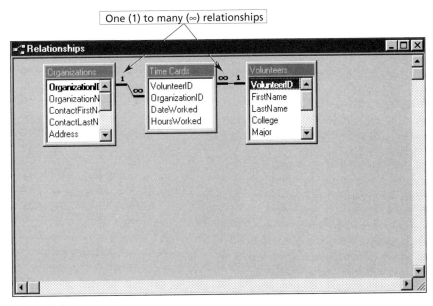

Figure 3.2

In the Volunteer Center database, you will set up one-to-many relationships among its tables. You will then be able to enter an identification code such as HH only once in the Organizations table, but that code will appear in the Time Cards table each time you add a record for a volunteer working at Habitat for Humanity. You will also be able to enter the social security number of a student only once in the Volunteers table, but that number will appear in the Time Cards table each time you record another volunteer activity for that student.

You can also enforce ***referential integrity,*** a set of rules that make sure relationships between records in related tables are valid. For example, if referential integrity is in force between the Organizations and Time Cards tables, you will not be able to enter an organization code in the Time Cards table unless that code has already been entered in the Organizations table.

You will enter data after you establish the field properties controlling data entry and define the appropriate relationships. You can enter data with or without the use of a form.

SETTING FIELD PROPERTIES

On-screen Help includes many topics related to field properties. Using Answer Wizard, you can gain a general understanding of five ways to customize fields in tables. You will then have most of the information you need to make changes in your tables.

To view on-screen Help about customized fields:

1 Start Access, and then select Cancel to close the Microsoft Access dialog box.

2 Choose Answer Wizard from the Help menu.

3 Type **field properties** in the Type your request box, and then select Search.

4 In the Tell Me About section, select *Examples of customized fields in tables,* and then select Display.
The Help screen shown in Figure 3.1 appears.

5 Click the vertical bar at the left end of *Require data entry,* and then read the explanation shown in Figure 3.3.

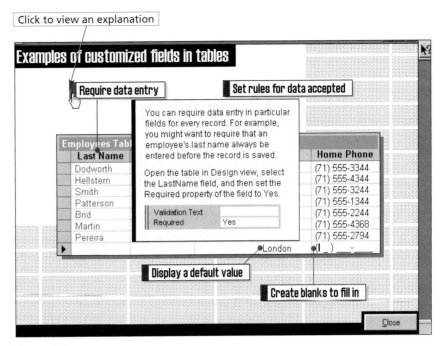

Figure 3.3

6 Click outside the explanation box.

7 Click the vertical bar at the left end of *Set the display format,* and then read the explanation shown in Figure 3.4.

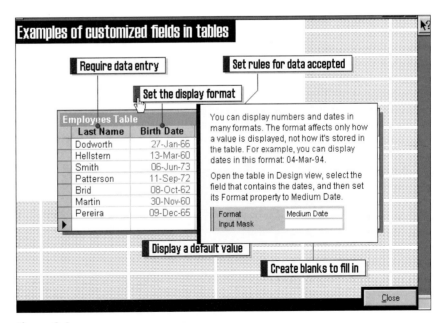

Figure 3.4

8 Click the vertical bar at the left end of *Create blanks to fill in,* and then read the explanation shown in Figure 3.5.

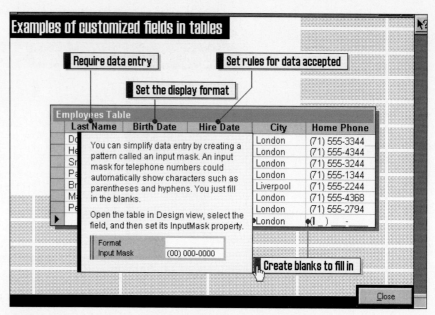

Figure 3.5

9 Click outside the explanation box.

10 Click the vertical bar at the left end of *Display a default value*, and then read the explanation shown in Figure 3.6.

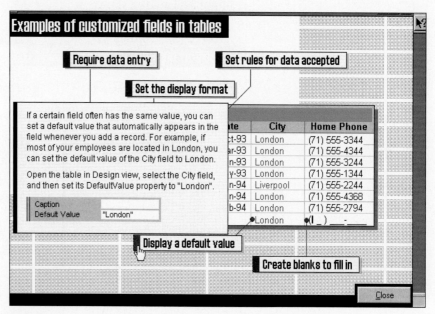

Figure 3.6

11 Click the vertical bar at the left end of *Set rules for data accepted*, and then read the explanation shown in Figure 3.7.

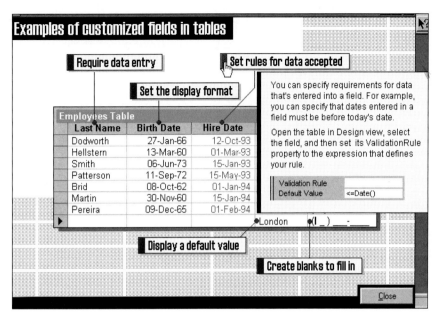

Figure 3.7

12 Select Close to exit on-screen Help.

In the following sections you will work in design view to set field properties in each table within the Volunteer Center database.

Designating Fields as Required

Every table has one or more essential fields, such as VolunteerID, FirstName, and LastName in the Volunteers table. Such a field should be set up as a *required field,* which means that Access will not save a new record in a table unless the associated data are present.

> **Tip** Other data you think are essential for desired outputs, such as e-mail name or birth date, may not be available when you want to enter a record in a table. If you do not designate the associated field(s) as required, you can enter the data you have and edit the record later.

You will set the Required property in the Field Properties section of a table in design view, as shown in Figure 3.8. Clicking the arrow at the right end of the Required box displays the two options Yes and No.

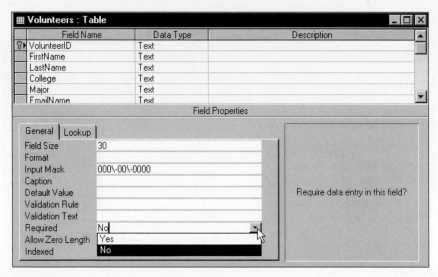

Figure 3.8

Tip Selecting Design in the Database dialog box displays the current table in design view, which allows you to edit field specifications. Selecting Open in the Database dialog box displays the current table in datasheet view, which allows you to add or edit data. To switch views, select the View icon that appears at the left end of the toolbar.

In the following steps you will specify as required only the most essential fields in the three tables of your Volunteer Center database.

To specify required fields:

1 Open the Volunteer Center database, and then open the Volunteers table in design view.
The first field VolunteerID is automatically selected.

2 Click in the Required box in the Field Properties section, and then click the arrow to display your options, as shown in Figure 3.8.

3 Select Yes to make VolunteerID a required field.

4 Set Required to Yes for the FirstName and LastName fields.

5 Close the table and save your changes.

6 Open the Organizations table in design view, and then set OrganizationName as a required field.

7 Close the table and save your changes.

8 Open the Time Cards table in design view, and then set all four fields as required fields.

9 Close the table and save your changes.

Specifying Formats and Input Masks

Access provides two field properties that produce similar results: Format and Input Mask. A *format* determines how a value is displayed, not how it is entered or stored in a table. You can apply a format to fields with AutoNumber, Number, Currency, Date/Time, Text, or Yes/No data types.

For example, Figure 3.4 shows the results of applying the Medium Date format to the Birth Date field. Figure 3.9 shows other predefined formats available for Date/Time fields.

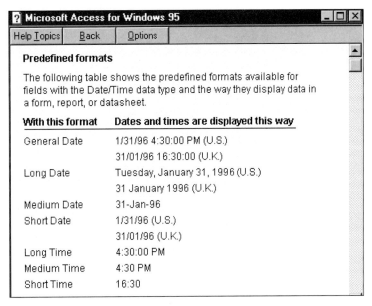

Figure 3.9

An *input mask* is a pattern controlling data entry, usually applied to text and date/time fields. The pattern may contain characters that separate data, such as parentheses and dashes, and characters that represent allowable data entry. For example, if you set up the input mask (000)000-0000 for a phone number field, Access will display the parentheses and dash, leaving blank spaces for you to enter a digit from 0 to 9 for each number in the area code and phone number. Figure 3.10 shows a Help screen that explains most of the input mask characters.

Character	Description
0	Digit (0 through 9, entry required; plus [+] and minus [-] signs not allowed).
9	Digit or space (entry not required; plus and minus signs not allowed).
#	Digit or space (entry not required; blank positions converted to spaces, plus and minus signs allowed).
L	Letter (A through Z, entry required).
?	Letter (A through Z, entry optional).
A	Letter or digit (entry required).
a	Letter or digit (entry optional).
&	Any character or a space (entry required).
C	Any character or a space (entry optional).
. , : ; - /	Decimal placeholder and thousands, date, and time separators. (The actual character used depends on the regional settings specified in the Windows Control Panel.)
<	Causes all characters that follow to be converted to lowercase.
>	Causes all characters that follow to be converted to uppercase.
!	Causes input mask to fill from right to left, rather than from left to right, when characters on the left side of the input mask are optional. You can include the exclamation point

Figure 3.10

Note that a zero in an input mask indicates required entry of a single digit, a 9 means that entry of a digit from 0 to 9 is optional, and an exclamation point causes an input mask to fill from the right as you enter data. Knowing these rules, you could change an input mask for a phone number to !(999)000-0000 if you anticipate that an area code will not be needed or available for some records.

You will set input masks in the Field Properties section of a table in design view. You can type your own data entry pattern or select among predefined patterns using *Input Mask Wizard.* In the following steps you will look at the Format and Input Mask properties set up by Table Wizard in the Volunteer Center database. You will also establish additional input masks in all three tables and adjust remaining Text field sizes to match those shown in the data dictionary.

Tip Make sure that common fields have the same Field Size and Input Mask properties in both tables.

To edit field size and input mask properties in the Organizations table:

1 Open the Organizations table in design view.

2 Change the field size of OrganizationID to 5.

3 Type **>CCCCC** in the Input Mask box, as shown in Figure 3.11.

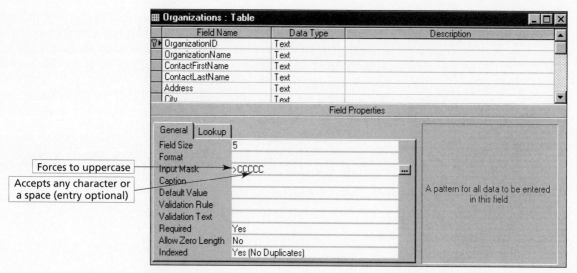

Figure 3.11

4 Select the State field.

5 Change Field Size to 2, and then type **>CC** in the Input Mask box.

6 Change other field sizes in the Organizations table to match those for Text fields in the data dictionary, as shown in Figure 2.1.

7 Close the table and save your changes.

To edit predefined properties for one field in the Volunteers table:

1 Open the Volunteers table in design view.

2 Change the field size of VolunteerID to 12.

3 Click within the Input Mask box in the Field Properties section.
A flashing cursor appears at the left end of the Input Mask box, and the Build button appears at the right end.

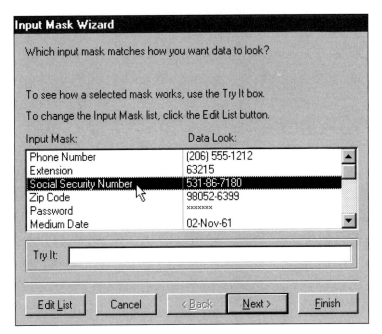

4 Click the Build button at the right end of the Input Mask box.

5 Select Yes if prompted to save the table.
A dialog box appears that asks you which input mask matches how you want data to look.

6 Select Social Security Number, as shown in Figure 3.12.

Figure 3.12

7 Select Next>.
A dialog box appears that asks if you want to change the input mask and set the placeholder character.

8 Select Next>.
A dialog box appears that asks how you want to store the data.

9 Select Without the symbols in the mask, as shown in Figure 3.13.

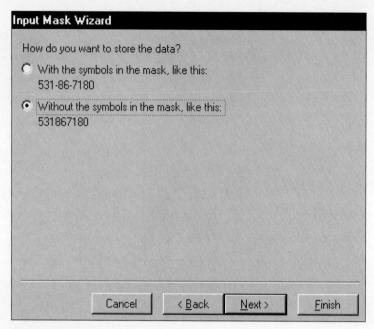

Figure 3.13

10 Select Next>, and then select Finish.

To view and edit other field properties in the Volunteers table:

1 Select the LocalPhone field.

2 Select the current input mask containing placeholders for area code, and then type **000\-0000** as the new input mask.

3 Change the field size of LocalPhone to 9.

4 Select the Birthdate field and note the Short Date format set by Table Wizard.

5 Select the HasCar field and note the Yes/No format set by Table Wizard.

6 Change other field sizes in the Volunteers table to match those for Text fields in the data dictionary, as shown in Figure 2.1.

7 Close the table and save your changes.

To edit field properties in the Time Cards table:

1 Open the Time Cards table in design view.

2 Select the VolunteerID field, click within the Input Mask box, and then select the Build button.

3 Select Yes if prompted to save the table.

4 Select Social Security Number as shown in Figure 3.12, and then select Next>.
A dialog box appears that asks if you want to change the input mask and set the placeholder character.

5 Select Next>, and then select Without the symbols in the mask, as shown in Figure 3.13.

6 Select Next>, and then select Finish.

7 Select the OrganizationID field, and then type **>CCCCC** in the Input Mask box.

8 Select the DateWorked field, and then select the Input Mask box.

9 Select the Build button, and then select Yes if prompted to save the table.

10 Select the predefined input mask Short Date, select Next>, and then select Finish.

11 Close the table and save your changes.

Setting Default Values

A *default value* appears automatically in a field when you add a new record. You can accept this value in the record or type a new one over it.

Setting default values will eliminate typing errors and save data entry time if the specified value is the one usually entered in the field. For example, the Organizations table of the Volunteer Center database includes City and State fields. Assume that most of the organizations served by the center are located in the city of Indianapolis and all of them are located in the state of Indiana. Setting Indianapolis and IN (the code for Indiana) as defaults will eliminate the need to enter those values in each new record. For the few times when the city is not Indianapolis, you can type the new name over the default.

A text default value must be enclosed in quotation marks, as shown for the State field in Figure 3.14. You will set several default values in the following steps.

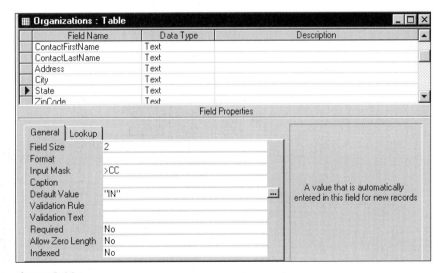

Figure 3.14

 To set a default value:

1 Open the Organizations table in design view.

2 Select the City field.

3 Type **"Indianapolis"** in the Default Value box (be sure to include the quotation marks).

4 Select the State field.

5 Type **"IN"** in the Default Value box, as shown in Figure 3.14.

6 Close the table and save your changes.

Now every time you add a record in the Organizations table, the City and State fields will already contain data. However, if you want to enter different data in either field, you can type over the default value.

Assigning Validation Rules and Text

Access provides some validation of data based on data type. For example, you cannot enter text in a number field or an invalid date in a date field. Access will halt data entry and display an error message if you enter a number other than 1 through 12 to represent a month, or you enter an invalid day such as 31 for the month of April.

You can also set your own validation rules in the Field Properties section of a table in design view. A *validation rule* determines whether or not data being entered in a field should be rejected. For example, a validation rule might specify that hours worked on a specific date cannot exceed 24. If you try to enter a number higher than 24, Access will not allow the data entry.

> **Tip** Although a validation rule is set up to reject data, you should write the rule in terms of what data are acceptable. For example, a validation rule concerning maximum hours in a day should be written as < =24, which means that acceptable hours are less than or equal to 24.

Validation text appears on the screen if attempted data entry violates a validation rule. If you do not specify validation text when you set up a validation rule, Access will supply a general error message.

In the following steps you will specify the validation rule and its associated text shown in Figure 3.15.

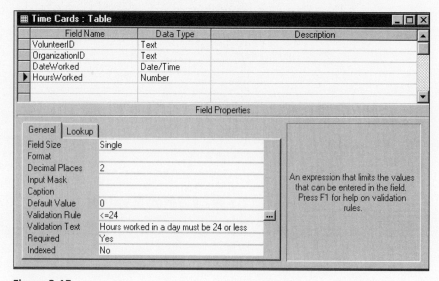

Figure 3.15

To work with validation settings in Field Properties:

1 Open the Time Cards table in design view.

2 Select the HoursWorked field.

3 Type `<=24` in the Validation Rule box.

4 Type `Hours worked in a day must be 24 or less` in the Validation Text box.

5 Check that your validation rule and text match those shown in Figure 3.15, and make corrections as necessary.

6 Close the Time Cards table and save your changes.

All essential field properties are now set. As soon as you specify relationships among the tables, you'll be ready to enter data.

 If necessary, you can close this database now. You can then exit Access and continue this project later.

DEFINING RELATIONSHIPS AMONG TABLES

You can specify relationships among tables by using the Relationships dialog box, accessed through the Relationships button on the toolbar. First you will add the tables you want to relate to the Relationships dialog box and then drag the key field from one table and drop it on the equivalent field in the other table. Figure 3.16 illustrates the process for establishing a relationship between the Organizations and Time Cards tables in the Volunteer Center database based on the common field OrganizationID.

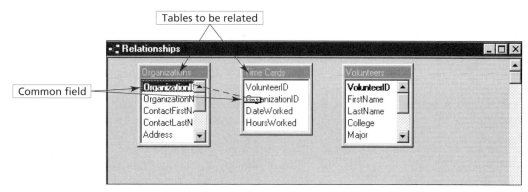

Figure 3.16

As soon as you release the mouse button from the drag-and-drop operation, Access will display the field and tables in the relationship and the relationship type. If the common field is a primary key in one table but not in the other table, the relationship type will be One-To-Many, as shown in Figure 3.17.

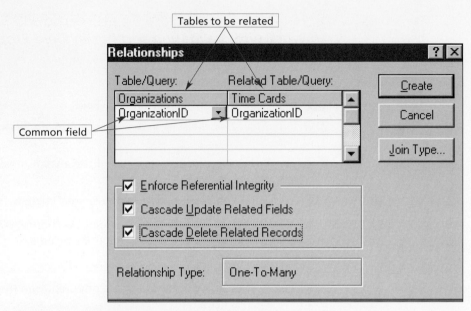

Figure 3.17

If you select Enforce Referential Integrity in the Relationships dialog box, Access applies a set of rules that makes sure relationships between records in related tables are valid. For example, if referential integrity is in force between the Organizations and Time Cards tables, you cannot enter a value for the organization code (OrganizationID) in the Time Cards table unless that value exists in the Organizations table. You also cannot change or delete an organization code in the Organizations table if there are records containing that code in the Time Cards table.

Checking the Enforce Referential Integrity box also gives you the option of updating related fields and deleting related records, actions that would normally be prevented by referential integrity rules. If you select Cascade Update Related Fields, Access will automatically update related records if you change a primary key. For example, if you were to change OrganizationID from MOW (Meals on Wheels) to MEALS in the Organizations table of the Volunteer Center database, Access would also change MOW to MEALS in each record of the Time Cards table. If you select Cascade Delete Related Records, Access will automatically delete related records if you delete a record in the primary table. For example, if you were to delete the record containing MOW in the Organizations table, Access would automatically delete all records containing MOW in the Time Cards table.

When you create a one-to-many relationship, Access displays a connecting line with two symbols, as shown in Figure 3.18. The 1 indicates that specific data can appear only once, while the ∞ symbol indicates the same data can appear many times. For example, you will enter the OrganizationID MOW only once in the Organizations table, but that same code can appear many times in the Time Cards table.

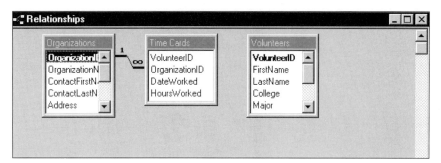

Figure 3.18

Figure 3.2 shows the relationships among tables in the Volunteer Center database. In the following steps you will create those relationships.

To add tables to the Relationships dialog box:

1 If necessary, start Access and open the Volunteer Center database.

2 Select Relationships in the toolbar (or select Relationships from the Tools menu).

A blank Relationships dialog box appears in the background, and you see the Show Table dialog box shown in Figure 3.19.

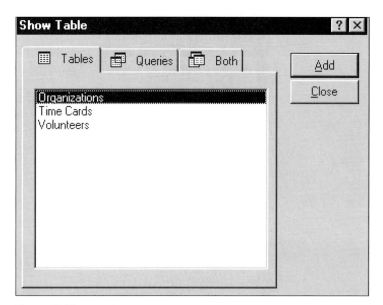

Figure 3.19

3 Select Add.

Access adds the Organizations table to the Relationships dialog box. You can see part of the field list in the background.

4 Select Time Cards, and then select Add.

5 Select Volunteers, and then select Add.

6 Select Close.

Three tables appear in the Relationships dialog box, as shown in Figure 3.20.

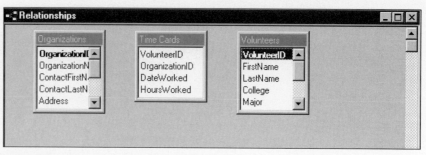

Figure 3.20

Tip You can also select a table by double-clicking its name. To select several tables at once, you can press and hold down (CTRL) click each table name you need, and then select Add.

To set relationships among tables:

1 Position the pointer on OrganizationID in the Organizations table, press and hold down the mouse button, and move the pointer to OrganizationID in the Time Cards table.
A small horizontal bar should appear on OrganizationID in the Time Cards table.

2 Release the mouse button.
The Relationships dialog box shown in Figure 3.21 appears.

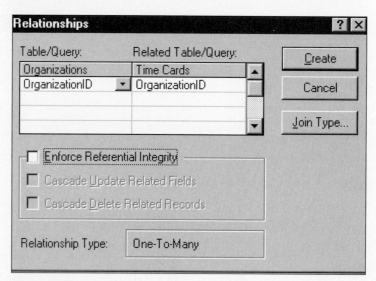

Figure 3.21

3 Select Enforce Referential Integrity.

4 Select Cascade Update Related Fields.

5 Select Cascade Delete Related Records.

Reminder Selected options appear with checkmarks.

6 Select Create.
Access creates a one-to-many relationship between the Organizations table and the Time Cards table based on the OrganizationID field, as shown in Figure 3.18.

Tip You can remove a relationship by clicking its connecting line in the Relationships dialog box and then pressing (DEL) If necessary, you can then specify another relationship.

7 Repeat the process described in steps 1 and 2 to connect the VolunteerID fields in the Time Cards and Volunteers tables.

Tip You can drag the VolunteerID field from the Volunteers table to the Time Cards table, or you can drag the field in the opposite direction. Access knows that VolunteerID is a primary key in the Volunteers table (primary keys appear boldface) and will set the one-to-many relationship in the proper direction.

8 Select the settings shown in Figure 3.22.

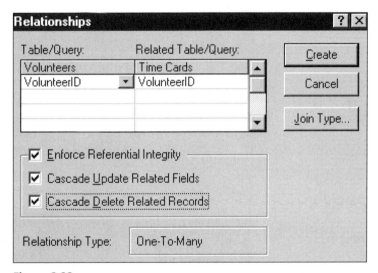

Figure 3.22

9 Select Create.
Access sets another one-to-many relationship, as shown in Figure 3.23.

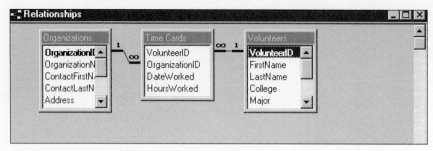

Figure 3.23

10 Close the Relationships dialog box and save your changes.

ENTERING AND EDITING DATA IN DATASHEET VIEW

In datasheet view, data are displayed in rows and columns. Each row is a complete record, and each column holds data for a field. Figure 3.24 shows the initial portions of three records in datasheet view. Moving the horizontal scroll bar allows you to see other fields.

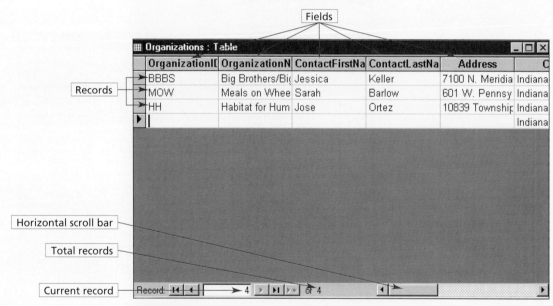

Figure 3.24

To enter data, you will click within the desired field and row and then start typing. You can press (TAB) or (ENTER) to move to the next field in the row. Generally, the data you enter in a table can be found on a *source document,* which is a standard paper form with spaces to enter details that vary from one record to the next. The Organizations Table Data Entry Form shown in Figure 3.25 is an example of a source document, in which data that you will enter in the Organizations table appear in italics.

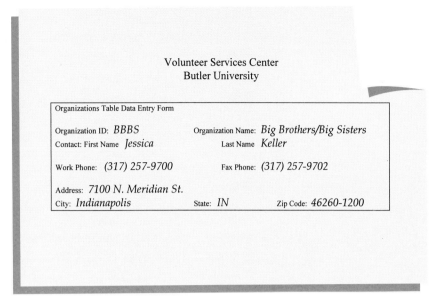

Figure 3.25

If you enforced referential integrity in one or more relationships, be sure to enter records in each table containing a primary key before you attempt to enter duplicate data in the related tables. In the Volunteer Center database, for example, you must enter records in the Organizations and Volunteers tables before you can enter social security numbers and organization codes in the Time Cards table.

In the following steps you will enter data for three records in the Organizations table of the Volunteer Center database. Data entry may seem a bit awkward because fields in the datasheet view are not in the same order as those in the source document.

To enter records in datasheet view:

1 Select the Organizations table in the Volunteer Center database, and then select Open.

An incomplete record 1 appears in datasheet view, as shown in Figure 3.26.

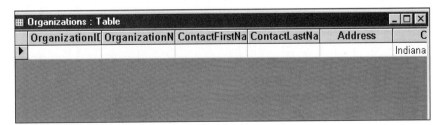

Figure 3.26

2 Type **bbbs** in the OrganizationID field, and then press ⌶TAB⌶

The letters in the OrganizationID field automatically appear uppercase due to the input mask controlling the field.

3 Type **Big Brothers/Big Sisters** in the OrganizationName field, and then press ⌶TAB⌶

Currently, the column is too narrow to display the entire entry; the contents scroll within the column as you type.

4 Type `Jessica` in the ContactFirstName field, and then press (TAB)

5 Type `Keller` in the ContactLastName field, and then press (TAB)

6 Type `7100 N. Meridian St.` in the Address field, and then press (TAB) three times to bypass the default entries in the City and State fields.

7 Type `462601200` in the ZipCode field, and then press (TAB)
Access automatically inserts the dash between the first five digits and the last four digits, as specified in the field's input mask.

8 Type `3172579700` in the WorkPhone field, and then press (TAB)
Access automatically inserts the parentheses around the area code and the dash between the first three digits and the last four digits of the phone number, as specified in the field's input mask.

9 Type `3172579702` in the FaxNumber field and press (TAB)
A blank record 2 appears.

10 Enter record 2 using Meals on Wheels data in the first of two source documents in Figure 3.27.

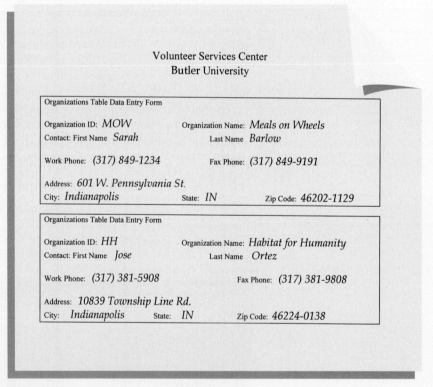

Figure 3.27

11 Enter record 3 using Habitat for Humanity data in the second source document in Figure 3.27.
The initial portions of three records appear as shown in Figure 3.24.

12 Close the Organizations table.

EXIT If necessary, you can close this database now. You can then exit Access and continue this project later.

Entering and Editing Data in a Form

The datasheet view of records is not easy to read if you cannot see all of the fields on one screen, as shown in Figure 3.24. A table may contain more fields than you want to work with during a routine editing session. The order of fields in datasheet view may not match the order of fields in the source document, thus slowing data entry.

You can improve the environment in which you add, edit, and view data by creating and using a form. Figure 3.28 illustrates a form displaying all fields for one record.

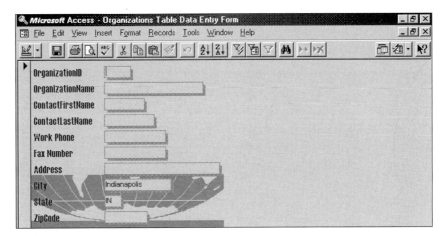

Figure 3.28

In Project 1 you entered data in one of the Music Collection forms you created by using Database Wizard. In this project you will create a form using Form Wizard, modify the form, and use the form to add more records to the Organizations table in the Volunteer Center database.

Creating a Form with Form Wizard

Form Wizard works much like Table Wizard, which you used in Project 2. You will start Form Wizard from the Forms tab in the Database window. First you will select each table or query containing the fields you need in the form (you will work with queries in Project 4). Then you will transfer the fields you want to include from the Available Fields box to the Selected Fields box, as shown in Figure 3.29. The order in which you transfer fields to the Selected Fields box is the order in which they will appear on the form.

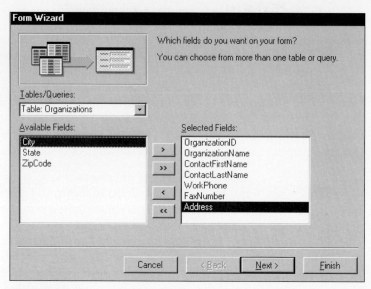

Figure 3.29

After selecting fields for the form, you will select among the following layouts: Columnar, Tabular, and Datasheet. If you want to view multiple records, one per row, you will select Tabular or Datasheet. If you want to view all fields for one record, you will select Columnar. In this view, fields display from top to bottom in a column, with additional columns added as necessary.

In the following steps you will use Form Wizard to create a columnar form to display data from the Organizations table in the Volunteer Center database. You will select the fields one at a time, so that the order of fields matches that shown in the Organizations Table Data Entry Form. Finally, you will add one record using this form.

To create a columnar form:

1 If necessary, start Access and open the Volunteer Center database.

2 Select the Forms tab, and then select New.
The New Form dialog box appears.

3 Select Form Wizard from the list at the right side of the box.

4 Click the arrow shown in Figure 3.30.

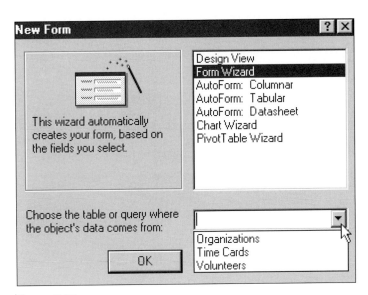

Figure 3.30

5 Select Organizations from the pull-down list, and then select OK. The initial Form Wizard dialog box appears as shown in Figure 3.31.

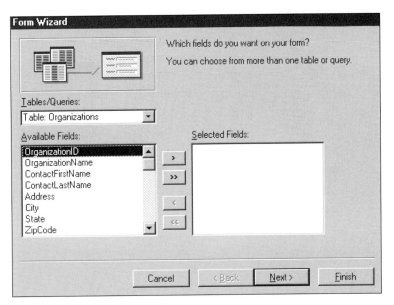

Figure 3.31

6 Select the following fields from the Available Fields box in the order given: OrganizationID, OrganizationName, ContactFirstName, ContactLastName, WorkPhone, FaxNumber, Address, City, State, and ZipCode.

> *Reminder*   To select a field, double-click its name in the Available Fields box, or highlight the field name and click the Next> button. To remove a field, double-click its name in the Selected Fields box, or highlight the field name and click the <Back button.

7 Check that your Selected Fields box includes the appropriate fields in the proper order as shown in Figure 3.32. Make changes as necessary.

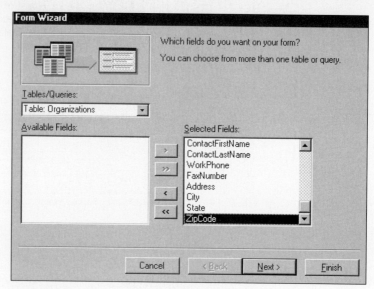

Figure 3.32

8 Select Next>.
Form Wizard displays a dialog box for selecting a layout.

9 Select Columnar, and then select Next>.
Form Wizard displays a dialog box for selecting a background style.

10 Select International, and then select Next>.
Form Wizard displays a dialog box for naming the form.

11 Enter the title and setting shown in Figure 3.33.

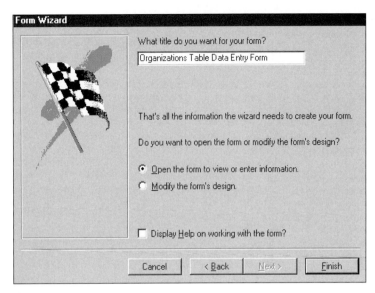

Figure 3.33

12 Select Finish.
Access displays the first record in the Organizations table in columnar form, as shown in Figure 3.34.

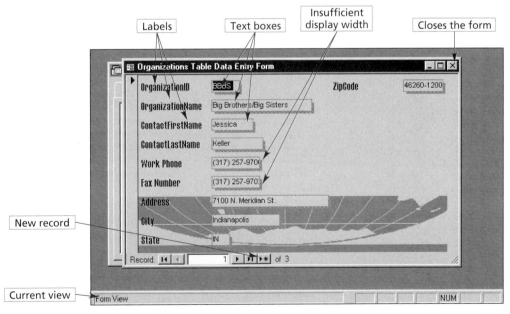

Figure 3.34

The contents of each field appear in text boxes down a column in the order selected. Descriptive labels appear to the left of the text boxes. Although the Work Phone and Fax Number text boxes on the form are not wide enough to display all the data, the field widths defined in the table structure are sufficient to store the data you enter.

To enter a record in the columnar form:

1 Click New Record, the last of the buttons at the bottom of the form.

2 Enter the data shown in Figure 3.35, pressing ⌈TAB⌉ or ⌈ENTER⌉ to advance to the next field.

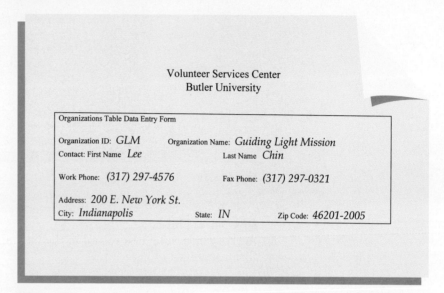

Volunteer Services Center
Butler University

Organizations Table Data Entry Form

Organization ID: *GLM*   Organization Name: *Guiding Light Mission*
Contact: First Name *Lee*   Last Name *Chin*

Work Phone: *(317) 297-4576*   Fax Phone: *(317) 297-0321*

Address: *200 E. New York St.*
City: *Indianapolis*   State: *IN*   Zip Code: *46201-2005*

Figure 3.35

3 Close the form by clicking the X button in the upper-right corner of the dialog box, as shown in Figure 3.34.
The name Organizations Table Data Entry Form appears on the Forms tab in the Database window.

Modifying a Form

You may want to make changes to a form created by Form Wizard, such as adding or deleting a field, moving one or more fields to make the form match a source document, or increasing the display width of a field. Perhaps you'd like to change a label describing a text box, add a background picture, or vary font style and size. You can make such changes to a form in design view.

Figure 3.36 shows the Organizations Table Data Entry Form in design view with the WorkPhone field selected for sizing. In the following steps you will slightly widen the display of the WorkPhone and FaxNumber fields so that all data are in view.

Tip If the Toolbox blocks part of the design work area, you can click its title and drag it to another location.

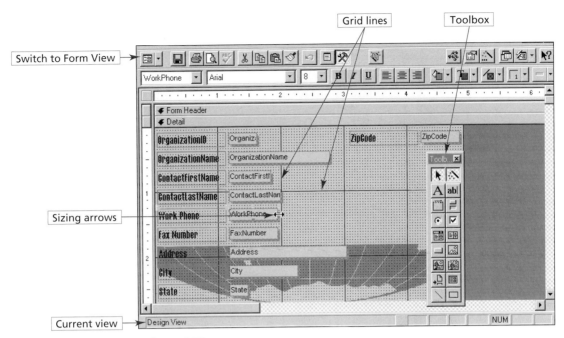

Figure 3.36

To size a text box on a form:

1 Open the Organizations Table Data Entry Form in design view.

2 Click Maximize in the upper-right corner to enlarge the work surface.

3 Click within the Work Phone text box to select it, and then move the pointer to the right border of the text box.
The sizing arrows appear as shown in Figure 3.36.

4 Drag the right side of the text box several spaces past the grid line on the right, and then release the mouse button.

5 Repeat steps 3 and 4 to increase the size of the Fax Number text box.

6 Click outside the Fax Number text box to deselect it.

7 Check that your Work Phone and Fax Number text boxes display widths similar to those shown in Figure 3.37, and resize if necessary.

Resized text boxes

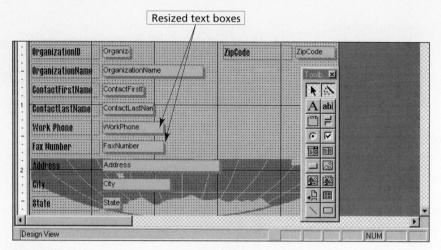

Figure 3.37

8 Switch to form view, click New Record, and then enter the record shown in Figure 3.38.

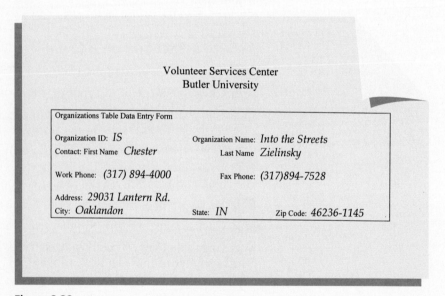

Figure 3.38

9 Close the form and save your design changes.

Data entry in the Organizations table is complete. In the final section of this project, you will create and use data entry forms for the other two tables in the Volunteer Center database.

COMPLETING DATA ENTRY

Generally, you can start data entry with actual data if a table has a primary key based on a single field and if that table has a small number of records in comparison to other tables. The Organizations table in the Volunteer Center database fits this description, and you can assume that it contains actual data.

If a table could have hundreds or thousands of records, such as the Volunteers or Time Cards table, respectively, you should start data entry with data that will test output. For example, suppose that student volunteers are enrolled in one of five colleges, and you want to group records by college in a report. To test grouping, it is sufficient to enter test data for just two colleges, with several volunteer records for each of those two colleges. You can then design and test the desired report to make sure that changes do not have to be made to the structure of the table. With careful planning, you can generally check for output problems with fewer than 50 test records. You can then delete the test records and enter actual data.

> **Tip** You should also include data that will test the data entry process. For example, try to leave a required field blank or attempt to enter duplicate data in a primary key field.

With minimal instruction in the following steps, you will create a data entry form for the Volunteers table and use the form to enter test data in 5 records. You will then enter test data in the Time Cards table, adding 25 records in datasheet view. Refer to instructions in prior sections if you cannot remember how to do a specific task.

 To create the Volunteers Table Data Entry Form:

1 Select the Forms tab, and then select New.

2 Make the wizard and table selections shown in Figure 3.39.

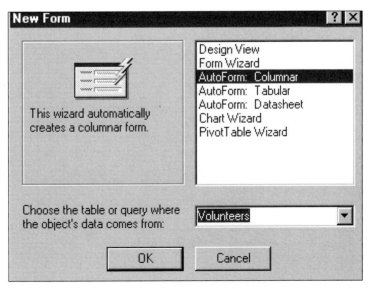

Figure 3.39

3 Select OK.

AutoForm Wizard automatically creates a form and displays the first record, as shown in Figure 3.40. The form displays all fields in the table in the same order as found in datasheet view, except the fields display down a column instead of across a row.

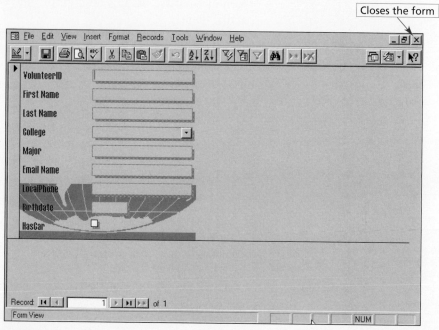

Figure 3.40

 To enter records and save the form:

1 Enter the VolunteerID, First Name, and Last Name data shown in Figure 3.41.

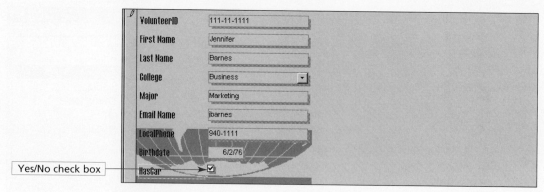

Figure 3.41

2 Click the arrow at the right end of the College text box, and select Business from the pull-down list.

3 Enter the Major, Email Name, LocalPhone, and Birthdate data shown in Figure 3.41.

Reminder   Enter leading zeros in dates. When you enter 060276, Access displays 6/2/76.

4 Click the HasCar check box to indicate Yes.
A checkmark appears in the box.

5 Enter the four additional records shown in Table 3.1.

Field	Record 2	Record 3	Record 4	Record 5
VolunteerID	222-22-2222	333-33-3333	444-44-4444	555-55-5555
FirstName	Tonya	Tom	Michael	Nathan
LastName	Wilson	Long	Barnes	Smith
College	Business	Arts & Sciences	Arts & Sciences	Business
Major	Accounting	Psychology	Biology	Marketing
EmailName	twilson	tlong	mbarnes	nsmith
LocalPhone	940-2222	940-3333	940-4444	940-5555
Birthdate	12/12/77	5/13/77	10/17/78	11/20/76
HasCar	Yes	No	Yes	No

Table 3.1

6 Click the X button in the upper-right corner of the form window to close the Volunteers form, and then select Yes when prompted to save changes to the design of the form.

7 Type **Volunteers Table Data Entry Form** in the Save As dialog box, and then select OK.
The names of two forms appear on the Forms tab of the Database window.

To enter records in the Time Cards table:

1 Select the Tables tab in the Database window, select the Time Cards table, and then select Open.

2 Enter the records shown in Table 3.2.

Record	VolunteerID	OrganizationID	Date Worked	Hours Worked
1	111-11-1111	BBBS	1/3/96	2.5
2	111-11-1111	MOW	1/5/96	4
3	111-11-1111	HH	1/15/96	10
4	111-11-1111	BBBS	1/17/96	4
5	222-22-2222	MOW	1/10/96	3
6	222-22-2222	HH	1/15/96	12
7	222-22-2222	BBBS	1/17/96	3
8	222-22-2222	HH	1/22/96	8
9	222-22-2222	IS	2/25/96	4
10	222-22-2222	BBBS	2/28/96	4
11	333-33-3333	MOW	2/6/96	3
12	333-33-3333	MOW	2/13/96	3.5
13	333-33-3333	MOW	2/20/96	3
14	333-33-3333	IS	2/25/96	8
15	333-33-3333	MOW	2/27/96	3.5
16	444-44-4444	GLM	1/13/96	6
17	444-44-4444	GLM	1/20/96	5
18	444-44-4444	GLM	1/27/96	8
19	444-44-4444	IS	2/25/96	5
20	555-55-5555	GLM	1/6/96	4
21	555-55-5555	GLM	1/13/96	10
22	555-55-5555	HH	1/15/96	6
23	555-55-5555	GLM	1/20/96	5.5
24	555-55-5555	HH	1/22/96	6
25	555-55-5555	IS	1/25/96	8

Table 3.2

Quick Fix If you get an error message that referential integrity rules require a matching record in a table, check that field sizes and input masks for the common fields are identical.

3 Close the table, and then close the database.

THE NEXT STEP

In this project you learned how to set most of the field properties in a table and set a one-to-many relationship between tables. As a next step, use on-screen Help to find out all you can about the Caption, Allow Zero Length, and Indexed field properties as well as the one-to-one and many-to-many relationships.

You also created columnar forms using Form Wizard and AutoForm Wizard. Try using the same techniques to create tabular forms. If you also take a look at datasheet forms, you'll have a better idea of your options to enter and edit data.

This concludes Project 3. You can either exit Access or go on to work the Study Questions, Review Exercises, and Assignments.

SUMMARY AND EXERCISES

Summary

- By setting field properties, you can help ensure that data are complete, accurate, and presented in a consistent manner.
- If you specify Required as a field property, Access will not save a record that does not contain the required data.
- The Format field property determines how a value is displayed, not how it is entered or stored in a table.
- The Input Mask property controls data entry through a pattern for allowable characters, such as (999)000-0000 for an optional area code with a dash automatically separating the first three and last four digits of a phone number.
- If you set Default Value as a field property, the value you specify appears automatically in a field when you add a new record.
- You can set Validation Rule and Validation Text field properties. A validation rule determines whether or not data being entered in a field should be rejected. Validation text appears on the screen if attempted data entry violates a validation rule.
- Tables are related if the same data can be entered in both tables. A one-to-many relationship exists if data restricted to one entry in one table can appear many times in its related table.
- Referential integrity refers to a set of rules that make sure relationships among records in related tables are valid.
- You can enter and edit data in datasheet view or a form. A form contains only the fields you specify in the order selected.
- Using Form Wizard, you can create a columnar, tabular, or datasheet form. You can modify a form in design view.

Key Terms and Operations

Key Terms
default value
format
input mask
Input Mask Wizard
one-to-many relationship
referential integrity
required field
source document
validation rule
validation text

Operations
Designate a field as
   required
Specify an input mask on your own
Select a predefined input mask
Set a default value
Specify a validation rule and
   associated text
Define a one-to-many relationship
   between tables
Enforce referential integrity
Enter data in datasheet view
Create columnar forms using Form
   Wizard and AutoForm Wizard
Modify a form by resizing a text box
Enter test data

Study Questions

Multiple Choice

1. Which is not a phase in developing and using a database management system?
   a. designing and creating the database
   b. entering and editing data
   c. selecting the font used to display data
   d. converting data into information

2. GIGO means
   a. garbage in, garbage out.
   b. general input, general output.
   c. that you cannot rely on information in reports if the data are wrong or missing.
   d. Both a and c.

3. Which is not an action that controls data entry?
   a. set the display format
   b. set rules for data accepted
   c. create blanks to fill in
   d. display a default value

4. Which is a true statement about required fields?
   a. Access will not save a record unless data in required fields are present.
   b. The Required property is set in the design view of a table.
   c. Data in a Required field cannot be edited later.
   d. Both a and b.

5. The Format property serves what purpose?
   a. determines how a value displays
   b. controls data entry
   c. is used with date/time fields only
   d. All of the above.

6. Which is not a true statement about default values?
   a. Default values appear automatically in a field when you add a record.
   b. A default value cannot be typed over.
   c. Setting a default value will save data entry time.
   d. Default values reduce typing errors.

7. Access validates data
   a. based on data type.
   b. based on validation rules you specify as field properties.
   c. by rejecting data and displaying an error message on the screen.
   d. All of the above.

8. If you select Enforce Referential Integrity,
   a. Access checks the integrity of the data entered in each data field.
   b. Access applies a set of rules that make sure relationships between records in related tables are valid.
   c. Access automatically spell checks data as it is entered.
   d. Both a and b.

9. When you enter and edit data in datasheet view,
   a. data display in rows and columns.
   b. data in each column represent a complete record.
   c. each row holds data for a field.
   d. Both b and c.

10. Which is not a layout offered by AutoForm Wizard?
   a. Columnar
   b. Tabular
   c. Object Linking and Embedding
   d. Datasheet

Short Answer

1. _____ integrity refers to a set of rules that make sure relationships between records in related tables are valid.

2. What field property would you set to prevent saving a new record in a table unless the associated data were present?

3. What field property, other than Input Mask, determines how data are displayed?

4. Which two data types are most associated with input masks?

5. Although a validation rule is set up to reject data, how should you write the rule?

6. How do you set a relationship between two tables?

7. How do you remove a relationship between two tables?

8. What two views allow you to enter data in a table?

9. What two benefits do default values provide?

10. You can use two methods to select a field name from the Available Fields box. Highlighting the field and clicking the Next> button is one method. What is the other method?

For Discussion

Answer the following discussion questions in the context of a new situation. Assume that you provide lawn care services during the summer. Your business is expanding, so you plan to set up a two-table Access database named Lawn Care to keep track of it. One table named Customers will contain one record per customer, with fields showing customer number, name, address, and phone number data. The other table named Services will track the type of service performed, date performed, time involved, and fee charged.

1. Discuss the purpose of the Required field property. What fields in the Customers and Services tables would likely be set as required fields?

2. What is an input mask? What input masks might you specify in the Lawn Care database?

3. What is a one-to-many relationship? Assume that such a relationship exists between the two tables in the Lawn Care database, based on the contents of a customer number field. Explain which table would be the "one" portion of the relationship and which table would be the "many" portion of the relationship.

4. Explain referential integrity. Give an example of data entry that would not be allowed if referential integrity were enforced in the Lawn Care database.

5. Describe two ways that you could enter a record in the Customers table.

Review Exercises

Project 2 review exercises involved creating three tables in the Job Search database, a multitable information system tracking job search efforts and results. In these review exercises you will modify several field properties, set relationships, create forms, and enter data.

Modifying Field Properties

1. Start Access and open the Job Search database.

2. Open the Companies table in design view, type >CCCCCCCCCC as the input mask for the CompanyID field, and specify that CompanyID is a required field.

3. Close the table, saving your changes.

4. Open the Applications table in design view, type >CCCCCCCCCC as the input mask for the CompanyID field, and specify that CompanyID is a required field.

5. Set a Short Date input mask for the SendDate and ResponseDate fields, and then close the table and save your changes.

6. Open the Interviews table in design view, type >CCCCCCCCCC as the input mask for the CompanyID field, and specify that CompanyID is a required field.

7. Set a Short Date input mask for the InterviewDate field and a Medium Time input mask for the StartTime field.

8. Close the table and save your changes.

Setting Relationships

1. Specify the relationships shown in Figure 3.42.

Tip If one or more tables do not appear when you select Relationships in the toolbar, you can select Show Table from the Relationships menu, and then add any missing tables before specifying the relationships.

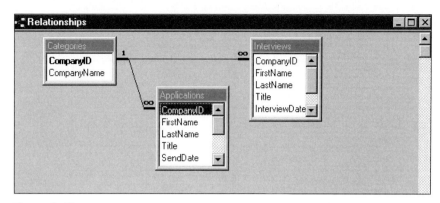

Figure 3.42

2. Close the Relationships dialog box and save your changes.

Creating Forms

1. Select the Forms tab, select New, and then select AutoForm: Columnar and the Companies table.

2. Adjust display widths of fields as needed, close the form, and save your changes using the name Enter company codes and names.

3. Repeat steps 1 and 2 to create a form based on the Applications table. Name the form Enter initial contacts and responses.

4. Repeat steps 1 and 2 to create a form based on the Interviews table. Name the form Enter interviews and results.

Using Forms to Enter Data

1. Open the Enter company codes and names form, enter the data shown in Table 3.3, and then close the form.

Record	Company ID	Company Name
1	ABCTECH	ABC Technologies, Inc.
2	SUN	Sun Landscaping
3	A1FLAG	A1 Flag Specialties, Inc.
4	KELLY	Kelly Personnel Services
5	ADP	ADP Processing, Inc.
6	SNELL	Snell & Snell Associates
7	WALKER	Walker Research

Table 3.3

2. Open the Enter initial contacts and responses form, enter the data shown in Tables 3.4 and 3.5, and then close the form.

Field	Record 1	Record 2	Record 3	Record 4
CompanyID	ABCTECH	SUN	A1FLAG	KELLY
FirstName	Sandra	Tom	Jeffrey	Karel
LastName	Bennett	King	Orris	Sander
Title	Personnel Manager	HR Director	HR Director	Office Manager
SendDate	04/21/97	04/21/97	04/21/97	04/21/97
OpenPosition	Data Entry	Lawn Care	Telemarketing	Data Entry
RatePerHour	8.75	10	9.50	9.25
InfoSource	Newspaper Ad	Networking	Newspaper Ad	Placement Office
ResponseDate	04/25/97	04/24/97	04/25/97	04/28/97
InterviewInvite	Yes	Yes	Yes	No

Table 3.4

Field	Record 5	Record 6	Record 7	Record 8
CompanyID	ADP	SNELL	WALKER	KELLY
FirstName	Peter	Susan	Lee	Karel
LastName	Osland	Rieber	Fountain	Sander
Title	Personnel Manager	HR Director	HR Director	Office Manager
SendDate	04/21/97	04/21/97	04/28/97	04/28/97
OpenPosition	Data Entry	Data Entry	Data Entry	Telemarketing
RatePerHour	9.50	11.25	11.00	8.25
InfoSource	Placement Office	Networking	Newspaper Ad	Newspaper Ad
ResponseDate	04/25/97	04/28/97		05/2/97
InterviewInvite	Yes	No		Yes

Table 3.5

3. Open the Enter interviews and results form, enter the data shown in Table 3.6, and then close the form.

Field	Record 1	Record 2	Record 3	Record 4
CompanyID	SUN	ABCTECH	ABCTECH	A1FLAG
FirstName	Tom	Jordan	Sandra	Sarah
LastName	Betts	Fields	Bennett	Fox
Title	Field Manager	Director of Research	Personnel Manager	Sales Director
InterviewDate	04/25/97	04/28/97	04/28/97	04/29/97
StartTime	9:30 AM	10:00 AM	1:30 PM	3:30 PM
Notes	Job offer made. I have one week to respond.	30 minute interview followed by tests. Second interview at 1:30.		

Table 3.6

Assignments

Writing Validation Rules

Using on-screen Help, find out how to write a validation rule for each of the following independent situations: a date must be in 1997, an entry must be a nonzero value, and a value must be three characters beginning with the letter *S*.

Viewing On-Screen Help on Relationships

Use Answer Wizard to look up information about relationships. Select *Determining the relationships for your database* in the Tell Me About section, and read the multiscreen display. Explain the examples used to illustrate a one-to-many relationship, a many-to-many relationship, and a one-to-one relationship.

Viewing On-Screen Help on Forms

In this project you created a data entry form. Explain two other types of forms, as described in the Tell Me About section of Answer Wizard's Help on forms.

Putting on a Fund-Raiser (Part Two)

Continue to develop the database for tracking fund-raising activities that you designed and created in Project 2. Set field properties and relationships as appropriate. Create a data entry form for each table. Enter a sufficient number of records to test desired outputs.

PROJECT 4: CONVERTING DATA INTO INFORMATION

Objectives

After completing this project, you should be able to:

▶ Find records matching a search condition

▶ Filter records by selection and form

▶ Create a select query using Simple Query Wizard

▶ Resize, hide, and unhide columns

▶ Sort records on one or more fields

▶ Print results

▶ Create reports using Report Wizard

CASE STUDY: COORDINATING VOLUNTEER ACTIVITIES III

Recall that developing and using a database management system generally involves three phases: designing and creating the database, entering and editing data, and converting data into information. In your job as a summer intern, you have completed the second phase by entering enough sample data to test output. Now you are ready to produce the information requested by volunteer center personnel during database design interviews.

Designing the Solution

The terms *data* and *information* are often used interchangeably, but in the context of database management they have different meanings. *Data* are the raw facts or assumptions stored in a database. *Information* is data presented in a usable form.

Creating information from data requires four steps: selecting, organizing, formatting, and displaying data stored in the database. First you will *select* the data you need from one or more tables. For example, to list volunteers and their phone numbers, you will work with only the Volunteers table in the Volunteer Center database. However, to report volunteer activity including the names of volunteers, the hours they worked, and the organizations involved, you will use the Volunteers, Time Cards, and Organizations tables. As part of the selection process, you can limit output to the fields and records you specify.

When you *organize* output you arrange records based on the contents of one or more fields. For example, if you were to list the names and dates worked of students who volunteered during the last month, you could arrange output in order by last name or by date worked.

In the context of converting data into information, *format* refers to arranging fields in a useful layout, with descriptive text to explain each element. For example, a telephone list will be easy to read if you display each name and number on one line, with the name preceding the phone number.

When you *display* information, you send output to the screen or a printer. Sometimes you can view the field contents on-screen to get the information you need, such as a student's e-mail address or a list of volunteer activities available at an organization. At other times you will need to print information, such as reports you have prepared for distribution outside the volunteer center.

The options on the toolbar shown in Figure 4.1 can help you convert data to information quickly. With little more than a click of a button, you can rearrange the order of records, *filter* records by specifying a condition for record selection, and find each record containing the data you specify.

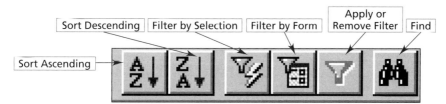

Figure 4.1

If your information needs are relatively complex or you want to save output specifications for reuse later, you can create queries and reports. A *query* allows you to display and analyze data in different ways, for example, to show fields from more than one table. A *report* provides an effective way to print professional-looking output based on a table or query. The names of queries and reports appear on their respective tabs in the Database window; the Reports tab is shown in Figure 4.2.

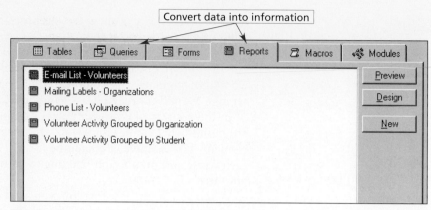

Figure 4.2

In this project you will first use toolbar buttons to vary the content and format of information displayed on the screen. You will also create simple queries and reports with the aid of wizards.

FINDING A MATCH

If you are looking for a particular value in a table, you can use the Find dialog box to enter your search conditions. You will specify what you want to find, where to search, and how much of the field to match in text boxes, as shown in Figure 4.3. You can also use check boxes to further restrict the search; for example, you can look only for data that matches the case typed in the Find What box or search only the current field. Access can search a single field much faster than it can search an entire table.

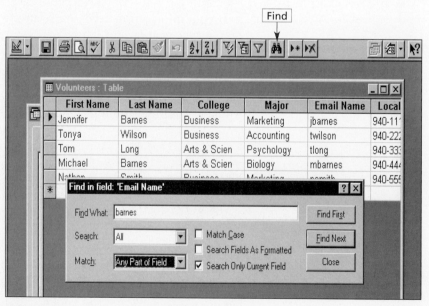

Figure 4.3

Tip If you don't know the exact value you want to find, you can use wildcard characters in the Find What box. You can use an asterisk (*) at the beginning or end of your search text to represent any number of characters. A question mark (?) represents any single alphabetic character. A number sign (#) represents any single numeric character.

In the following steps you will locate specific records using the Find dialog box. You will also move a column to a different location in the table so that the results of a find operation are more meaningful.

To find a match to any part of a field:

1 Start Access and open the Volunteer Center database.

2 Open the Volunteers table in datasheet view.

3 Click within the Email Name column.

4 Select Find in the toolbar.
The Find in field dialog box opens.

5 Type **barnes** in the Find What box.

6 Select Any Part of Field from the Match pull-down list.

7 Change other settings as necessary to match those shown in Figure 4.3.

8 Select Find First.
Access highlights *barnes* in the Email Name field of the first record found (*jbarnes* for *Jennifer Barnes*).

9 Select Find Next.
Access highlights *barnes* in the Email Name field of the second record found (*mbarnes* for *Michael Barnes*).

10 Select Find Next.
Access tells you the search is over.

11 Select OK, and then select Close.

To find a match at the start of a field:

1 Click within the Birthdate column, and then select Find in the toolbar.

2 Type **10** in the Find What box, and then select Start of Field from the Match pull-down list.

3 Select Find First.
Access highlights 10/17/78 in the first record containing 10 at the start of the Birthdate field, as shown in Figure 4.4. The name of the volunteer with this October birthday is not visible.

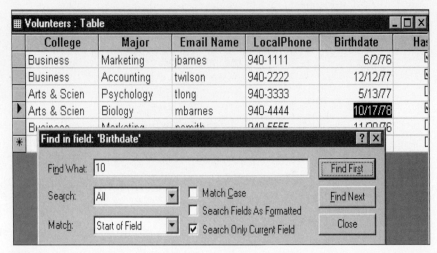

Figure 4.4

4 Select Find Next, select OK, and then select Close.

To move a column and repeat a find operation:

1 Click within the column heading Birthdate, and then press and hold down the mouse button.

A small rectangle at the bottom of the pointer indicates a move operation, as shown in Figure 4.5.

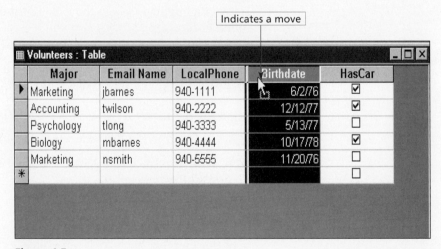

Figure 4.5

2 Drag the pointer to the left until the thick vertical bar appears between the Last Name and College columns, as shown in Figure 4.6.

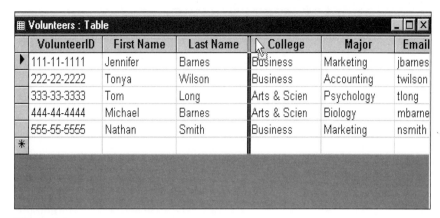

Figure 4.6

3 Release the mouse button.
Access inserts the Birthdate column between the Last Name and College columns, as shown in Figure 4.7.

Volunteers : Table					
VolunteerID	First Name	Last Name	Birthdate	College	Ma
111-11-1111	Jennifer	Barnes	6/2/76	Business	Marketi
222-22-2222	Tonya	Wilson	12/12/77	Business	Accour
333-33-3333	Tom	Long	5/13/77	Arts & Scien	Psychc
444-44-4444	Michael	Barnes	10/17/78	Arts & Scien	Biology
555-55-5555	Nathan	Smith	11/20/76	Business	Marketi

Figure 4.7

4 Select Find in the toolbar, and then select Find First.
Access again highlights 10/17/78, which you can now see is the birthdate of Michael Barnes.

5 Close the dialog box.

6 Close the table without saving your changes.

USING FILTERS TO SELECT RECORDS

Rarely do you want to view or print every record in a database table. In fact, most database tables become so large that it is not practical to view or print every record. The term *filter* is used for both the means and the process of limiting the records that are selected to those that meet specific criteria.

Access provides three ways to filter records: Filter By Selection, Filter

By Form, and the Advanced Filter/Sort window. In the following steps you will view general information about each method.

To view on-screen Help about filters:

1 Choose Answer Wizard from the Help menu.

2 Type **filters** in the Type your request box, and then select Search.

3 In the Tell Me About section, select *What are filters and how do they work?*, and then select Display.

The Help screen shown in Figure 4.8 appears.

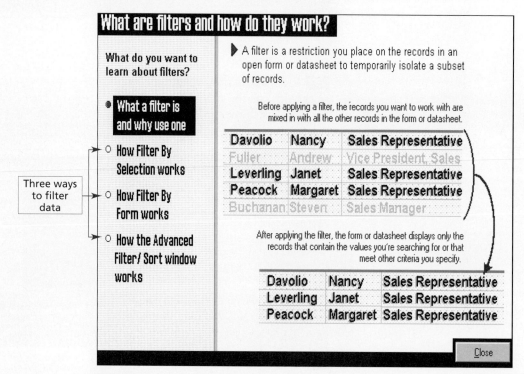

Figure 4.8

4 Read the definition of a filter and study the example of filtered records.

5 Select How Filter By Selection works, and study the example.

6 Select How Filter By Form works, and study the example.

7 Select How the Advanced Filter/Sort window works, and study the example.

8 Select Close.

Filter By Selection and Filter By Form are the easiest ways to filter records. You will work with both of these methods in the following sections.

Filtering by Selection

Using Filter By Selection, you can limit display to those records that meet one search condition at a time. To use this method, you must be able to find and select an example of the value you want the filtered records to contain.

Tip Once you display a set of records that meet your first search condition, you can select another value from within that set. For example, if you filtered records in the Volunteers table to show individuals enrolled in the College of Business, you could then filter those records to show marketing majors within the college.

You can specify your search condition in form or datasheet view. In the following steps you will filter records by selecting a value in datasheet view.

To filter by selection:

1 Open the Time Cards table in datasheet view.

2 Select BBBS in any cell of the OrganizationID field, as shown in Figure 4.9.

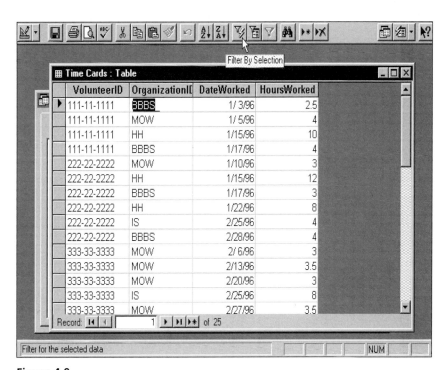

Figure 4.9

3 Select Filter By Selection in the toolbar.
Only the four records containing BBBS in the OrganizationID field appear on the screen, as shown in Figure 4.10.

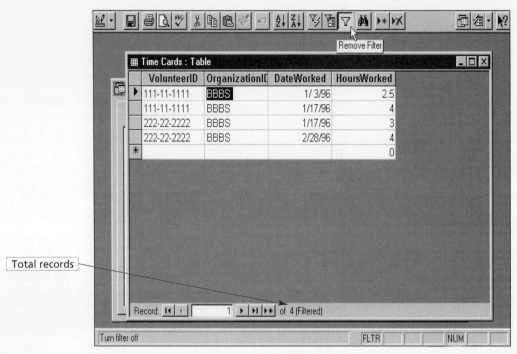

Figure 4.10

4 Select Remove Filter in the toolbar.
Access removes the filter. The record counter shows 25 records again.

5 Select HH in any cell of the OrganizationID field, and then select Filter By Selection.
Only the five records containing HH in the OrganizationID field appear on the screen.

6 Select 1/15/96 in any cell of the DateWorked field, and then select Filter By Selection.
Of the original five records containing HH in the OrganizationID field, only three records remain that display 1/15/96 as the date worked.

7 Select Remove Filter in the toolbar.

8 Close the table without saving your changes.

Filtering by Form

Using Filter By Form, you can limit display to those records that meet one or more search conditions. You can specify multiple conditions as *And criteria,* which means that all conditions must be met for a record to be selected. For example, you might restrict records to those showing volunteer activities for a specific organization on a specific date. Both the organization and date conditions must be met before a record will be selected. You can also specify multiple conditions as *Or criteria,* which means that a record will be selected if any one of the conditions is met, such as working for one organization or another.

When you use the Filter By Form feature, your search criteria are not limited to matching values found in a form or table. You can also use an *expression,* which is a combination of symbols and values that produces a result. For example, you might use the expression >=8 to select records showing hours worked greater than or equal to 8.

Selecting Filter By Form from the toolbar opens a window displaying a blank view of your form or datasheet. Clicking any field and then clicking the arrow at the right end of that field displays a list of values stored in the field. In Figure 4.11, for example, you see the unique entries in the Last Name field of the Volunteers table. You will specify your criteria by selecting from a field list or by typing a value or expression in the blank space below a field name.

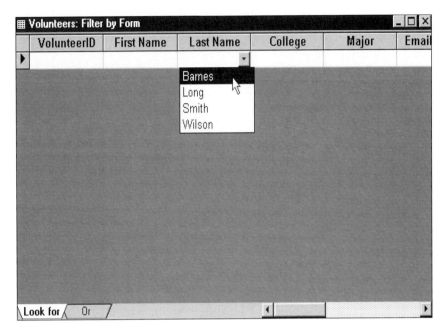

Figure 4.11

If you do not select Or in the lower-left corner of the Filter By Form window, Access will select only those records meeting all search conditions. If you select Or, Access will select a record if any condition is met. In the following steps you will open a Filter By Form window from datasheet view and work with various combinations of search criteria.

Tip When setting a filter, be sure to delete unwanted search criteria that carry over from prior specifications by selecting (highlighting) each search condition and pressing (DEL)

To filter by form with a single exact-match search condition:

1 Open the Volunteers table in datasheet view.
Five records appear as shown in Figure 4.12.

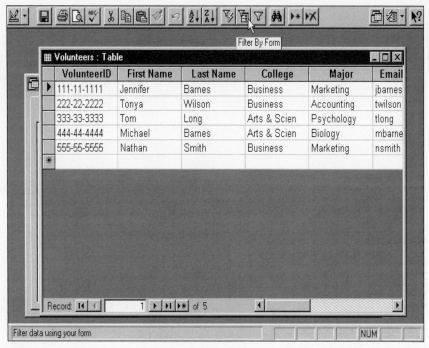

Figure 4.12

2 Select Filter By Form in the toolbar.
The Filter by Form window appears.

3 Click within the Last Name field, and then click the arrow at the right end of the field.
The unique last names appear in a pull-down list, as shown in Figure 4.11.

4 Select Barnes.
Access displays a text search condition encased in quotation marks, as shown in Figure 4.13.

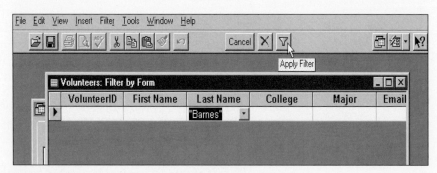

Figure 4.13

5 Select Apply Filter in the toolbar.
Two records display with last name Barnes.

You could have executed this exact-match search on one field more quickly by using Filter By Selection. The remaining examples, however, require a more advanced filtering process.

To filter by form with two exact-match search conditions, both of which must be met:

1 Select Filter By Form.

2 Click within the Major field, and then select Marketing from the pull-down list.
Your search criteria should match those shown in Figure 4.14.

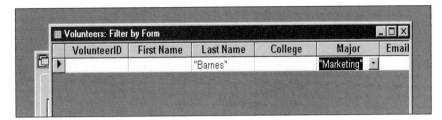

Figure 4.14

3 Select Apply Filter.
One record meeting both criteria is displayed.

4 Close the table without saving the changes.

To filter by form with an expression:

1 Open the Time Cards table in datasheet view.
The record counter indicates 25 records.

2 Select Filter By Form.

3 Type **>=8** beneath the HoursWorked field name, as shown in Figure 4.15.

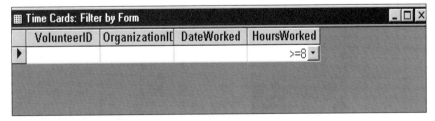

Figure 4.15

4 Select Apply Filter.
The seven records meeting the search condition are displayed as shown in Figure 4.16.

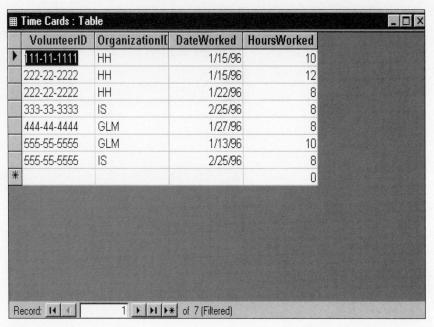

Figure 4.16

To filter by form with two exact-match search conditions, either one of which causes a record to be selected:

1 Select Filter By Form.

2 Delete the search condition > = 8 from the HoursWorked field.

3 Select HH from the OrganizationID pull-down list.

4 Click Or in the bottom-left corner of the window.

5 Select MOW from the OrganizationID pull-down list.

The screen now looks like Figure 4.17.

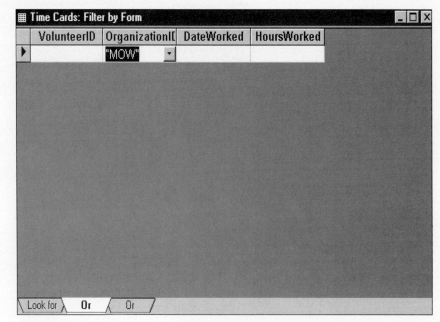

Figure 4.17

6 Select Apply Filter.

The 11 records meeting either search condition are displayed as shown in Figure 4.18.

VolunteerID	OrganizationIC	DateWorked	HoursWorked
111-11-1111	MOW	1/ 5/96	4
111-11-1111	HH	1/15/96	10
222-22-2222	MOW	1/10/96	3
222-22-2222	HH	1/15/96	12
222-22-2222	HH	1/22/96	8
333-33-3333	MOW	2/ 6/96	3
333-33-3333	MOW	2/13/96	3.5
333-33-3333	MOW	2/20/96	3
333-33-3333	MOW	2/27/96	3.5
555-55-5555	HH	1/15/96	6
555-55-5555	HH	1/22/96	6
			0

Record: 1 of 11 (Filtered)

Figure 4.18

7 Close the table without saving your changes.

EXIT If necessary, you can close this database now. You can then exit Access and continue this project later.

USING QUERIES TO SELECT AND ORGANIZE DATA

Filters allow you to restrict display of records in a single table. What if you want to view and print specified fields instead of entire records? What if those fields are not all in the same table? You can meet these information needs using queries, as explained in on-screen Help.

To view on-screen Help about queries:

1 If necessary, start Access and open the Volunteer Center database.

2 Choose Answer Wizard from the Help menu.

3 Type **queries** in the Type your request box, and then select Search.

4 In the Tell Me About section, select *Queries: What they are and how they work,* and then select Display.

The Help screen shown in Figure 4.19 appears.

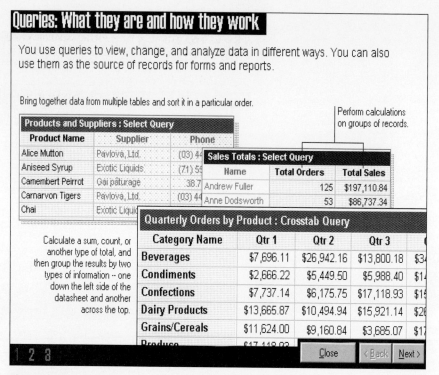

Figure 4.19

5 Read the general introduction to queries, and then select Next> in the lower-right corner or 2 in the lower-left corner.
The second of three screens appears.

6 Study the diagram showing how a query can pull data from more than one table and display information in the order you specify.

7 Select Next> or 3 to view the final Help screen, and then select Close.

As explained in on-screen Help, a ***select query*** retrieves data from one or more tables. Figure 4.20 shows a select query in datasheet view that displays information from the three tables in the Volunteer Center database.

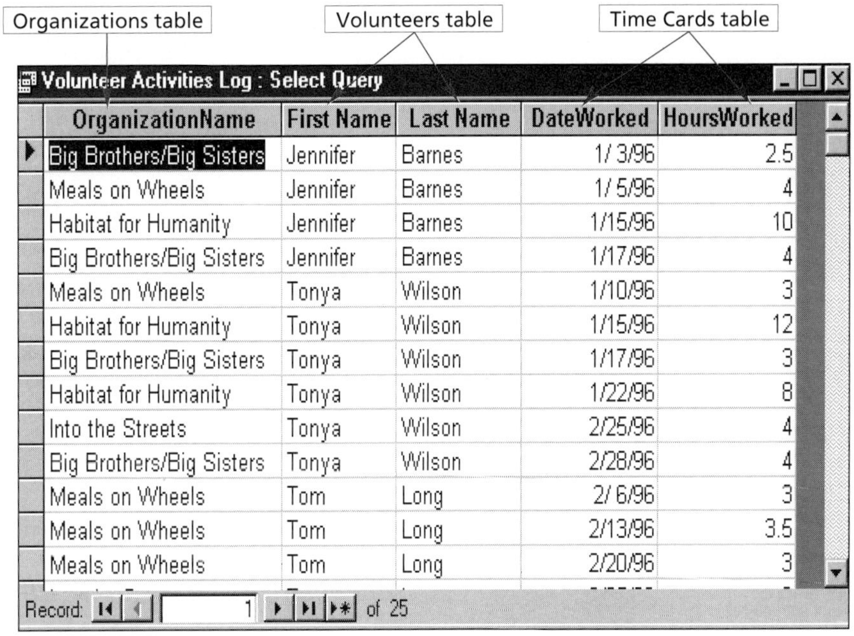

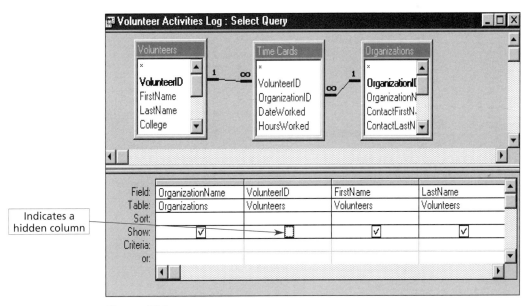

Figure 4.20

You can switch between the datasheet and design views of a query. Design view shows tables and relationships in the top half of the screen and a columnar display of fields and related tables in the bottom half, as shown in Figure 4.21. The Sort, Show, and Criteria rows allow you to sort records in the query, hide or unhide columns, and limit the view to records meeting search criteria.

Figure 4.21

Access provides **Simple Query Wizard** to guide you as you create a select query. You can modify the results by hiding one or more fields, changing column width, changing the order of fields, and sorting records.

Using Simple Query Wizard

Simple Query Wizard works much like Form Wizard, which you used in Project 3. You will start Simple Query Wizard from the Queries tab in the Database window. Then you will select each table containing fields you need in the query and transfer the fields you want to include from the Available Fields box to the Selected Fields box. The order in which you transfer fields to the Selected Fields box is the order in which they will appear in datasheet and design views.

In the following steps you will use Simple Query Wizard to create a query pulling data from the three tables in the Volunteer Center database.

To create a select query using Simple Query Wizard:

1 Select the Queries tab in the Volunteer Center Database window, and then select New.

2 Select Simple Query Wizard, as shown in Figure 4.22, and then select OK.

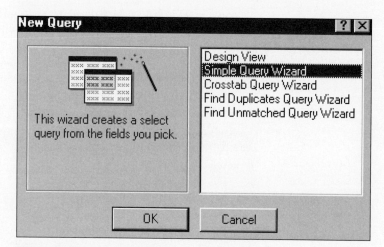

Figure 4.22

3 Select the Organizations table from the Tables/Queries pull-down list if that table name does not already appear in the Tables/Queries box in the Simple Query Wizard dialog box.

4 Double-click OrganizationName in the Available Fields box. OrganizationName appears in the Selected Fields box.

5 Select the Volunteers table from the Tables/Queries pull-down list.

6 Select VolunteerID, FirstName, and LastName from the Available Fields box.

The specifications on the screen should match those shown in Figure 4.23.

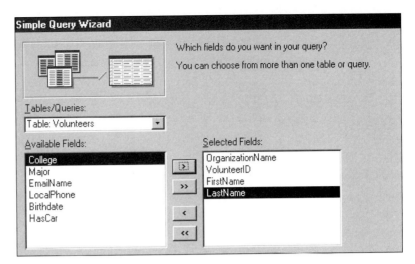

Figure 4.23

7 Select the Time Cards table from the Tables/Queries pull-down list.

8 Select DateWorked and HoursWorked from the Available Fields box. The specifications on the screen should match those shown in Figure 4.24.

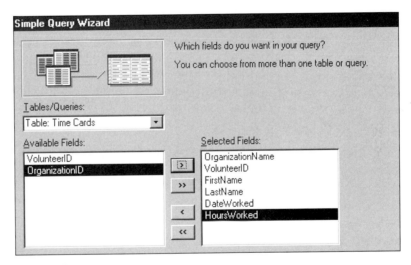

Figure 4.24

9 Select Next>.
Simple Query Wizard prompts you to specify a detail or summary query.

10 Select Detail, and then select Next>.

11 Type **Volunteer Activities Log** in the What title do you want for your query box.

12 Select the Open the query to view information button, and then select Finish.
Access displays a datasheet showing data pulled from three tables as shown in Figure 4.25.

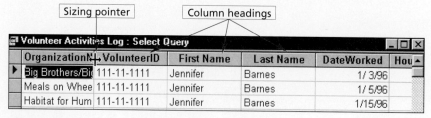

Figure 4.25

Resizing and Hiding Columns

You can adjust the size of columns to take up more or less space in datasheet view. In Figure 4.25, for example, the first column could be widened to show the full names of the organizations. Reducing the width of the other columns would allow more information to be displayed.

You will resize a column in datasheet view by dragging the right edge of its column heading in either direction until the column is the desired width. If you double-click the right edge of a column heading, Access automatically sizes the column to fit its data or column heading, whichever is larger. Choosing Column Width from the Format menu and then selecting Best Fit serves the same purpose.

> **Tip** To avoid excess space created by a long column title, such as HoursWorked, you can select the field's Caption box in design view and type a smaller description, such as Hrs.

Figure 4.26 shows you where to position the pointer to change the width of the first column in the Volunteer Activities Log query.

Figure 4.26

> **Tip** You cannot use Undo to restore original column widths. To undo column width changes, you must close the datasheet without saving layout changes.

Some data should be kept confidential, such as social security numbers and pay rates. You can store such data in a table or query and hide or unhide columns displaying the data as necessary. You will find commands to hide and unhide columns on the Format menu. You can also hide a column by deselecting its Show box in design view, as shown for the VolunteerID field in Figure 4.21.

Caution   When you save changes to a query, Access deletes hidden columns from the query. To avoid deletion, choose Unhide Columns from the Format menu, and check the boxes in front of the fields you want to keep. You can also select the appropriate Show boxes in design view.

In the following steps you will widen the first column in the Volunteer Activities Log query and narrow the other columns. You will also hide the VolunteerID column showing social security numbers.

To adjust the widths of columns in datasheet view:

1 Position the pointer on the right edge of the OrganizationName column heading, as shown in Figure 4.26.

2 Double-click the mouse.
The OrganizationName column automatically widens to display the longest organization name.

3 Position the pointer on the right edge of the First Name column heading.

4 Drag the pointer to the left to reduce column size, as shown in Figure 4.27.

OrganizationName	VolunteerID	First Name	Last Name	DateWork
Big Brothers/Big Sisters	111-11-1111	Jennifer	Barnes	1/
Meals on Wheels	111-11-1111	Jennifer	Barnes	1/
Habitat for Humanity	111-11-1111	Jennifer	Barnes	1/1

Volunteer Activities Log : Select Query

Figure 4.27

5 Release the mouse button.

6 Repeat steps 3 through 5 to reduce the size of the Last Name column.

To hide a column in datasheet view and save your changes:

1 Click within the VolunteerID field.

2 Choose Hide Columns from the Format menu.
The VolunteerID column disappears, as shown in Figure 4.20.

3 Close the query, and select Yes when prompted to save your changes.

Sorting on One or More Fields

It is often necessary to view records in a sequence different from that in which they were entered and stored in the database. Reordering of records is based on the contents of a field, which you can arrange in ascending or descending order. For example, you might organize records by last name in ascending order or by date in descending order.

The Sort Ascending and Sort Descending buttons on the toolbar shown in Figure 4.1 allow you to reorder records based on the contents of a single field. To sort on more than one field, you will use the query design view shown in Figure 4.21.

Fields controlling a multiple sort do not have to be adjacent to each other, but their columns must be in order of importance from left to right. For example, to sort records in the Volunteer Activities Log query by date worked and then by last name within each date worked, you would have to position the DateWorked field to the left of the LastName field.

In the following steps you will use both the query design view and a sort button to sort records in the Volunteer Activities Log query based on the contents of a single field. You will then rearrange columns and sort on two fields.

To sort on one field in query design view:

1 Open the Volunteer Activities Log query in design view.

Tip The tables and the relationships among tables appear in the top half of the Select Query window. Your tables may appear in a different order that makes it harder to view the relationships. You can change the order by dragging a table by its title to a new location.

2 Click the arrow at the right end of the Sort box in the OrganizationName column to display the Sort pull-down list, as shown in Figure 4.28.

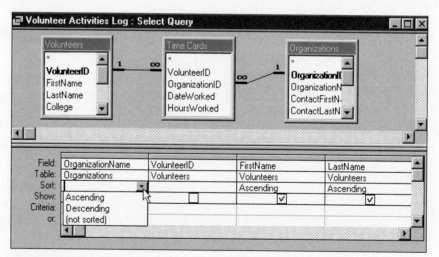

Figure 4.28

3 Select Ascending.

4 Switch to datasheet view to see the records listed in alphabetical order by organization name, as shown in Figure 4.29.

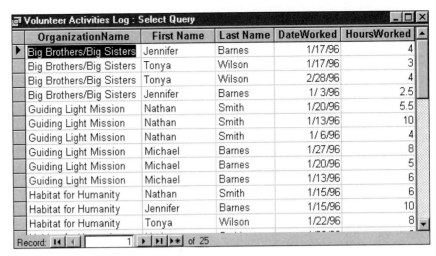

Figure 4.29

To sort on one field using a Sort button:

1 Select the DateWorked column.

2 Select Sort Ascending in the toolbar.
Records appear in order by date, starting with the earliest date.

To sort on more than one field:

1 Switch to query design view.

2 Display the Sort pull-down list in the OrganizationName column, and select (not sorted).

3 Select the LastName column by clicking LastName at the top of the column.
Access highlights the entire column.

4 Position the pointer on the narrow bar above LastName, as shown in Figure 4.30.

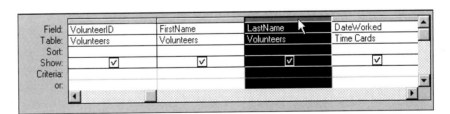

Figure 4.30

5 Drag and drop the column to the left of the FirstName column.

6 Select the Sort settings for LastName, FirstName, and DateWorked shown in Figure 4.31.

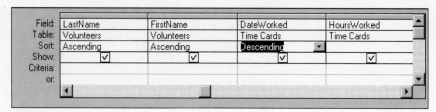

Field:	LastName	FirstName	DateWorked	HoursWorked
Table:	Volunteers	Volunteers	Time Cards	Time Cards
Sort:	Ascending	Ascending	Descending	
Show:	☑	☑	☑	☑
Criteria:				
or:				

Figure 4.31

7 Switch to datasheet view to see the sorted records, as shown in Figure 4.32.

Records appear in order by last name (*Barnes* before *Long*), and then by first name within last name (*Jennifer Barnes* before *Michael Barnes*). For each student, the records then appear in order of date worked, with the most recent first.

Closes the query

Volunteer Activities Log : Select Query				
OrganizationName	Last Name	First Name	DateWorked	HoursWorked
Big Brothers/Big Sisters	Barnes	Jennifer	1/17/96	4
Habitat for Humanity	Barnes	Jennifer	1/15/96	10
Meals on Wheels	Barnes	Jennifer	1/ 5/96	4
Big Brothers/Big Sisters	Barnes	Jennifer	1/ 3/96	2.5
Into the Streets	Barnes	Michael	2/25/96	5
Guiding Light Mission	Barnes	Michael	1/27/96	8
Guiding Light Mission	Barnes	Michael	1/20/96	5
Guiding Light Mission	Barnes	Michael	1/13/96	6
Meals on Wheels	Long	Tom	2/27/96	3.5
Into the Streets	Long	Tom	2/25/96	8
Meals on Wheels	Long	Tom	2/20/96	3
Meals on Wheels	Long	Tom	2/13/96	3.5
Meals on Wheels	Long	Tom	2/ 6/96	3

Record: |◄ ◄ 1 ► ►| ►* of 25

Figure 4.32

Printing Results

Up to this point you viewed the results of find, filter, and query operations in a window on the screen. You can also print any of these results immediately by selecting Print in the toolbar, or you can open Page Setup and Print dialog boxes through the File menu to change settings before you print.

Figure 4.33 shows the Page Setup dialog box. You can select the Margins tab to change the top, bottom, left, and right margins. On the Page tab you can make changes to the orientation, paper, and printer.

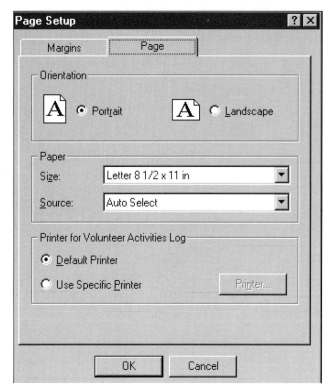

Figure 4.33

Figure 4.34 shows the Print dialog box. After you make changes as needed to the print range and the number of copies, you will select OK to begin printing.

In the following steps you will print all the records in the Volunteer Activities Log query at default settings.

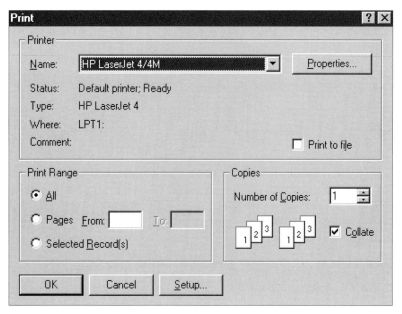

Figure 4.34

To print the current query results and close the query:

1 Select Print in the toolbar.

The records appear in a datasheet layout on paper. Access adds the name of the query as a title, places the current date in the upper-right corner, and places the page number bottom center.

2 Close the query by clicking the X button in the upper-right corner of the Select Query window, as shown in Figure 4.32, and select Yes when prompted to save your changes.

EXIT

If necessary, you can close this database now. You can then exit Access and continue this project later.

CREATING REPORTS WITH REPORT WIZARD

Filters and queries both produce lists of records, one record per row, with field names as column headings. You may, however, prefer to present data in a more formal manner. You can, for example, create output containing several title lines and header or footer information that appears at the top or bottom of each page in a multiple-page printout. You can also group similar records, create new fields based on data in existing fields, calculate subtotals as well as grand totals of numeric fields, generate mailing labels, and present data in a graph. These features are available in reports, as explained through on-screen Help.

To view on-screen Help about reports:

1 If necessary, start Access and open the Volunteer Center database.

2 Choose Answer Wizard from the Help menu.

3 Type **reports** in the Type your request box, and then select Search.

4 In the Tell Me About section, select *Reports: What they are and how they work,* and then select Display.

The Help screen shown in Figure 4.35 appears.

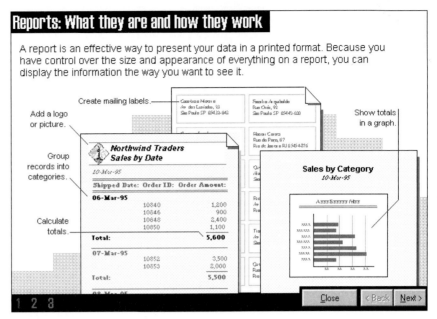

Figure 4.35

5 Read the general introduction to reports, and then select Next>.

6 Study the sample report showing which parts are stored in the report's design and which parts pull data from the database.

7 Select Next> to view the third of three Help screens, which shows a sample report in design view.

8 Select Close.

Access is a powerful database management product that allows you to design your own reports as well as take advantage of predefined features available through Report Wizard. This wizard presents a series of screens for selecting the content and appearance of a report. After you select the table or query containing the data you need, you will select fields in the order you want them to appear and specify the sort order of records. You can then select vertical or tabular layout, portrait or landscape orientation, and tell Access to adjust field widths so all fields fit on a page. You will finish your report specifications by choosing among predefined styles and naming the report.

> **Tip**   If the report you have in mind will contain all fields in order from a table or query, you can select AutoReport: Columnar or AutoReport: Tabular to create a report without responding to screen prompts.

In the following sections you will use Report Wizard to create three reports of increasing complexity for the Volunteer Center database.

Creating a List

During the database design process, users identified desired outputs, one of which was a list showing how to contact volunteers. Creating a four-column report that pulls last name, first name, local phone number, and e-mail name data from the Volunteers table will meet this information need.

To select fields and the sort order using Report Wizard:

1 Select the Reports tab, and then select New.

2 Select Report Wizard, and then select the Volunteers table, as shown in Figure 4.36.

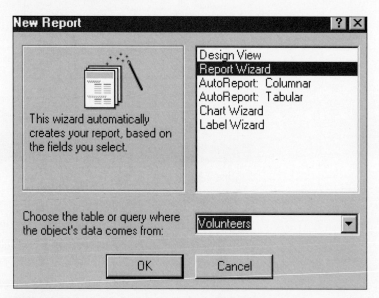

Figure 4.36

3 Select OK.

4 Select LastName, FirstName, LocalPhone, and EmailName from the Available Fields box, and then select Next>.

Reminder You can select a field by double-clicking its name or by highlighting its name and clicking the > button.

A Report Wizard screen appears, asking if you want to add grouping levels.

5 Select Next>.

6 Click the arrow at the right end of the first sort field to display a pull-down list, as shown in Figure 4.37.

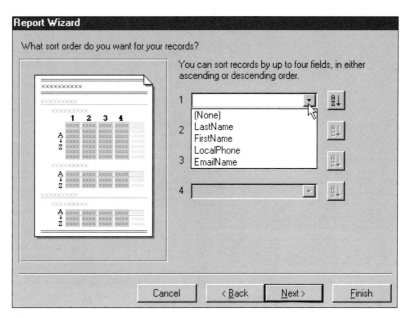

Figure 4.37

7 Select LastName.

8 Display the second sort field pull-down list, and then select FirstName.

9 Select Next>.

To complete the specifications and print the report:

1 Check that your settings match those shown in Figure 4.38, and then select Next>.

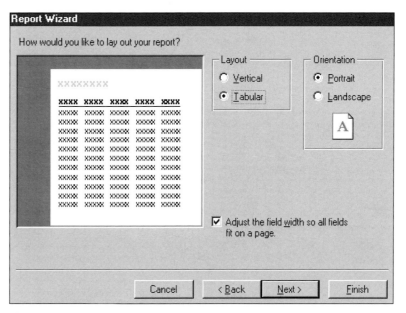

Figure 4.38

2 Select Formal as the style, and then select Next>.

3 Type **Volunteer Contact List** as the title of the report.

4 Select Preview the report, and then select Finish.

Report Wizard creates the report and displays it on the screen as shown in Figure 4.39.

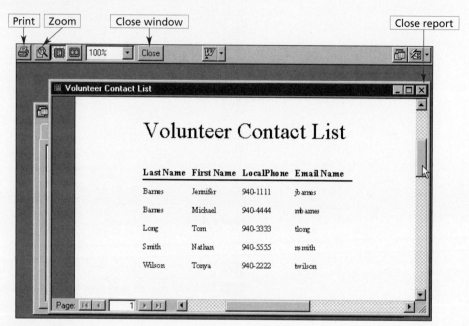

Figure 4.39

5 Select Print in the toolbar.

6 Close the report.

The report named Volunteer Contact List appears under the Reports tab in the Database window.

> **Tip** If you close the report by clicking the X button in the upper-right corner of the window, the Database window reappears. Selecting Close from the toolbar displays the report in design view, so you will need to close that window to return to the Database window.

Summarizing Information

Sometimes listing records row after row without a break produces all the information you need, such as an alphabetized list of volunteers and their phone numbers. Other outputs provide more information if similar records are grouped. Figure 4.40, for example, shows part of a two-page report in which records appear grouped by volunteer.

Volunteer Time Card Summary Report

First Name	Last Name	DateWorked	HoursWorked
Jennifer	Barnes		
		1/ 3/96	2.5
		1/ 5/96	4
		1/15/96	10
		1/17/96	4

Summary for 'VolunteerID' = 111111111 (4 detail records)
Sum   20.5

Tonya	Wilson		
		1/10/96	3
		1/15/96	12
		1/17/96	3
		1/22/96	8
		2/25/96	4
		2/28/96	4

Summary for 'VolunteerID' = 222222222 (6 detail records)
Sum   34

Tom	Long		
		2/ 6/96	3
		2/13/96	3.5
		2/20/96	3
		2/25/96	8
		2/27/96	3.5

Summary for 'VolunteerID' = 333333333 (5 detail records)
Sum   21

Figure 4.40

On your own or by using Report Wizard, you can provide summary information based on the contents of a field, such as the total number of hours worked by each volunteer shown in Figure 4.40. You can also display the minimum and maximum values in a field, the average of all numbers in a field, and a percent of the total for each group.

In the following steps you will use Report Wizard to create the report shown in Figure 4.40. This report pulls data from two tables.

To select fields from two tables:

1 Select the Reports tab, and then select New.

2 Select Report Wizard, select the Volunteers table, and then select OK.

3 Select FirstName and LastName from the Available Fields box.

4 Display the Tables/Queries pull-down list, and then select the Time Cards table.

5 Select DateWorked and HoursWorked from the Available Fields box. Your field selections should match those shown in Figure 4.41.

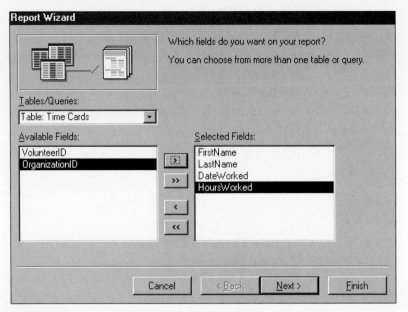

Figure 4.41

6 Select Next>.
Report Wizard asks how you want to view your data.

7 Select Next> to accept viewing your data by volunteers.
Report Wizard asks if you want to add any grouping levels.

8 Select Next> to accept grouping on volunteer name.

To specify the sort order and complete the report specifications:

1 Display the first sort box pull-down list and select DateWorked.
Your setting for sort order of detail records should match that shown in
Figure 4.42.

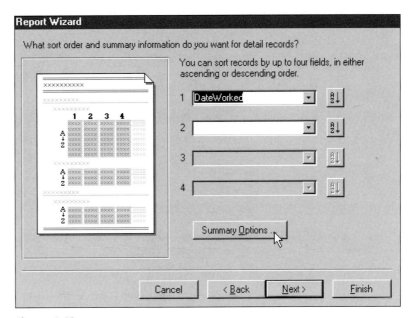

Figure 4.42

2 Select Summary Options.

3 Select the settings shown in Figure 4.43, and then select OK.

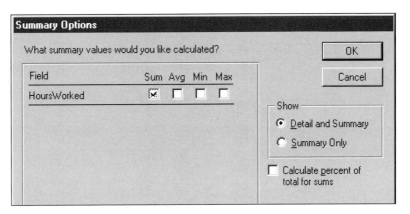

Figure 4.43

4 Select Next>.

5 Select Stepped layout, Portrait orientation, and Adjusts the field width so all fields fit on a page.

6 Select Next>.

7 Select Formal style, and then select Next>.

8 Type **Volunteer Time Card Summary Report** as the title of the report.

9 Select Preview the report, and then select Finish.
Report Wizard creates the report and displays it on the screen.

10 Use vertical and horizontal scroll bars to view the report.

11 Select Print in the toolbar.
Access prints the report, part of which is shown in Figure 4.40.

12 Close the report.
Volunteer Time Card Summary Report appears under the Reports tab in the Database window.

Using Subgroups in a Report

Occasionally you may want to group records within a group. In the previous report a group consisted of the dates and hours worked by one volunteer. Suppose you want to know the number of hours each student worked for a specific organization, as well as the total hours overall. You can display this information by grouping on the contents of the last name and first name fields and then subgrouping on the contents of the organization field name.

In the following steps you will use Report Wizard to create a report with subgroups. This report pulls data from three tables.

> **Tip** You could copy the previous report and then modify it in design view to include subgroupings, but using Report Wizard to create a new report is easier. On-screen Help provides information about saving a database object.

To select fields from three tables:

1 Select the Reports tab, and then select New.

2 Select Report Wizard, select the Volunteers table, and then select OK.

3 Select FirstName and LastName from the Available Fields box.

4 Display the Tables/Queries pull-down list, and then select the Organizations table.

5 Select OrganizationName from the Available Fields box.

6 Display the Tables/Queries pull-down list, and then select the Time Cards table.

7 Select DateWorked and HoursWorked from the Available Fields box. Your field selections should match those shown in Figure 4.44.

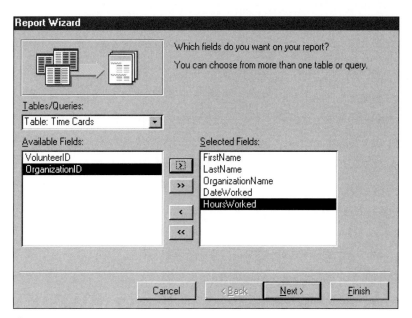

Figure 4.44

8 Select Next>.
Report Wizard asks how you want to view your data.

9 Select Next> to accept viewing your data by volunteers.
Report Wizard asks if you want to add any grouping levels.

10 Double-click OrganizationName to select it.
Your grouping levels should match those shown in Figure 4.45.

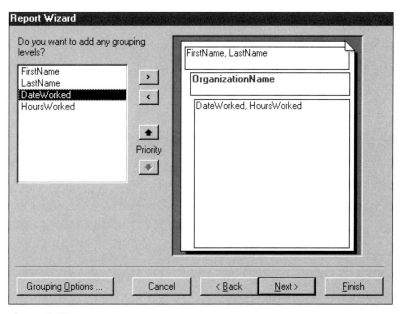

Figure 4.45

11 Select Next>.

To specify sort order and complete the report specifications:

1 Display the first sort box pull-down list and select DateWorked.

2 Select Summary Options, check Sum, and then select OK.

3 Select Next>.
Database Wizard displays layout and orientation options.

4 Select Next> to accept the current layout and orientation settings.

5 Select Next> to accept the current style setting.

6 Type `Volunteer Time Report by Organization` as the title of the report.

7 Select Preview the report, and then select Finish.
Report Wizard creates the report and displays it on the screen.

8 Use vertical and horizontal scroll bars to view the report.

9 Select Print in the toolbar.
Access prints the report, part of which is shown in Figure 4.46.

Volunteer Time Report by Organization

First Name	Last Name	OrganizationName	DateWorked	HoursWorked
Jennifer	*Barnes*			
		Big Brothers/Big Sisters		
			1/ 3/96	2.5
			1/17/96	4
		Summary for 'OrganizationName' = Big Brothers/Big Sisters (2 detail records)		
		Sum		6.5
		Habitat for Humanity		
			1/15/96	10
		Summary for 'OrganizationName' = Habitat for Humanity (1 detail record)		
		Sum		10
		Meals on Wheels		
			1/ 5/96	4
		Summary for 'OrganizationName' = Meals on Wheels (1 detail record)		
		Sum		4
Summary for 'VolunteerID' = 111111111 (4 detail records)				
Sum				20.5
Tonya	*Wilson*			
		Big Brothers/Big Sisters		
			1/17/96	3
			2/28/96	4
		Summary for 'OrganizationName' = Big Brothers/Big Sisters (2 detail records)		
		Sum		7
		Habitat for Humanity		
			1/15/96	12
			1/22/96	8
		Summary for 'OrganizationName' = Habitat for Humanity (2 detail records)		
		Sum		20
		Into the Streets		
			2/25/96	4

Figure 4.46

10 Close the report.

Volunteer Time Report by Organization appears under the Reports tab in the Database window.

11 Close the database.

THE NEXT STEP

In this project you created filters, queries, and reports to convert data into information. In the process you also sorted output based on the contents of one or more fields and printed results.

As a next step, you might look into other features in each area. For example, learn how to set up complex select and sort criteria using the Advanced Filter/Sort window. Discover the purpose of a cross-tab query. Make changes to the layout of a report in design view, such as rearranging fields and adding a picture or logo. Determine the results you can achieve using Chart Wizard and Label Wizard. You can also set up your own switchboard system to execute common tasks.

This concludes Project 4. You can either exit Access or go on to work the Study Questions, Review Exercises, and Assignments.

SUMMARY AND EXERCISES

Summary

- Data are the raw facts or assumptions stored in a database. Information is data presented in a usable form.
- You can create information using techniques to select, organize, format, and display data.
- Find operations and filters allow you to focus on records in one table that meet specified criteria. A find operation moves the cursor to the next record meeting the search condition. A filter hides records that do not meet search criteria.
- You can filter by selection or filter by form, or you can specify both sort and filter conditions in the Advanced Filter/Sort window.
- Use a query instead of a filter if you want to restrict display of fields as well as records. A select query can retrieve data from more than one table.
- Sort Ascending and Sort Descending buttons on the toolbar allow you to reorder records based on the contents of a single field. You can sort on more than one field using query design view.
- Access provides a variety of wizards to help you create queries and reports, including Simple Query Wizard and Report Wizard.
- Reports present data in a more formal way than queries or filters. Report features include title lines, header or footer information, groups of similar information, subtotals and grand totals of numeric fields, and new fields based on data in existing fields.

Key Terms and Operations

Key Terms	**Operations**
And criteria	Find a match
data	Filter by selection
expression	Filter by form
filter	Create a select query
information	Resize a column
Or criteria	Hide a column
query	Sort on one or more fields
report	Print results
select query	Create a list
Simple Query Wizard	Summarize information
	Use subgroups in a report

Study Questions

Multiple Choice

1. Which feature would you use to locate each occurrence of a particular value?

   a. Search
   b. Find
   c. Replace
   d. Locate

2. If you do not know the exact value you are looking for in a table, which of the following symbols can you use to substitute for more than one character in your search condition?

   a. #
   b. $
   c. ?
   d. None of the above.

3. You can limit screen display to those records that meet one or more search conditions at a time by using Filter By

   a. Query
   b. Form
   c. Selection
   d. Sort

4. Which of the following is true about resizing or hiding columns?

   a. To avoid excess space created by a long column title, you can use a smaller title in the field's Caption property.
   b. When you save changes to a query, Access removes hidden columns from a query.
   c. To avoid removal of hidden columns, unhide the columns before saving changes to a query.
   d. All of the above.

5. Fields controlling a multiple-field sort

   a. must be adjacent to each other.
   b. must be in order of importance from left to right in the table.
   c. must contain the same data type.
   d. All of the above.

6. Which of the following is true about sorting data?
   a. You often need to view records in a sequence different from that in which they were entered and stored in the database.
   b. Reordering of records is based on the contents of a field.
   c. You can arrange records in ascending or descending order.
   d. All of the above.

7. Which of the following is not one of four actions concerning the conversion of data into information as described in this project?
   a. selecting
   b. saving
   c. formatting
   d. displaying

8. Which of the following would be valid search criteria in a table containing city and state fields?
   a. filtering for city Indianapolis and state Indiana
   b. filtering for city Indianapolis and city Cincinnati
   c. Both a and b.
   d. Neither a nor b.

9. Which Wizard can you use to create a select query?
   a. Select Query Wizard
   b. Simple Query Wizard
   c. Cross-tab Query Wizard
   d. None of the above.

10. Which is a true statement about using Report Wizard to create output?
    a. You can create a simple list of data.
    b. You can group and summarize data on a common field of data.
    c. You can subgroup but not summarize data within an existing group.
    d. Both a and b.

Short Answer

1. What term describes data presented in a usable form?

2. In this project you read about four actions to convert data into information. Which of the four actions refers to arranging data based on the contents of one or more fields?

3. What options do you have to display fields from more than one table?

4. What wildcard character in a search condition accepts any single number?

5. After you display a set of records that meet your first search condition, you can select another value from within that set. Give an example other than the one provided in the text.

6. When using Filter By Form, you can enter a search condition as an expression. What expression would tell Access to select only those records in which a value was less than or equal to 50?

7. What wizard would you use to create formal displays of your data, complete with titles, headers, and footers?

8. Use a _____ to specify a condition for record selection, and find each record containing the data you specify.

9. A _____ provides an effective way to print professional-looking output based on a table or query.

10. Sorting data in reverse order (z to a) or from the largest to the smallest (9 to 0) is called _____ order.

For Discussion

Answer the following discussion questions assuming that you have created a two-table Access database named Lawn Care. One table named Customers contains one record per customer, with fields showing customer number, name, address, and phone number data. The other table named Services tracks the type of service performed, date performed, time involved, and fee charged.

1. Assume that your Customers table has over 200 records, including 3 customers with the last name Smith. Describe how you could quickly look up the phone number of Joseph Smith.

2. What steps would you take to produce a list of customers and their phone numbers, arranged in order by customer last name and then by first name within duplicate last names?

3. You can filter records based on two exact-match search conditions, either one of which would cause a record to be selected and you can filter records based on two exact-match search conditions, both of which must be met before a record is selected. Give an example of each related to the Lawn Care database.

4. A query can retrieve data from more than one table. Describe a query you might create involving both tables of the Lawn Care database. Explain also how to print query results.

5. You can group and sort records using Report Wizard. Describe a report you might create exhibiting grouped and sorted records. Explain also the steps involved in using Report Wizard to create the report.

Review Exercises

In Project 3 review exercises you modified field properties, set relationships, created forms, and entered data in the Job Search database. In these review exercises you will convert data into information by finding matches, setting filters, and creating queries and reports.

Finding Matches

1. Start Access, open the Job Search database, and open the Applications table in datasheet view.

2. Click within the OpenPosition column, select Find in the toolbar, and specify Data Entry as the search condition.

3. Find each occurrence of Data Entry.

4. Find each occurrence of News at the beginning of the InfoSource field.

Filtering by Selection

1. Display the Applications table in datasheet view, select (highlight) Data Entry in one of the OpenPosition fields, and then select Filter By Selection in the toolbar.

2. Within the records limited to Data Entry positions, select Newspaper Ad in one of the InfoSource fields, and then select Filter By Selection again.

3. Remove the filter.

Filtering by Form

1. Display the Applications table in datasheet view, and select Filter By Form in the toolbar.

2. Specify Data Entry or Lawn Care as the open position, and then select Apply Filter.

3. Check that only records containing Data Entry or Lawn Care in the OpenPosition field appear on the screen, and then remove the filter.

4. Use Filter By Form to display only those records for which the rate per hour is greater than or equal to $10, and then remove the filter.

5. Close the table without saving your changes.

Creating a Query

1. Start Simple Query Wizard and select the CompanyName field from the Companies table.

2. Select the OpenPosition, SendDate, and ResponseDate fields from the Applications table.

3. Name the detail query Applications Log, and then view the results.

4. Sort on company name, adjust column widths as necessary, and then print the results.

5. Close the table without saving your changes.

Creating a Report

1. Start Report Wizard, select the Companies table, and then select the CompanyName field.

2. Select the Applications table, and then select the OpenPosition, RatePerHour, ResponseDate, and InterviewInvite fields.

3. View data by Companies, and set up grouping on OpenPosition and sort in descending order on RatePerHour.

4. Select Stepped layout, Portrait orientation, and Adjust the field width so all fields fit on a page.

5. Select the style of your choice, and then name the report Responses Grouped by Job Type.

6. Preview, print, and close the report.

Assignments

Exploring Other Wizards

You now have experience using Answer, Database, Table, Lookup, Simple Query, Form, and Report Wizards. Use on-screen Help to learn about four other wizards, including Chart Wizard and Label Wizard. Write a few sentences describing the purpose of each of the four wizards.

Comparing Select Queries and Filters

Select queries and filters both restrict display of records to those meeting specified criteria. Display Answer Wizard, enter select queries as the search condition, and then select *Similarities and differences between select queries and filters* in the Tell Me About section. Summarize your findings.

Learning about Action Queries

In this project you used Simple Query Wizard to create a select query. Now use on-screen Help to learn about action queries. Write a paragraph summarizing your findings.

Putting On a Fund-Raiser (Part Three)

Using the fund-raising database you created in prior assignments, convert data into information. Find and filter records in one table at a time. Create and save one or more queries that pull data from multiple tables. Preview, print, and save a variety of reports consistent with desired outputs identified in the database design phase.

PROJECT 5:   REVISITING QUERIES

Objectives

After completing this project, you should be able to:

▶ Specify multiple criteria

▶ Create a calculated field

▶ Use a function in an expression

▶ Select a predefined calculation

▶ Analyze data using a crosstab query

CASE STUDY: TRACKING SALES

Assume that you are an Arts Administration major combining business interests with creative abilities. Recently you formed a small company named Designer Tees to provide income while you attend school. You set up a World Wide Web site to market your product, t-shirts customized with your own designs. You also set up an Access database to track sales. You now have data for three months that you want to examine.

Designing the Solution

First you should understand how data are organized and identify your current information needs. Your relatively small operation does not require a complex information system that includes inventory management. You buy plain t-shirts in five sizes and three colors as needed, add the requested designs, and ship the orders at customers' expense. Four of your friends help you to process orders received by phone or fax, and you pay them a small commission on each sale. Your Designer Tees database includes four tables: Customers, Orders, Salesperson, and Products. Figure 5.1 shows the fields in each table and the relationships among the tables.

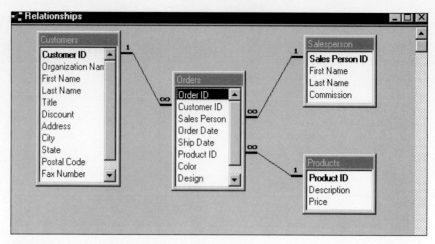

Figure 5.1

You can examine your data using select and *crosstab queries*. As you saw in Project 4, a select query allows you to retrieve data from one or more tables by specifying which fields and records you want to see. You can also create new information based on existing data. For example, if you store data about the price of a product, the quantity ordered, and the discount offered to a customer, you can create information about the amount due on an order.

A ***crosstab query*** displays summary data in spreadsheet form, with row and column headings based on fields in a table or query. The individual cells contain calculated data. For example, you might create a crosstab query that counts the number of orders processed by each salesperson for each customer.

In this project you will create a variety of select queries and one crosstab query. You will start by creating queries with multiple search conditions.

SPECIFYING MULTIPLE CRITERIA

In Project 4 you used Filter By Form to view records containing data that matched a single search condition, all search conditions (And criteria), and any one of multiple conditions (Or criteria). You also specified an expression as the filter (the expression $> = 8$ for hours worked). You can produce similar results by creating select queries that you can save and run again.

Figure 5.2 shows the work surface you can use to select fields, specify sort order, enter search criteria, and set up calculations. Tables and relationships appear in the upper half of the query design view. You can indicate your query specifications in the design grid in the lower half.

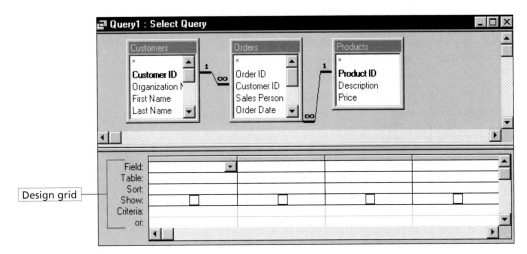

Figure 5.2

When you run a query, fields appear in the order you picked them. You will select a field by dragging its name from a table in the upper half to a column in the design grid.

> **Tip** Use the vertical scroll bar at the upper-right edge of the design view to display other tables. Use the vertical scroll bar within a table to see other fields. If you select a field in error, highlight its name in the design grid and press (DEL)

To begin querying the Designer Tees database, you will display orders by a specific organization (a single exact-match search condition), look at orders for a specific organization for which the quantity ordered was greater than or equal to 8 (And criteria), and then view orders for either the golf or tennis design (Or criteria).

> **Tip** Appendix A lists the data in all four tables of the Designer Tees database. If the database is not available, you can reconstruct it by referring to Figure 5.1 and Appendix A.

To open a database and display query design view:

1 Start Access and open the Designer Tees database.

2 Select the Queries tab, and then select New.
The New Query dialog box appears.

3 Select Design View, and then select OK.
The Show Table dialog box appears.

4 Add the Customers, Orders, and Products tables.

5 Close the Show Table dialog box.
Access displays a query design view similar to the one shown in Figure 5.2. Three tables appear in the upper half of the view.

To select fields from multiple tables:

1 Drag Organization Name, the second field in the Customers table, to the Field row of the first column of the design grid. (Do not release the mouse button yet.)

A small horizontal bar appears in the first column, as shown in Figure 5.3.

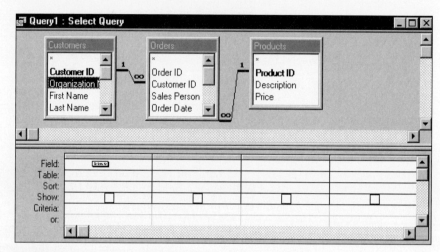

Figure 5.3

2 Release the mouse button.

Access displays the selected field and its table in the first column, as shown in Figure 5.4.

The checkmark in the Show box indicates the field will appear in query results.

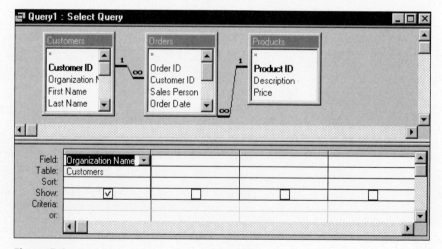

Figure 5.4

3 Drag the field name Customer ID from the Customers table to the Field row of the second column.

4 Click the Show row in the Customer ID column.
The checkmark disappears, indicating the field will not appear in query results.

5 Drag the field name Order Date from the Orders table to the third column.

6 Drag the field name Description from the Products table to the fourth column.

7 Use the horizontal scroll bar on the design grid to display the next blank column.

8 Drag the field name Quantity Ordered from the Orders table to the fifth column.

9 Check that the last four field specifications match those shown in Figure 5.5, and make corrections as necessary.

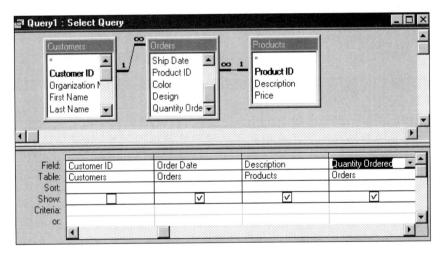

Figure 5.5

To specify sort order, enter a search condition, and run the query:

1 Display the Sort pull-down list in the Order Date column, and then select Ascending.

2 Select the Criteria row in the Customer ID column.

3 Type ="GLENL"
The criteria specification should match that shown in Figure 5.6 including the quotation marks.

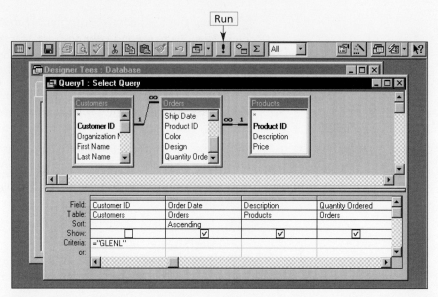

Figure 5.6

4 Select the Run button on the toolbar or switch to datasheet view. Selected fields from the eight records matching the GLENL search condition appear in datasheet view, as shown in Figure 5.7.

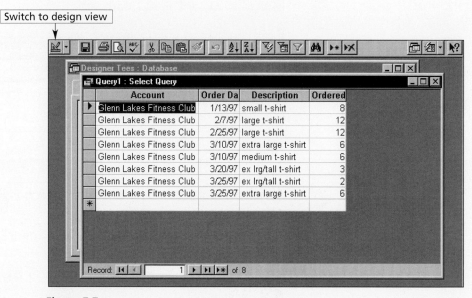

Figure 5.7

5 Switch to query design view.

To add another search condition and run the revised query:

1 Select the Criteria row in the Quantity Ordered column.

2 Type **>=8**

3 Check that your criteria match those shown in Figure 5.8, and make corrections as necessary.

Closes the query

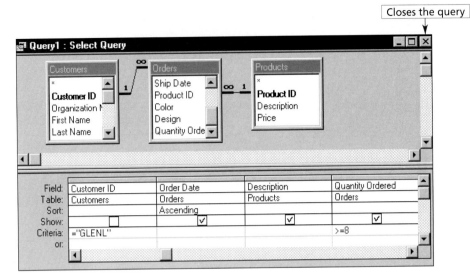

Figure 5.8

4 Run the query by selecting the Run button on the toolbar or switching to datasheet view.
Selected fields from the three records matching both search conditions (GLENL customer ID and order quantity equal to or greater than 8) appear in datasheet view.

5 Switch to query design view.

To modify and save the query:

1 Delete $>= 8$ in the Criteria row of the Quantity Ordered column.

2 Type **="HOLE1"** in the Criteria row of the Customer ID column to replace = "*GLENL*".

3 Run the query.
Selected fields from the six records matching the HOLE1 search condition appear in datasheet view.

4 Switch to query design view.

5 Close the query.

6 Select Yes when prompted to save changes to the query.

7 Type **Orders from one customer** as the query name in the Save As dialog box, and then select OK.
The name you specified appears in the Queries folder, as shown in Figure 5.9. Whenever you want to view orders for one customer, you can open this query, replace the last entry in the Customer ID Criteria row with your new search condition, and run the query.

Figure 5.9

To specify Or criteria in a query:

1 Select the Queries tab if it is not already selected, and then select New.

2 Select Design View, and then select OK.

3 Add the Customers, Orders, and Products tables, and then close the Show Table dialog box.

4 Drag the following fields to the columns indicated:
Column 1   Customer ID from the Customers table
Column 2   Order Date from the Orders Table
Column 3   Description from the Products Table
Column 4   Color from the Orders Table
Column 5   Design from the Orders Table
Column 6   Quantity Ordered from the Orders Table

5 Select the Criteria row in the Design column, and then type `="golf"`

6 Select the Or row in the Design column, and then type `="tennis"`
The last four search conditions should match those shown in Figure 5.10.

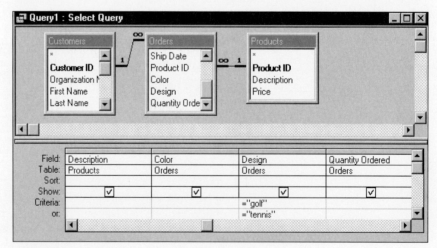

Figure 5.10

7 Run the query.
Selected fields from the eight records containing either golf or tennis as the design appear in datasheet view, as shown in Figure 5.11.

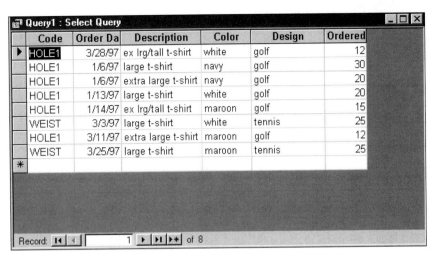

Code	Order Da	Description	Color	Design	Ordered
HOLE1	3/28/97	ex lrg/tall t-shirt	white	golf	12
HOLE1	1/6/97	large t-shirt	navy	golf	30
HOLE1	1/6/97	extra large t-shirt	navy	golf	20
HOLE1	1/13/97	large t-shirt	white	golf	20
HOLE1	1/14/97	ex lrg/tall t-shirt	maroon	golf	15
WEIST	3/3/97	large t-shirt	white	tennis	25
HOLE1	3/11/97	extra large t-shirt	maroon	golf	12
WEIST	3/25/97	large t-shirt	maroon	tennis	25

Figure 5.11

8 Switch to query design view.

To delete current criteria and save the field specifications:

1 Delete both criteria in the Design column.

2 Close the query.

3 Select Yes when prompted to save changes to the query.

4 Type **Order details** as the query name in the Save As dialog box, and then select OK.

The name you specified appears in the Queries folder, as shown in Figure 5.12. Whenever you want to view orders for specific sizes, colors, and/or designs, you can open this query, type your criteria in the appropriate rows, and run the query.

Figure 5.12

EXIT If necessary, you can close this database now. You can then exit Access and continue this project later.

CREATING CALCULATED FIELDS

Some of your information needs may not be met by viewing existing data. For example, you may have data on quantity ordered, price, and discount allowed, but you want to compute the total amount due. Perhaps you have data about order and ship dates, but you would like to know if you are meeting your goal of shipping within two weeks. Access allows you to create new information based on existing data by setting up *calculated fields* in queries.

A ***calculated field*** creates new data or presents existing data in a different way. For example, you can create a calculated field to perform a mathematical calculation on two Number type fields or join two Text type fields. You can view data resulting from a calculated field in a query or report, but the field is not part of the database structure stored on disk.

You will create a calculated field by defining some calculation in an expression. Although you can type each character in the expression yourself, as you did in Project 4 when you entered >=8 in a Filter By Form operation, you may find it easier to set up a complex expression using the Expression Builder dialog box shown in Figure 5.13.

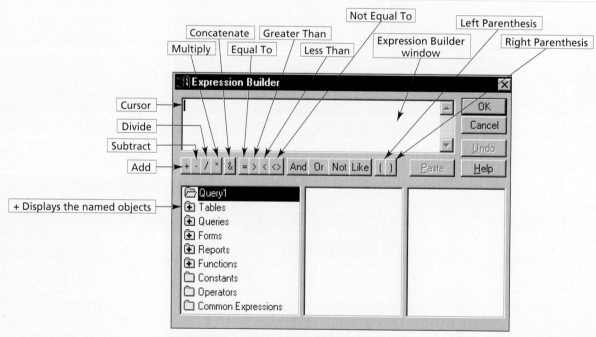

Figure 5.13

You will enter an expression in the Expression Builder window portion of the dialog box. Selecting a button below that window copies the word or symbol on the button to the current cursor position in the window. The three columns below the buttons are display areas from which you can select other portions of an expression. In the following sections you will glimpse the power of calculated fields by creating and running three queries that contain expressions.

Using Arithmetic Operators

If you select a button below the Expression Builder window, Access will paste a *mathematical, comparison, logical,* or *string operator* in the Expression Builder window. A **mathematical operator** performs a calculation such as addition (+), subtraction (−), multiplication (*), or division (/). You will use a **comparison operator** (also known as a *relational operator*) to specify the scope of a search, such as finding data that are equal to (=), greater than (>), less than (<), not equal to (<>), or like stated criteria. A **logical operator** specifies a logical relationship of inclusion or exclusion. For example, the logical operators And and Not restrict the number of records retrieved. The logical operator Or broadens the number of records retrieved. A **string operator** performs a calculation on alphanumeric characters, such as connecting two Text fields using the Concatenate (&) button.

When several mathematical operators appear in an expression, each part is evaluated according to the rules of operator precedence, which include performing multiplication and division before addition and subtraction.

> **Tip** You can use parentheses to override the order of precedence. Operations within parentheses are always performed before those outside. If you need more information, use Answer Wizard to view on-screen Help on the topic of Operator Precedence.

For the Designer Tees database, you will calculate two fields containing one or more of the arithmetic operators shown on the buttons in Figure 5.13. One calculated field will compute the amount due on an order by multiplying quantity ordered by the discounted selling price. The other calculated field will compute a salesperson's commission by multiplying the results of the first calculated field by the salesperson's commission percentage.

> **Tip** You may find it helpful to write out the basic calculation before you begin. For example, the expression to compute total due on a t-shirt order would have the following general format:
>
> $$\text{Quantity Ordered} \times \text{Price} \times (1 - \text{Discount})$$
>
> You should also check that results calculate properly. For example, if a customer who gets a 25 percent discount orders 30 shirts at $30 each, the total due should be $675.

In the following steps you will build the first of two expressions containing fields and arithmetic operators.

To start a query and access the Expression Builder dialog box:

1 If necessary, load Access and open the Designer Tees database.

2 Select the Queries tab, and then select New.

3 Select Design View, and then select OK.

4 Add all four tables, and then close the Show Table dialog box.

5 Drag the Customer ID field to the Field row in the first column.

6 Drag the Order Date field to the Field row in the second column.

7 Select the Field row in the third column.

8 Select the Build button on the toolbar.

The Expression Builder dialog box appears as shown in Figure 5.13.

To build an expression to calculate totals:

1 Select Tables by double-clicking its folder icon marked with a plus sign.

A list of tables in the Designer Tees database appears as shown in Figure 5.14.

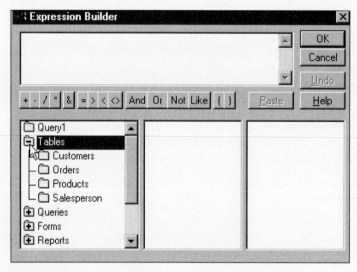

Figure 5.14

2 Select the Products table by double-clicking its folder icon.

A list of fields in the Products table appears in the middle column, as shown in Figure 5.15.

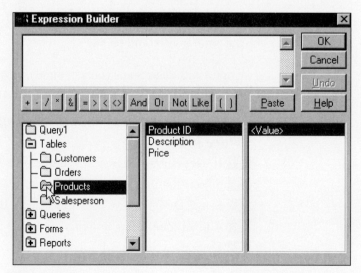

Figure 5.15

3 Select the Price field by double-clicking its name.

[Products]![Price] appears in the Expression Builder window, indicating that you have selected the Price field from the Products table.

4 Select ∗ (the Multiply button, shown in Figure 5.13).

The expression you are building should match that shown in Figure 5.16.

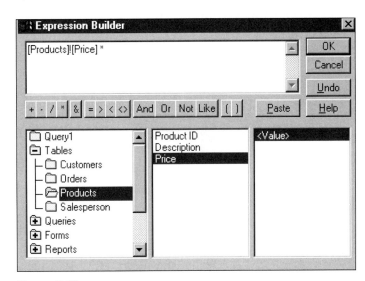

Figure 5.16

5 Select the Orders table, and then select the Quantity Ordered field.

6 Select ∗ (the Multiply button).

The expression you are building should match that shown in Figure 5.17.

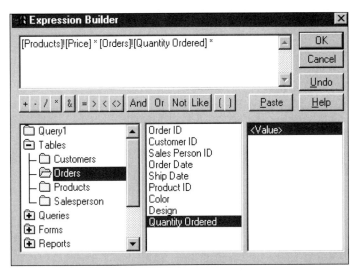

Figure 5.17

7 Select ((the Left Parenthesis button).

8 Type **1**

9 Select − (the subtract button).

10 Select the Customers table, and then select the Discount field.

11 Select) (the Right Parenthesis button).

The expression you entered should match that shown in Figure 5.18.

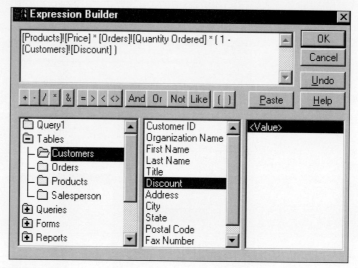

Figure 5.18

12 Select OK.

The Expression Builder dialog box closes, and query design view reappears. The Field row in the third column displays the end of the new expression.

To name the expression, run the query, and check the results:

1 Click in the Field row of another column, and then select the Field row in the third column again.

The beginning of the expression appears, preceded by *Expr1*, the name Access assigns to a calculated field.

2 Select only the *Expr1* portion of the expression, and then type
Total Due

Total Due replaces Expr1 as the name of the calculated field.

3 Run the query.

4 Select any cell in the Order Date column, and then select Sort Ascending in the toolbar.

Your query results should match those shown in Figure 5.19.

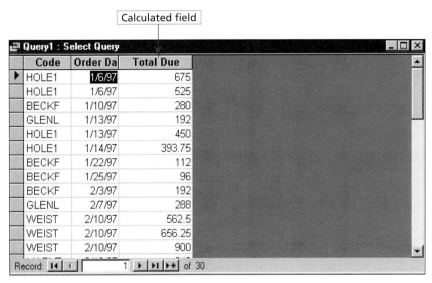

Figure 5.19

A check of data related to the initial HOLE1 order on 1/6/97 would show that 30 shirts were ordered at $30 each. Applying HOLE1's 25 percent discount to the original $900 bill would result in a total due of $675. A check of data related to the BECKF order on 1/10/97 would show that 10 shirts were ordered at $35 each. Applying BECKF's 20 percent discount to the original $350 bill would result in a total due of $280. Be sure to randomly check the results of calculations in your own queries.

Reminder   The calculated field appears only when you run the query. The field does not become part of the database.

To close the query, saving your changes:

1 Switch to query design view.

2 Close the query.

3 Select Yes when prompted to save changes to the query.

4 Type **Order totals and commissions** as the query name in the Save As dialog box, and then select OK.

The name you specified appears in the Queries folder.

Using a String Operator

You will use the string operator & (ampersand sign) in an expression to concatenate text fields. For example, selecting a first name field, selecting the Concatenate button (&), and then selecting the last name field will cause both names to display together. If you also type " " (a quote mark, a space, and then another quote mark) before the last name field in the expression, the two names will appear with a space between them.

In the following steps you will modify the Order totals and commissions query to include a fourth column displaying the salesperson's first and last names and a fifth column to compute commission on the order.

To combine two text fields in an expression and run the query:

1 Open the Order totals and commissions query in design view.

2 Select the Field row in column four, and then select Build in the toolbar.

3 Select Tables, and then select the Salesperson table.

4 Select First Name from the list of fields in the middle column. [*Salesperson*] *!* [*First Name*] appears in the Expression Builder window.

5 Select & (the Concatenate button, the fifth button from the left). The expression you are building should match that shown in Figure 5.20.

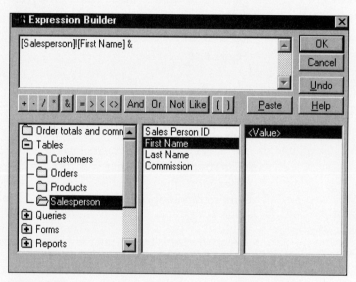

Figure 5.20

6 Type " " (include a space between the double quotes).

7 Select the & button again.

8 Select *Last Name* from the list of fields. The expression you entered should match that shown in Figure 5.21.

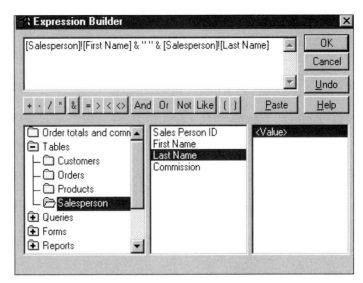

Figure 5.21

9 Select OK to close the Expression Builder dialog box.
Query design view reappears with a calculated field defined in column four.

To name the expression and run the query:

1 Click in the Field row of another column, and then select the Field row in the fourth column again.
The beginning of the expression appears, preceded by *Expr1*.

2 Select only the *Expr1* portion of the expression, and then type
Salesperson
Salesperson replaces Expr1 as the name of the calculated field.

3 Run the query.
The first and last names of salespersons appear in one field, as shown in Figure 5.22.

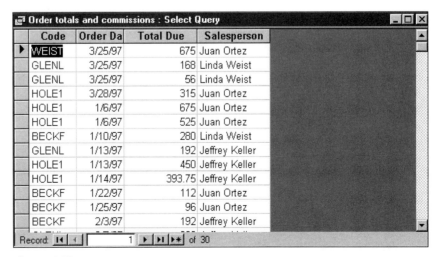

Figure 5.22

To add a field computing commissions:

1 Switch to query design view.

2 Select the entire *Total Due* expression in the Field row in the third column.

3 Choose Copy from the Edit menu.

4 Select the Field row in the fifth column.

5 Choose Paste from the Edit menu.

6 Select Build in the toolbar.

The *Total Due* expression automatically appears in the Expression Builder window, as shown in Figure 5.23.

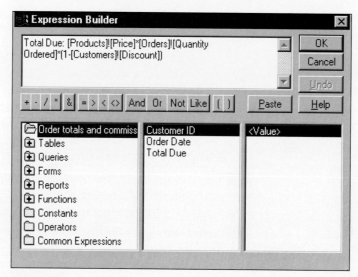

Figure 5.23

7 Select ∗ (the Multiply button).

8 Select the Salesperson table, and then select the Commission field.

9 Select the original expression name, *Total Due*, as shown in Figure 5.24.

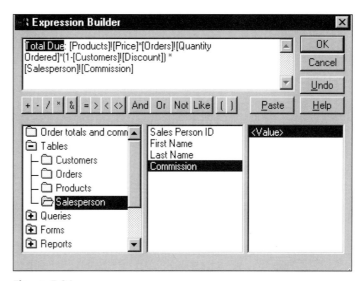

Figure 5.24

10 Type **Commission** to rename the expression.

11 Select OK to close the Expression Builder dialog box.
Query design view reappears with a calculated field defined in column five.

To run the query and check the results:

1 Run the query.
Five columns of data appear in datasheet view.

2 Select any cell in the Order Date column, and then select the Sort
Ascending button on the toolbar.
The commissions earned by salespersons appear in the fifth column, as
shown in Figure 5.25.

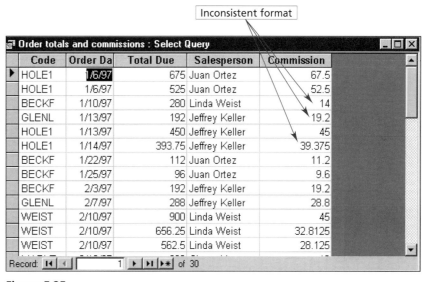

Figure 5.25

A check of data related to the initial HOLE1 order on 1/6/97 would show that Juan Ortez processed the order. Applying Juan's 10 percent commission rate to the $675 due would result in a $67.50 commission. A check of data related to the BECKF order on 1/10/97 would show that Linda Weist processed the order. Applying Linda's 5 percent commission rate to the $280 due would result in a $14 commission. Be sure to randomly check the results of calculations in your own queries.

To change the format of calculated fields and view the results:

1 Switch to query design view.

2 Select *Total Due* at the beginning of the expression in the third column's Field row.

3 Choose Properties from the View menu.

4 Display the Format pull-down menu, as shown in Figure 5.26.

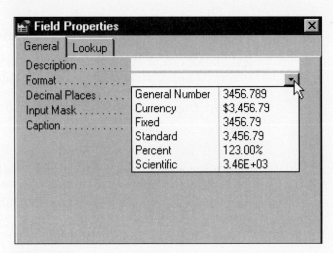

Figure 5.26

5 Select Standard, and then close the Field Properties dialog box.

6 Select *Commission* at the beginning of the expression in the fifth column's Field row, and then repeat steps 3 through 5.

7 Run the query.
All amounts for total due and commission appear with two decimal places.

8 Switch to design view and close the query, saving your changes.

EXIT If necessary, you can close this database now. You can then exit Access and continue this project later.

Working with Functions

A *function* is a program that returns a single value. Access provides over 100 built-in functions that you can use to create expressions. Figure 5.27

shows several categories of functions in the middle column and some of the functions within the Date/Time category in the third column.

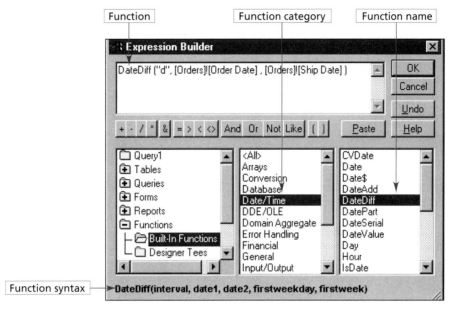

Figure 5.27

Syntax refers to required form and content. A function includes the function name followed by information items within parentheses. The information items must be separated by commas. The DateDiff function shown in Figure 5.27 displays the interval between two specified dates. You can choose among a variety of intervals including year, quarter, month, week, day, and hour.

You will select a function to paste in the Expression Builder window the same way you selected a field. Figure 5.28 illustrates the effect of selecting the DateDiff function.

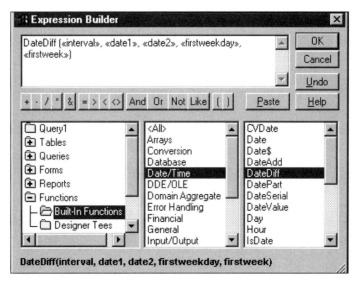

Figure 5.28

An item with double angle brackets will be replaced with the appropriate data or field specification. For example, replacing <<interval>> with "d" and replacing <<date1>> and <<date2>> with order date and ship date fields, respectively, would create an expression calculating the number of days to ship an order.

Tip If you eliminate the last two specifications, <<firstweekday>> and <<firstweek>>, Access uses Sunday for the first day in a week and January 1 for the first day of a year.

In the following steps you will create a query in the Designer Tees database that shows the difference between order date and ship date. You will then modify the query to show only those orders for which it took more than two weeks to ship.

To paste a function into the Expression Builder window:

1 If necessary, load Access and open the Designer Tees database.

2 Select the Queries tab, and then select New.

3 Select Design View, and then select OK.

4 Add the Orders table and close the Show Table dialog box.

5 Drag the Customer ID, Order Date, and Ship Date fields in the order given to the Field row in the first three columns.

6 Select the Field row in the fourth column, and then select the Build button on the toolbar.

7 Select Functions in the first column, and then select Built-In Functions. Function categories appear in the middle column, and a list of all available functions appears in the third column.

8 Click Date/Time in the middle column to display only the Date/Time functions in the third column.

Quick Fix If you double-click Date/Time instead of single-clicking it, Access automatically selects the first Date/Time function CVDate, which you do not want. Select the resulting expression in the Expression Builder window and press `DEL` or immediately click the Undo button in the Expression Builder dialog box.

9 Double-click the function name DateDiff.
The syntax for the DateDiff function appears in the Expression Builder window, as shown in Figure 5.28.

To modify the initial function expression:

1 Select <<*interval*>> by clicking between the double-angle brackets surrounding the word *interval*.

2 Type **"d"** (be sure to include the quotation marks).
The function you are building should match that shown in Figure 5.29.

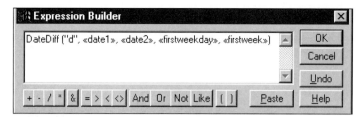

Figure 5.29

3 Select <<*date1*>>

4 Select Tables, select the Orders table, and then select the Order Date field.

The function you are building should match that shown in Figure 5.30.

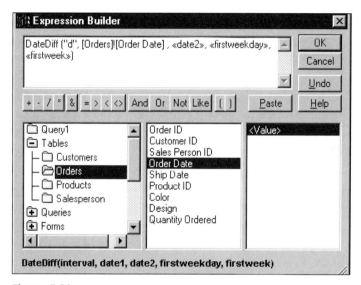

Figure 5.30

5 Select <<*date2*>>

6 Select the Ship Date field.

The function you are building should match that shown in Figure 5.31.

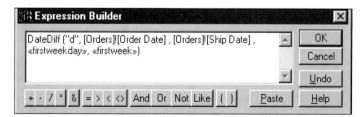

Figure 5.31

7 Select the <<*firstweekday*>>,<<*firstweek*>> portion of the function and press [DEL]

8 Delete remaining commas and spaces, if any, but do not remove the right parenthesis at the end of the expression.

9 Check that your revised function matches that shown in Figure 5.32, and make corrections as necessary.

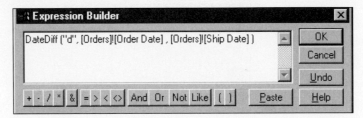

Figure 5.32

10 Select OK to close the Expression Builder dialog box and restore query design view.

To name the field and run the query:

1 Display *Expr1* at the beginning of the Field row in the fourth column.

2 Select *Expr1* and type **Ship Days**

3 Run the query.

The number of days between each order date and ship date appears in the Ship Days column, as shown in Figure 5.33.

Custome	Order Da	Ship Date	Ship Days
WEIST	3/25/97	4/7/97	13
HOLE1	1/6/97	1/17/97	11
HOLE1	1/13/97	1/24/97	11
BECKF	2/3/97	2/18/97	15
GLENL	2/7/97	2/18/97	11
WEIST	2/10/97	2/20/97	10
MARKT	2/18/97	3/3/97	13
GLENL	2/25/97	3/13/97	16
WEIST	3/3/97	3/14/97	11
WEIST	3/3/97	3/14/97	11
MARKT	3/14/97	3/24/97	10
WEIST	3/25/97	4/7/97	13
WEIST	2/10/97	2/20/97	10

Record: 1 of 30

Figure 5.33

Quick Fix If an error message appears when you try to run the query, you did not enter one or more portions of the function correctly. Switch to query design view, select Build in the toolbar, and modify the function as necessary. The most common errors include missing parentheses and commas.

To specify a search condition in the query:

1 Switch to query design view.

2 Type **>14** in the Criteria row of the Ship Days column, as shown in Figure 5.34.

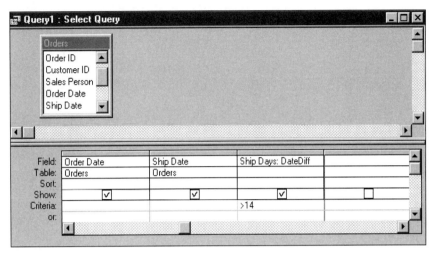

Figure 5.34

3 Run the query.
The results indicate that the orders for BECKF on 2/3/97 and GLENL on 2/25/97 were not shipped within 14 days.

4 Switch to query design view, close the query, and select Yes when prompted to save changes to the query.

5 Type **Orders exceeding 2-week shipment** as the query name, and then select OK.
The name you specified appears in the Queries folder.

USING PREDEFINED CALCULATIONS

Access provides a variety of predefined calculations that you can use in queries. You can enter your choice in the Total row in query design view. Figure 5.35 shows the pull-down menu from which you can make your selection.

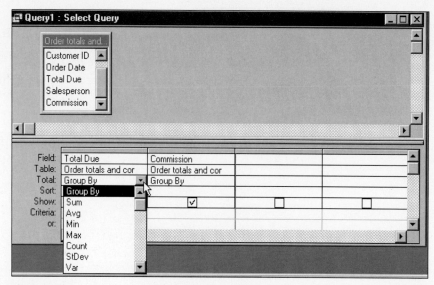

Figure 5.35

In the following sections you will create a query based on an existing query. The new query will display total sales and total commissions for orders in the Designer Tees database. You will then duplicate the query and modify it to show total sales and total commissions for each salesperson.

To specify a predefined calculation in a query:

1 Check that Queries is the current folder in the Database dialog box, and then select New.

2 Select Design View, and then select OK.

3 Select the Queries tab in the Show Table dialog box.

4 Add the Order totals and commissions query, and then select Close.

5 Drag the Total Due and Commission field names in the order given to the Field row in the first and second columns.

6 Select the Totals button on the toolbar.
Access inserts a row named Total below the Table row as shown in Figure 5.36.

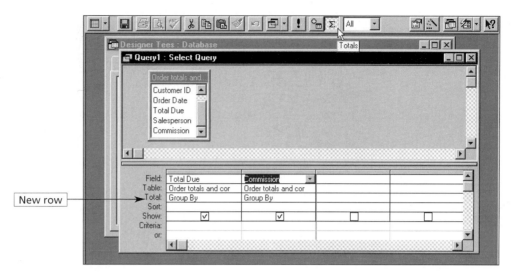

Figure 5.36

7 Select the Total row in the first column and then display the pull-down list shown in Figure 5.35.

8 Select Sum.

9 Repeat steps 7 and 8 to set up the same predefined calculation in the Commission column.

Your settings should match those shown in Figure 5.37.

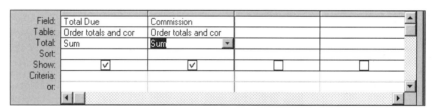

Figure 5.37

10 Choose Properties from the View menu, and set a Standard format for both fields.

To run the query and save the query design:

1 Run the query.

2 Drag the right edge of the cell containing the column name SumOfTotal Due to the right until you can see the complete name.

3 Repeat Step 2 to display the complete name SumOfCommission. Your query results should match those shown in Figure 5.38.

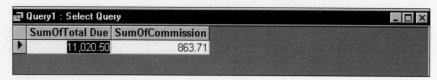

Figure 5.38

4 Close the query and save your specification using the name Summarize total sales and commissions.

To duplicate an existing query:

1 Select the query name Summarize total sales and commissions.

2 Select Copy in the toolbar.

3 Select Paste in the toolbar.

4 Type `Summarize sales and commissions by salesperson` in the Paste As dialog box, and then select OK.

To group records by salesperson before calculating totals:

1 Open the Summarize sales and commissions by salesperson query in design view.

2 Drag the Salesperson field name in the upper portion of the dialog box to the Field row in the first column.
Salesperson becomes the first field, and the other two fields shift to the right, as shown in Figure 5.39.

![Summarize sales and commissions by salesperson : Select Query window]

Figure 5.39

3 Run the query or switch to datasheet view.
Access automatically calculates total due and commission for each salesperson, as shown in Figure 5.40.

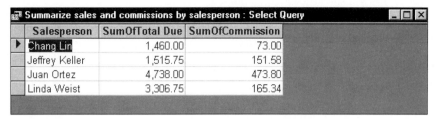

Figure 5.40

4 Close the query, saving your changes.

ANALYZING DATA WITH CROSSTAB QUERIES

A crosstab query calculates summary data based on the contents of two fields, displays the results in a spreadsheet format, and automatically provides column and row headings that describe the contents of the two fields. For example, Figure 5.41 shows the results of running a crosstab query that counts orders by each salesperson for each customer. The individual counts total 30, the number of records currently stored in the Orders table of the Designer Tees database.

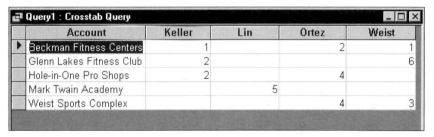

Figure 5.41

Answer Wizard provides an example of a crosstab query that sums data. Viewing that information will help you to understand how to use crosstab queries to analyze your own data.

To view on-screen Help about crosstab queries:

1 Choose Answer Wizard from the Help menu.

2 Type **crosstab query** in the request box, and then select Search.

3 Select Example of a crosstab query in the *Tell Me About* section, and then select Display.
The first of two Help screens appears.

4 Read the information on the initial Help screen, and note how much easier it is to compare data in the crosstab query than in the original table.

5 Select Next>.

6 Read the information on the second Help screen, with emphasis on how to create a crosstab query using the query design grid.

7 Select Close.

Access provides *Crosstab Query Wizard* to guide you through the process of creating a crosstab query. Prompts appear for the table or query name, the fields for row headings, the fields for column headings, the field for the body, and the title.

> **Tip** If you are already working in query design view to select fields from multiple tables, you can easily insert a Crosstab row and provide the necessary information without the aid of Crosstab Query Wizard.

In the following steps you will create a crosstab query that produces the results shown in Figure 5.41.

To create a crosstab query:

1 Check that Queries is the current folder in the Database dialog box, and then select New.

2 Select Design View, and then select OK.

3 Add the Customers, Orders, and Salesperson tables to the query, and then close the Show Table dialog box.

4 Select the Query Type button on the toolbar to display the pull-down menu shown in Figure 5.42.

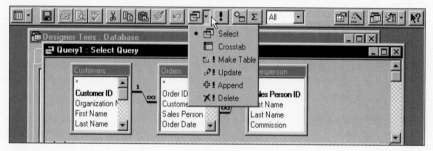

Figure 5.42

5 Select Crosstab.
The Show row disappears from the design grid, and Access inserts Total and Crosstab rows after the Table row.

6 Drag the Organization Name (Customers table), Last Name (Salesperson table), and Order ID (Orders table) field names to the Field row in the first three columns.

7 Select the Crosstab row in the first column, and then display the Crosstab pull-down list shown in Figure 5.43.

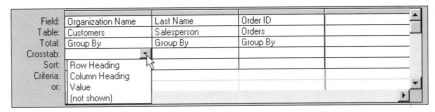

Figure 5.43

8 Select Row Heading from the pull-down list.

9 Select Column Heading from the Crosstab pull-down list in the second column.

10 Select Value from the Crosstab pull-down list in the third column.

11 Select Count from the Total pull-down list in the third column.
The query specifications should match those shown in Figure 5.44.

Figure 5.44

 To run the query, check the results, and save the query:

1 Run the query or switch to datasheet view.
The query results should match those shown in Figure 5.41.

2 Check that the counts total 30, the number of records in the Orders table.

3 Close the query and save your specifications using the name Order counts by customer and salesperson.
Access displays a different icon to indicate a crosstab query, as shown in Figure 5.45.

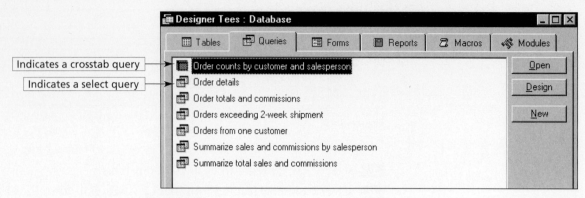

Figure 5.45

4 Close the database.

THE NEXT STEP

In this project you created a variety of select queries in which you specified multiple criteria, created calculated fields, worked with a function, and selected a predefined calculation. You also learned to create summary data using a crosstab query.

The Query Type pull-down menu shown in Figure 5.42 lists Make Table, Update, Append, and Delete in addition to Select and Crosstab. Those queries help you to maintain a database, and you will work with them in Project 7.

As a next step, you might use on-screen Help to reinforce existing knowledge and also read information on other query features. As a starting point, use Answer Wizard to look up information on calculated fields and then study the topic *Performing calculations in a query-an overview*. You will find it easier to understand the lengthy narrative description having been through the process of specifying calculations several times. For a new topic, learn about parameter queries and see if you can set one up.

Don't overlook trying out variations of the query specifications you have already made. Queries often provide the starting point for reports, and you'll find it easier to present the information you need in an eye-catching format if you are already comfortable with pulling the appropriate data together.

This concludes Project 5. You can either exit Access or go on to work the Study Questions, Review Exercises, and Assignments.

SUMMARY AND EXERCISES

Summary

- You can specify multiple criteria in a select query by entering your specifications in one or more Criteria rows in query design view.
- A calculated field creates new data or presents existing data in a different way. You can view data resulting from a calculated field in a query or report, but the field is not part of the database structure stored on disk.
- You can set up a calculated field by using the Expression Builder dialog box to enter the appropriate combination of fields and operators.
- A mathematical operator performs a calculation such as addition (+), subtraction (-), multiplication (*), or division (/).
- You will use a comparison operator to specify the scope of a search, such as finding data that are equal to (=), greater than (>), less than (<), not equal to (<>), or like stated criteria.
- A logical operator specifies a logical relationship of inclusion or exclusion, and a string operator performs a calculation on alphanumeric characters.
- A function is a program that returns a single value such as the number of days between two dates. Access provides over 100 built-in functions that you can use to create expressions.
- You can select a predefined calculation such as Count or Average when working in query design view.
- A crosstab query calculates summary data based on the contents of two fields, displays the results in a spreadsheet format, and automatically provides column and row headings that describe the contents of the two fields.

Key Terms and Operations

Key Terms
calculated field
comparison operator
crosstab query
Crosstab Query Wizard
function
logical operator
mathematical operator
string operator
syntax

Operations
Specify multiple criteria
Create a calculated field
Enter a function
Select a predefined calculation
Create a crosstab query

Study Questions

Multiple Choice
1. A select query allows you to
    a. retrieve data from one or more tables.
    b. specify which fields and records you want to see.
    c. create new information based on existing data.
    d. All of the above.

2. Which is not a true statement about a crosstab query?
   a. A crosstab query displays summary data in spreadsheet form.
   b. Only data stored in one or more tables appear when you run a crosstab query.
   c. Calculated data appear when you run a crosstab query.
   d. All of the above.

3. The / symbol indicates a _____ operator.
   a. logical
   b. mathematical
   c. comparison
   d. string

4. Which is not a true statement about queries?
   a. When you run a query, fields appear in the order you selected them.
   b. You can add a field to a query by dragging its name from a table in the upper half of the screen to a column in the query design grid.
   c. If a field specification already exists in a column in the query design grid, specifying another field at that location replaces the existing one.
   d. All of the above.

5. From query design view you can run a query by
   a. switching to datasheet view.
   b. selecting the button with a question mark in the toolbar.
   c. Both a and b.
   d. None of the above.

6. Which is not a true statement about a calculated field in a query?
   a. The calculated field becomes part of the database structure stored on disk when you save the query.
   b. A calculated field can display existing data in a new way.
   c. A calculated field can create new data from existing data.
   d. You can view data resulting from a calculated field in a query or report.

7. Which of the following expressions would evaluate to 12?
   a. 2 + 5*7-5
   b. (2 + 5)*(7-5)
   c. 2 + 5*(7-5)
   d. None of the above.

8. Which is a true statement about functions?
   a. A function is a program that returns a single value.
   b. Functions are limited to arithmetic operations.
   c. Access has over 100 built-in functions.
   d. Both a and c.

9. Syntax refers to
   a. the required form and content of a function.
   b. the name of the button that opens the Expression Builder dialog box.
   c. the name of a function.
   d. None of the above.

10. Assume that city and state data are stored in two separate fields. Which of the following symbol-and-character combinations would concatenate the two fields with a comma after the city and a space before the state?
   a. &," "&
   b. &,&" "&
   c. ","&" "
   d. None of the above.

Short Answer

1. Assume that a table named Salary Update includes the two fields Base Pay and Percent Raise, and that you want to create a calculated field that computes the new base pay after the raise. What expression would produce the required calculation?

2. Access provides a number of small programs that return a single value such as the number of days between two dates. What term describes these programs?

3. Provide two examples of comparison operators.

4. What type of query produces summary data arranged in spreadsheet form?

5. Name the feature that you can use to paste fields and operators in a calculation you are constructing.

6. What symbol(s) denotes a not equal relationship?

7. What do double angle brackets surrounding a word indicate if they appear within a function you pasted into an expression?

8. What term describes connecting two text fields?

9. If an error message appears when you try to run a query containing a function, what might you look for as the most common errors?

10. Name the type(s) of query you created in this project.

For Discussion

1. Explain And and Or logic as they relate to specifying multiple criteria in a query. Provide examples.

2. What is a calculated field? Describe the process to create one.

3. What is a function? Provide examples of functions in three categories other than Date/Time.

4. In this project you worked with a predefined calculation to total sales and commissions for each salesperson. Explain how you might use two of the other predefined calculations.

5. How does a crosstab query differ from a select query?

Review Exercises

Project 5 involved creating queries that displayed data based on one or more of the four tables in the Designer Tees database: Products, Customers, Orders, and Salesperson. In these review exercises you will apply what you have learned to similar situations.

Using And and Or Criteria in a Query

1. Start Access, open the Designer Tees database, and open the Order details query in query design view.

2. Delete existing criteria, if any, and then specify criteria to display orders for large navy t-shirts (Description is large t-shirt and Color is navy).

3. Run the query, verify that the results are accurate, and make corrections as necessary.

4. Modify the query design to display orders for large or extra large navy t-shirts.

5. Run the query, verify that the results are accurate, and make corrections as necessary.

6. Close the query without saving your changes.

Creating a Calculated Field

1. Create a new query containing the fields Order ID, Customer ID, and Order Date from the Orders table.

2. Select the Field row in the fourth column, and open the Expression Builder dialog box.

3. Create an expression that adds the number 14 to the Order Date field from the Orders table, and then name the expression Ship By.

4. Type `>=3/15/97` as the Order Date criteria.

5. Run the query.

6. Verify that only orders on or after 3/15/97 are displayed and that the new Ship By field adds 14 days to each Order Date.

7. Print your results (optional), and then close the query without saving your changes.

Selecting a Predefined Calculation

1. Create a new query containing the fields Customer ID and Quantity Ordered from the Orders table.

2. Type `=HOLE1` as the Customer ID criteria.

3. Run the query to view the orders from the customer identified as HOLE1.

4. Switch to query design view, and then select Totals in the toolbar.

5. Select Max from the Total pull-down list in the Quantity Ordered field.

6. Run the query to view the highest number of t-shirts in one size that were ordered by customer HOLE1.

7. Switch to query design view, and select Min from the Total pull-down list in the Quantity Ordered field.

8. Run the query to view the lowest number of t-shirts in one size that were ordered by customer HOLE1.

9. Close the query without saving your changes.

Creating a Crosstab Query

1. Open the Order totals and commissions query in design view.

2. Choose Save As from the File menu, and save the query within the current database under the name Commission totals by customer and salesperson.

3. Delete the Order Date and Total Due fields.

Reminder   To delete a field in the query design grid, select it by clicking the narrow bar above the field name, and then press ⌐DEL⌐

4. Select Crosstab from the Query Type pull-down menu in the toolbar.

5. Specify the Total and Crosstab settings shown in Figure 5.46, and then run the query.

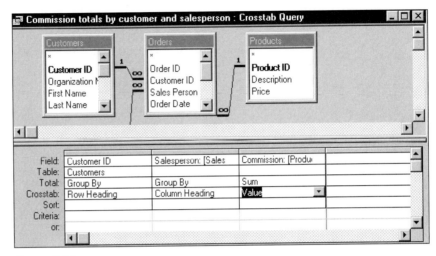

Figure 5.46

6. Close the query and save your changes.

Assignments

Learning about the Between/And Operator

Use Answer Wizard to look up information about the Between operator. If you then select *Retrieve a range of records using a query* in the *How Do I* section, you will see an example of using Between/And in an expression. What is that example? Also explain how you might use the Between/And operator to restrict record display in the Designer Tees database.

Learning about the Like Operator

Use Answer Wizard to look up information about the *Like operator*, and then select *Examples of criteria expressions for queries or filters* in the *Tell Me About* section. Scroll to the *What do you want to do?* section, and then select *See examples of expressions that use wildcard characters*. What are some of the sample expressions that include the Like operator? Also explain how you might use the Like operator to restrict record display in the Designer Tees database.

Finding Top Values

Use on-screen Help to learn about the Top Values pull-down menu in the toolbar, and summarize your findings. Also give an example of how you might use this feature when working with the Designer Tees database.

Putting on a Fund-Raiser (Part Four)

Using the fund-raising database you created in prior assignments, create a variety of select queries that meet information needs identified in the database design phase. Verify query results, print (optional), and save your specifications. One or more queries should specify multiple criteria, include a function in an expression, create a calculated field, or select among predefined calculations. If appropriate for your data, create and save a crosstab query, also.

PROJECT 6: REVISITING REPORTS

Objectives

After completing this project, you should be able to:

► Work within bands to create or modify a report

► Edit, size, and move a control

► Add and align a control

► Specify sort order, format, and font size in report design view

► Enhance a report with lines and special effects

► Use Label Wizard to create mailing labels

CASE STUDY: TRACKING SALES II

As you continue to manage your small company named Designer Tees, you turn your attention to information needs that cannot be met with queries alone. Your first priority is to create a report that groups order details by customer. You would also like to set up mailing labels.

Designing the Solution

You can reduce design time by using Report Wizard to set up fields, labels, and calculations in a report and then making minor adjustments on your own. Figure 6.1 shows part of a multiple-page sales summary report created by Report Wizard. The handwritten comments describe the changes you want to make to the original design.

Shorten the title

~~Data for the~~ Sales Summary by Customer ~~Report~~

Right align the field name on two lines

Center the field name on two lines

Organization Name	Discount	Order ID	Description	Ordered	Price	Total Sale
Beckman Fitness Centers						
	20.00%	970008	large t-shirt	8	$30.00	192
	20.00%	970002	ex lrg/tall t-shirt	10	$35.00	280
	20.00%	970007	small t-shirt	4	$30.00	96
	20.00%	970006	ex lrg/tall t-shirt	4	$35.00	112

Add a special effect to each organization name

Summary for 'Organization Name' = Beckman Fitness Centers (4 detail records)
Sum **680**
Percent **6.17%**

Sort by Order ID within each organization

Show numbers in currency format like the Price data

Glenn Lakes Fitness Club

	20.00%	970014	medium t-shirt	6	$30.00	144
	20.00%	970014	extra large t-shirt	6	$35.00	168
	20.00%	970012	large t-shirt	12	$30.00	288
	20.00%	970017	ex lrg/tall t-shirt	3	$35.00	84
	20.00%	970019	ex lrg/tall t-shirt	2	$35.00	56
	20.00%	970003	small t-shirt	8	$30.00	192
	20.00%	970019	extra large t-shirt	6	$35.00	168
	20.00%	970009	large t-shirt	12	$30.00	288

Add a vertical line to draw attention to summary information

Alter the report design so that the percentage discount only appears once for each customer

Summary for 'Organization Name' = Glenn Lakes Fitness Club (8 detail records)
Sum **1388**
Percent **12.59%**

Figure 6.1

The enhancements you have in mind involve several areas in the report. Viewing on-screen information can help you to understand how Access organizes a report in sections.

To view on-screen Help about the sections in a report:

1 Start Access and open the Designer Tees database.

2 Choose Answer Wizard from the Help menu.

3 Type **report sections** in the Type your request box, and then select Search.

4 In the *Tell Me About* section, select *Sections of a report,* and then select Display.
The first of three Help screens about report sections appears.

5 Read the general introduction to report sections, and then select Next> in the lower-right corner or 2 in the lower-left corner.
The second of three Help screens appears, showing the five sections controlling all multipage reports.

6 Click the vertical bar to the left of *Report header,* as shown in Figure 6.2, and read about the purpose of the initial section in a report.

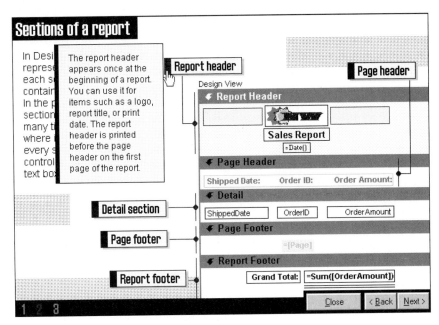

Figure 6.2

7 Click each of the other four vertical bars to view information about the page header, detail, page footer, and report footer sections.

8 Select Next> or 3 to view the third of three Help screens, which explains the advantages of grouping records.

9 Click the vertical bar to the left of *Group header,* as shown in Figure 6.3.

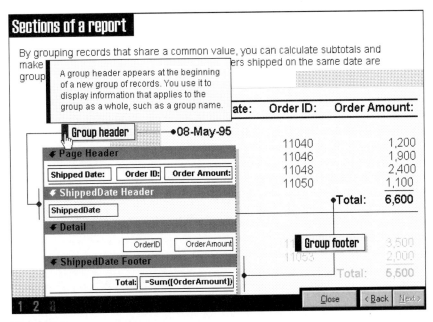

Figure 6.3

10 After reading about the purpose of a group header, select Close.

Report Wizard creates reports based on tables or queries. If you want to place restrictions on which records appear in a report, you need to create a query first, and then use Report Wizard to create a report based on the query. If record selection criteria are not needed, use Report Wizard to create a report based on fields in one or more tables.

Tip If a report will include a calculated field, you may find it easier to set up the expression in a query than to enter the expression in report design view.

The report you have in mind includes the calculated field Total Sale (see Figure 6.1). This field already exists as Total Due in your Order totals and commissions query. You could make a copy of this query and then delete, add, and rearrange fields as necessary. You might find it takes less time, however, to create a new query instead of modifying an existing one.

In the following sections you will create a query and then use Report Wizard to produce a report based on the query.

Tip Steps do not include detailed instructions for creating a calculated field and renaming an expression. If necessary, review the detailed steps provided in Project 5.

To create a query pulling data from three tables:

1 Select the Queries tab, and then select New.

2 Select Design View, and then select OK.

3 Add the Customers, Orders, and Products tables, and then close the Show Table dialog box.

4 Drag the following fields to columns one through six in the query design grid in the order shown:
Organization Name (Customers table)
Discount (Customers table)
Order ID (Orders table)
Description (Products table)
Quantity Ordered (Orders table)
Price (Products table)

5 Select the next blank column, and then select the Build button on the toolbar.

6 Build the expression Quantity Ordered * Price * (1-Discount), and check that the calculation matches that shown in the Expression Builder window shown in Figure 6.4.

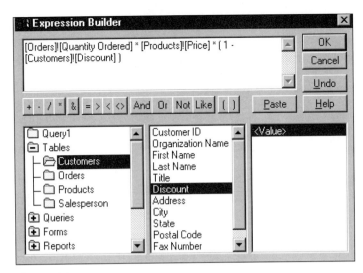

Figure 6.4

7 Make changes as necessary, and then select OK to close the Expression Builder window.

8 Change the name of the calculated field from *Expr1* to **Total Sale.**

9 Run the query.
The query results should include the fields and values shown in Figure 6.5.

Account	Discount	Order ID	Description	Ordered	Price	Total Sale
Weist Sports Complex	25.00%	970018	large t-shirt	30	$30.00	675
Glenn Lakes Fitness Club	20.00%	970019	extra large t-shirt	6	$35.00	168
Glenn Lakes Fitness Club	20.00%	970019	ex lrg/tall t-shirt	2	$35.00	56
Hole-in-One Pro Shops	25.00%	970020	ex lrg/tall t-shirt	12	$35.00	315
Hole-in-One Pro Shops	25.00%	970001	large t-shirt	30	$30.00	675
Hole-in-One Pro Shops	25.00%	970001	extra large t-shirt	20	$35.00	525
Beckman Fitness Centers	20.00%	970002	ex lrg/tall t-shirt	10	$35.00	280
Glenn Lakes Fitness Club	20.00%	970003	small t-shirt	8	$30.00	192
Hole-in-One Pro Shops	25.00%	970004	large t-shirt	20	$30.00	450
Hole-in-One Pro Shops	25.00%	970005	ex lrg/tall t-shirt	15	$35.00	393.75
Beckman Fitness Centers	20.00%	970006	ex lrg/tall t-shirt	4	$35.00	112
Beckman Fitness Centers	20.00%	970007	small t-shirt	4	$30.00	96
Beckman Fitness Centers	20.00%	970008	large t-shirt	8	$30.00	192
Glenn Lakes Fitness Club	20.00%	970009	large t-shirt	12	$30.00	288
Weist Sports Complex	25.00%	970010	medium t-shirt	25	$30.00	562.5
Weist Sports Complex	25.00%	970010	large t-shirt	40	$30.00	900
Weist Sports Complex	25.00%	970010	extra large t-shirt	25	$35.00	656.25
Mark Twain Academy	20.00%	970011	small t-shirt	10	$30.00	240

Record: |◀| ◀ | 1 | ▶ |▶|▶*| of 30

Figure 6.5

10 Switch to query design view, make changes as necessary, and then close the query.

11 Respond Yes when prompted to save the query.

12 Type **Data for the Sales Summary by Customer Report** as the query name in the Save As dialog box, and then select OK.

To create a report based on a query using Report Wizard:

1 Select the Reports tab, and then select New.
The New Report dialog box appears.

2 Select Report Wizard, and then select Data for the Sales Summary from the table or query pull-down list.

3 Check that the specifications match those shown in Figure 6.6, and then select OK.

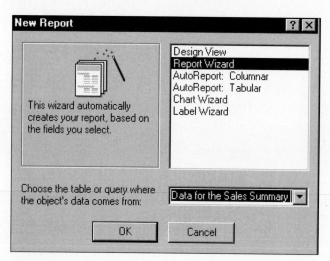

Figure 6.6

4 Click the >> button to transfer all fields in the order listed from the Available Fields box to the Selected Fields box, and then select Next>.
Access asks if you want to add any grouping levels.

5 Select Organization Name.

6 Check that your specifications match those shown in Figure 6.7, and then select Next>.
Access asks what sort order and summary information you want for detail records.

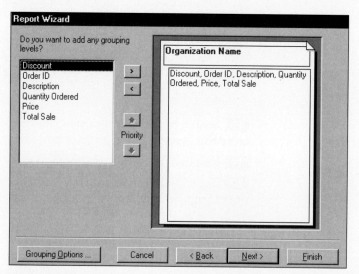

Figure 6.7

7 Select Summary Options.
The Summary Options dialog box appears.

8 Select the summary value Sum for Total Sale, select Detail and Summary in the Show section, and check the Calculate percent of total for sums box, as shown in Figure 6.8.

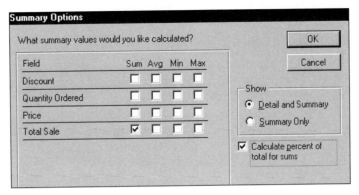

Figure 6.8

9 Select OK to restore display of the sort order screen, and then select Next>.
Access asks how you would like to lay out your report.

10 Select the settings shown in Figure 6.9, and then select Next>.

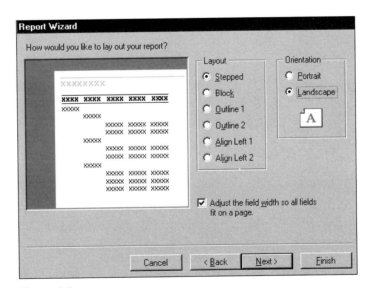

Figure 6.9

11 Select the Formal style, and then select Finish.
The new report appears in preview mode. Because you selected Finish instead of Next>, Access skipped the last Report Wizard screen and automatically assigned the name of the query to the new report.

12 Use scroll bars to view the report preview, and check that it includes the layout and content shown in Figure 6.1.

13 Choose Close from the File menu.

The report you created using Report Wizard appears with the name *Data for the Sales Summary by Customer Report* in the Reports tab of the Database window.

WORKING IN REPORT DESIGN VIEW

A powerful database management system product will allow you to design your own output as well as take advantage of standard layouts. If you open an Access report in design view, you will see a set of *bands,* which run horizontally across the entire width of the report design work surface. You use bands to position data and descriptive text within specific portions of the report. Figure 6.10 shows the position of the bands and other characteristics of the report design work surface.

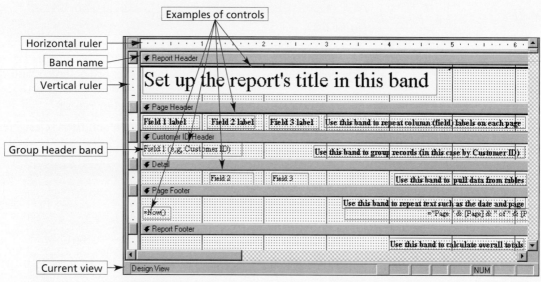

Figure 6.10

You should be somewhat familiar with sections of a report after viewing on-screen Help about the topic. Of the six bands shown in Figure 6.10, two are report bands and two are page bands. You will use the **Report Header band** to enter text or an object such as a company logo that will appear once at the beginning of the report. The **Report Footer band** lets you define text or calculations that appear once at the bottom of the last page in a report. Page bands allow you to enter text that appears at the top or bottom of each page. The **Page Header band** allows you to define text that will appear on page tops; the **Page Footer band** allows you to define text for page bottoms. For those reports in which each column displays data from a different field, you will use the Page Header Band to enter column headings.

You will use the **Detail band** in the middle to specify the fields you want to see in the report. If you decide to display similar records together, you can specify the field on which to group in the **Group Header band,** which appears just above the Detail band. Access displays the name of the field instead of the word *Group* in the band name. For example, Figure 6.10 shows that records will be grouped by Customer ID.

A curved down arrow appears to the left of each band name and points to the band work surface on which you can enter one or more controls. A **control** is an object such as a label, text box, check box, image, or line that you can place on a form or report to display data from a field or enhance the appearance of the report. For example, in Figure 6.10 the control in the Report Header band is a label describing the report's title. The = NOW( ) control at the left end of the Page Footer band is a text box that displays the current date. The rulers framing the top and left edges of the report design surface help you to position controls.

Tip Before you make major changes to a report's design, make a copy of the report under another name. If your revisions proceed as planned, you can delete the extra copy when you are finished. However, if you encounter major problems, you can start over with the original design.

In the following steps you will create another copy of the report you want to revise. You will then make the changes annotated on Figure 6.1.

To make a copy of a report:

1 Select Data for the Sales Summary by Customer Report on the Reports tab in the Database window.

2 Select the Copy button on the toolbar.

3 Select the Paste button on the toolbar.
The Paste As dialog box appears.

4 Type **Sales Summary by Customer** in the Report Name text box, and then select OK.

Two names appear on the Reports tab in the Database window. You will make your revisions to the report named Sales Summary by Customer. However, you will keep the report named Data for the Sales Summary by Customer Report until you are satisfied that the revised report works properly.

Quick Fix While learning to work with bands in report design view, do not be discouraged if you make one or more mistakes. If you think it would be easier to start over than correct the errors, repeat the previous steps to make a copy of the original report and specify that you want the copy to replace the one containing errors.

Using the Toolbox

When you work in report design view, you can use the buttons shown in Figure 6.11. These buttons make up the **toolbox,** which you can use to add controls to a report.

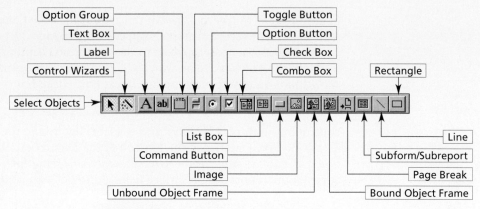

Figure 6.11

Label and text box are the basic controls. You can type literal text in a *label control*, such as the title for a report in the Report Header band or a descriptive field name in the Page Header band. A *text box control* displays data pulled from a table or calculated field. The controls in the Detail band are text boxes. The other buttons set up data entry, data validation, graphic, and picture controls.

If the toolbox does not appear when you open a report in report design view, you can display it by selecting Toolbox in the Standard toolbar, as shown in Figure 6.12, or by choosing Toolbox from the View menu.

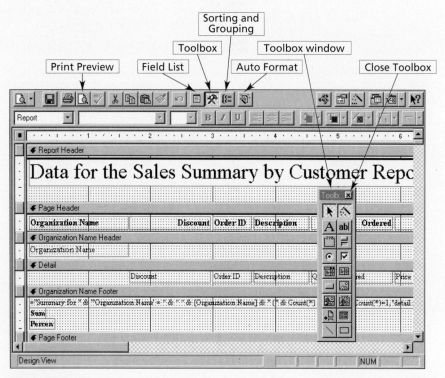

Figure 6.12

In Figure 6.12 you see a two-column toolbox window on the report design surface. You can move and size the toolbox, or you can anchor it to a border. The toolbox shown in Figure 6.11 is the layout that results if you anchor it to a border.

> **_Tip_**   You can see more of the design work surface if you turn off the toolbox display until you need to add a control. Choosing Toolbox from the View menu removes the toolbox (the checkmark in front of Toolbox disappears). You can also close the toolbox by clicking the Close button in the upper-right corner of the Toolbox window, as shown in Figure 6.12.

Editing, Sizing, and Moving a Control

You can edit, size, and move controls using techniques that apply to any Windows object. For example, you can select a control by clicking anywhere within the control. Sizing handles will appear as shown in Figure 6.13.

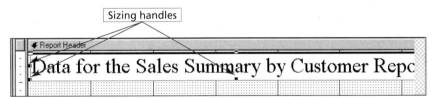

Figure 6.13

The pointer switches to a two-directional arrow when you position it on a sizing handle, and you can increase or decrease the size of the object by moving the pointer in the desired direction. The pointer switches to an open hand symbol when you position it on a border between sizing handles. You can then drag the selected control to a new location.

If you click within a control that's already selected, an insertion point appears inside the control, as shown in Figure 6.14. When the insertion point is active, you can enter or edit text.

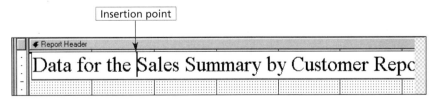

Figure 6.14

In the following steps you will open an existing report in report design view, edit the title in the Report Header band, and move a line control in the Page Header band.

To change the title of a report:

1 Open the Sales Summary by Customer report in report design view. Your screen should display the six bands shown in Figure 6.12.

2 Close the toolbox if one appears.

3 Select the label control in the Report Header band. Sizing handles appear as shown in Figure 6.13.

4 Click within the label control. The insertion point appears.

5 Select *Data for the* (including the space after *the*), as shown in Figure 6.15, and then press ⟨DEL⟩

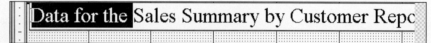

Figure 6.15

6 Select *Report* at the end of the title (including the space before *Report*), and then press ⟨DEL⟩

7 Click outside the label control box. The title appears as Sales Summary by Customer instead of Data for the Sales Summary by Customer Report.

To add space within a band and move a separator line:

1 Move the pointer to the top edge of the Organization Name Header bar. The shape of the pointer changes to a cross with arrows on each end of the vertical bar, as shown in Figure 6.16.

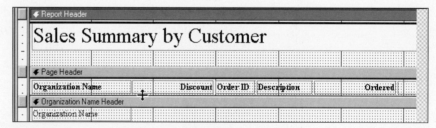

Figure 6.16

2 Drag the Organization Name Header bar down approximately one-half inch, as shown in Figure 6.17.

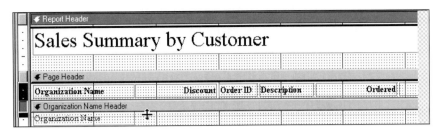

Figure 6.17

3 Release the mouse button.
Extra space appears within the Page Header band, as shown in Figure 6.18.

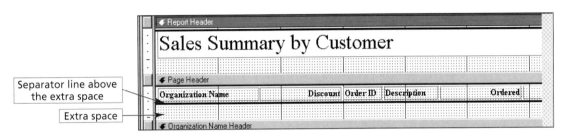

Figure 6.18

4 Click the bold black separator line shown in Figure 6.18.
The pointer changes to a hand, as shown in Figure 6.19.

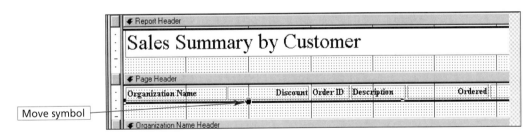

Figure 6.19

5 Drag the hand symbol down approximately one-fourth inch, and then release the mouse button.
The separator line appears below the extra space, as shown in Figure 6.20.

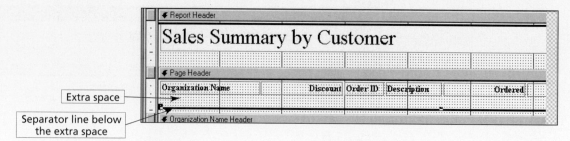

Extra space

Separator line below the extra space

Figure 6.20

6 Click outside the line to deselect it.

Adding and Aligning a Control

The steps you take to add a control will vary according to the type of control. Controls can be *bound, unbound,* and *calculated.* A **bound control** pulls data from a table or query. The most common type of bound control is a text box. Examples of bound controls in Figure 6.12 include the Organization Name control in the Organization Name Header band and the Discount control in the Detail band. To add a bound control, you will display the field pull-down list in the toolbar and select a field, drag it to the appropriate position in a report band, and then release the mouse button.

An **unbound control** does not have a data source. The most common type of unbound control is a label, such as a report title, but other objects, including lines and pictures that are not stored in the database, belong in this category. To add an unbound control, you will first select the appropriate tool from the toolbox, such as Label shown in Figure 6.21. You will then position the pointer where you want the upper-left edge of the control to start, drag it to the end point, and then release the mouse button.

New label control   Label

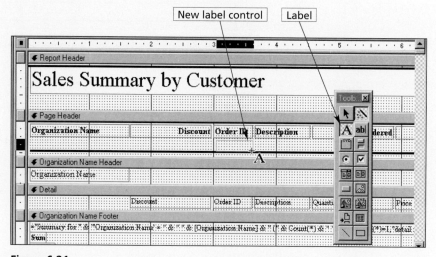

Figure 6.21

A *calculated control* uses an expression as its source of data. In Figure 6.21, the controls in the Organization Name Footer band are calculated controls. A text box is the most common type of control for displaying a calculated value. You can type the expression in a text box yourself or use the Expression Builder window to construct it.

Setting alignment for a control involves a two-step process: moving the control to the desired position within a band and then selecting Align Left, Center, or Align Right in the toolbar.

In the following steps you will revise two column headings in the Page Header band by adding two unbound controls, editing two others, and aligning the results.

To add an unbound control:

1 Display the toolbox and then select Label.

2 Position the pointer just under the lower-left corner of the Order ID control in the Page Header band, click and drag the pointer down and to the right as shown in Figure 6.21, and then release the mouse button.

3 Type **ID** in the new box, as shown in Figure 6.22.

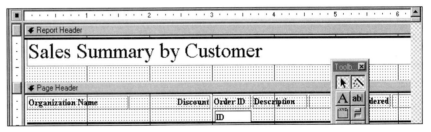

Figure 6.22

4 Click outside the new box to deselect it.
The new box shrinks in width to fit around the ID text.

5 Resize the width of the new box to match the width of the Order ID box above.

6 Select the original Order ID control in the Page Header band, and edit the text to read *Order* instead of *Order ID*.

7 Click outside the original box to deselect it, and then close the toolbox.

To center label controls:

1 Select the Order control in the Page Header band, and then select the Center button on the toolbar.

2 Select the ID control in the Page Header band, and then select Center. The revised column heading formed by two label controls appears as shown in Figure 6.23.

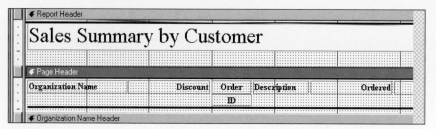

Figure 6.23

To revise another column heading and save your changes:

1 Use the horizontal scroll bar to view the Total Sale column in the report.

2 Repeat previously described procedures to add an unbound label control in the extra space just below the Total Sale control in the Page Header band.

3 Type **Sale** in the new label.

4 Edit the original label to read *Total* instead of *Total Sale*.

5 Right align both labels, as shown in Figure 6.24.

Figure 6.24

6 Close the report, saving your changes.

EXIT   If necessary, you can close this database now. You can then exit Access and continue this project later.

Specifying a Sort

If you specify sorting and grouping through Report Wizard, Access automatically moves the fields used for sorting and grouping to the left end of the report. However, if you set up sorting in report design view, the sort fields do not change position. You can use the Sorting and Grouping button (see Figure 6.12) on the toolbar to specify a sort. You can also choose Sorting and Grouping from the View menu.

Currently the records in the Sales Summary by Customer report are grouped by organization name, but within each group the records are not sorted. In the following steps you will specify a sort on the Order ID field.

To specify a sort in report design view:

1 If necessary, load Access, open the Designer Tees database, and then open the Sales Summary by Customer report in report design view.

2 Select the Sorting and Grouping buttons on the toolbar.

The Sorting and Grouping dialog box opens as shown in Figure 6.25. The Group Header and Group Footer properties for Organization Name are set to Yes.

Grouping symbol →

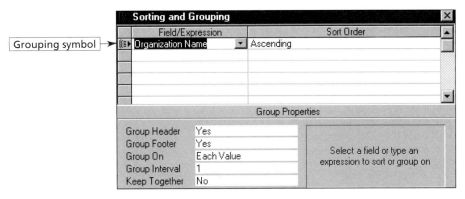

Figure 6.25

3 Select the next blank Field/Expression row in the Sorting and Grouping dialog box.

4 Display the Field/Expression pull-down list, and then select Order ID.

The specifications should match those shown in Figure 6.26.

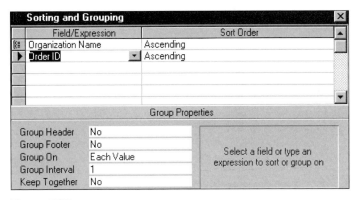

Figure 6.26

5 Close the Sorting and Grouping dialog box.

6 Select Print Preview (see Figure 6.12) to preview your report.

Records within each group should appear in ascending order on Order ID number, as shown for Beckman Fitness Centers in Figure 6.27.

Sales Summary by Customer

Organization Name	Discount	Order ID	Description
Beckman Fitness Centers			
	20.00%	970002	ex lrg/tall t-shirt
	20.00%	970006	ex lrg/tall t-shirt
	20.00%	970007	small t-shirt
	20.00%	970008	large t-shirt

Summary for 'Organization Name' = Beckman Fitness Centers (4 detail records)
Sum
Percent

Figure 6.27

7 Use the horizontal scroll bar to view data in the Total Sale field. The format of Total Sale amounts is not consistent with the currency format assigned to price amounts.

8 Close the report preview.

9 Save the changes to your report, but do not exit report design view.

Changing Number Format

You can change a field's properties in report design view by first selecting the field and then choosing Properties from the View menu. To change the Format property, you will then select the Format tab, as shown in Figure 6.28, and select the desired setting from a pull-down list.

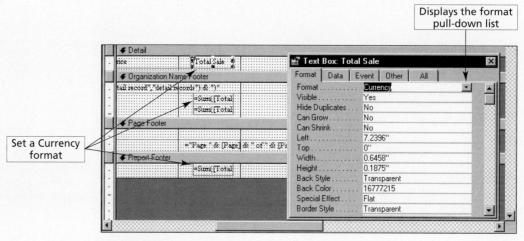

Displays the format pull-down list

Set a Currency format

Figure 6.28

All data in the Total Sale column of the Sales Summary by Customer report should appear in dollars and cents to be consistent with the price information. In the following steps you will apply the Currency format three times, as shown in Figure 6.28: to the Total Sale control in the Detail band, to the first =SUM control in the Organization Name Footer band (this control calculates total sales for the group), and to the =SUM control in the Report Footer band (this control calculates the total of all sales).

To change the Format property of a field in report design view:

1 Use the vertical and horizontal scroll bars to view the lower-right portion of the Sales Summary by Customer report in the left half of the window, as shown in Figure 6.28.

2 Select the Total Sale control in the Detail band.
Sizing handles appear around the Total Sale control.

3 Choose Properties from the View menu.
The Text Box: Total Sale dialog box opens.

4 Select the Format tab.

5 Display the Format pull-down list, and then select Currency.
The format specification should match that shown in Figure 6.28.

6 Select the first (top) =Sum control in the Organization Name Footer band.
The title of the dialog box changes to Text Box: Sum Of Total Sale.

7 Display the Format pull-down list, and then select Currency.

8 Select the =Sum control in the Report Footer band.
The title of the dialog box changes to Text Box: Total Sale Grand Total Sum.

9 Display the Format pull-down list, select Currency, and then close the dialog box.

10 Click outside the selected control, and then preview the report.

11 Check that both Price and Total Sale amounts appear with dollar signs and two decimal places, and then close the report preview.

12 Save the changes to your report, but do not exit report design view.

Changing Font Size

The font size that Report Wizard applies to controls in the Detail band is smaller than the font size assigned to the controls in a Group Header band. If you move a control from one band to another, it may be necessary to change the font size to match other controls in that band. You can change font type and size in report design view by first selecting the control you want to change and then selecting from Font Type and Font Size pull-down menus in the toolbar.

In the following steps you will move the Discount control from the Detail band to the Organization Name Header band. This action will eliminate repeating the customer's percentage discount information for each order. You will then increase the font size applied to the Discount control to match the size assigned to the Organization Name control in the same band.

To move a control from one band to another:

1 Select the Discount control in the Detail band.

2 Move the pointer to the edge of the control until the pointer changes to an open hand symbol, as shown in Figure 6.29.

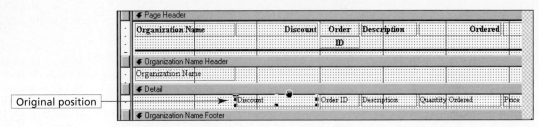

Original position

Figure 6.29

3 Drag the Discount control directly above its present position to the Organization Name Header band, and then click outside the Discount control to deselect it.

The Discount control appears to the right of the Organization Name control in the Organization Name Header band, as shown in Figure 6.30.

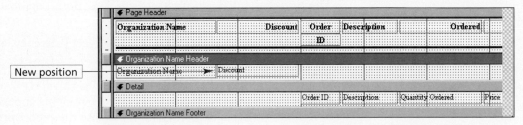

New position

Figure 6.30

4 Preview the report.

A customer's percentage discount appears once, as shown in Figure 6.31, instead of for every record, as shown in Figure 6.27. However, the discount percentage displays in a smaller font size than the associated organization name.

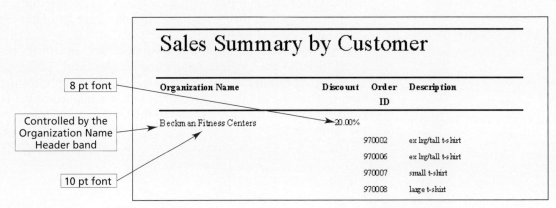

8 pt font

Controlled by the Organization Name Header band

10 pt font

Figure 6.31

5 Close the report preview.

To change font size in report design view:

1 Select the Discount control in the Organization Name Header band.

2 Display the Font Size pull-down menu on the Formatting toolbar.

3 Select 10, and then click outside the Discount control to deselect it.

4 Save the changes to your report, but do not exit design view.

Adding Lines and Special Effects

The Formal report format you selected through Report Wizard automatically placed three horizontal lines on a report to separate the sections. One appears above the report title, and the other two appear above and below the area containing column headings. You can add a line as well by selecting Line from the toolbox, positioning the pointer at your desired starting point, and dragging the pointer to the ending point.

> *Tip*   To delete a line, click anywhere on the line to select it, and then press ⌈DEL⌉

Access also provides a number of special effects that you can use to draw attention to selected portions of a report. The effects include Raised, Sunken, Etched, Shadowed, and Chiseled. The initial steps to apply a special effect are the same as those for selecting a number format. You will then select Special Effect on the Format tab and make your selection from a pull-down list.

Figure 6.32 illustrates the final changes you will make to the design of your Sales Summary by Customer report. For emphasis you will offset three controls from the left edge of the report and draw attention to them with a vertical line. You will also apply the Sunken special effect to organization names.

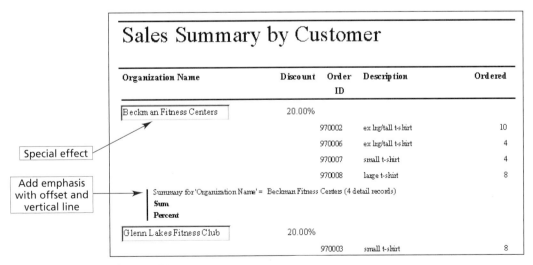

Figure 6.32

To indent controls and add a vertical line.

1 Add extra space at the left end of the Organization Name Footer band by moving each of the three controls about one-half inch to the right, as shown in Figure 6.33.

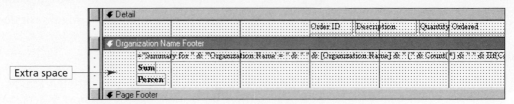

Extra space

Figure 6.33

2 Display the toolbox, and then select Line.

3 Position the pointer near the top of the extra space in the Organization Name Footer band and just left of the first control.

4 Drag the pointer down to form a short vertical line that nearly extends to the bottom of the extra space, as shown in Figure 6.34.

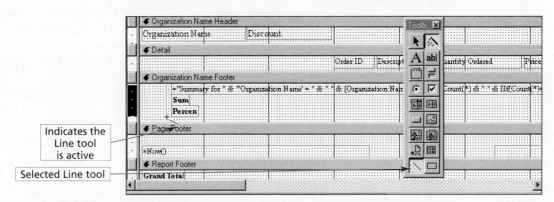

Indicates the Line tool is active

Selected Line tool

Figure 6.34

5 Release the mouse button, then click outside the line to deselect it.

To add special effects to a control:

1 Select the Organization Name control in the Organization Name Header band.

2 Choose Properties from the View menu.

3 Select Special Effect on the Format tab, and then display the pop-up list shown in Figure 6.35.

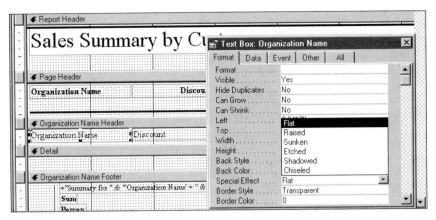

Figure 6.35

 Select Sunken, and then close the Text Box: Organization Name dialog box.

To preview, save, and print the revised report:

1 Preview the report.

2 Check that your report includes the offset labels, vertical line, and special effect shown in Figure 6.32.

3 Close the report preview, make changes as necessary in report design view, and then save your changes.

4 Select the Print button on the toolbar (optional).
Access prints a three-page report showing orders grouped by customer. The current date appears in the lower-left corner of each page, and the current page number out of the total pages appears in the lower-right corner. Summary information about total sales and percent of total sales appears after each group of records, and a grand total of all sales appears at the end.

5 Close the report.
The names of two reports appear on the Reports tab in the Database window.

Now that you know the revised report works properly, you can delete the original.

To delete a report:

 Select Data for the Sales Summary by Customer Report on the Reports tab.

2 Press (DEL)

3 Select Yes to any prompts related to deleting the report.
One report named Sales Summary by Customer appears on the Reports tab.

 If necessary, you can close this database now. You can then exit Access and continue this project later.

CREATING LABELS

Mailing labels may be the most commonly used labels. Preparers of bulk mailing can produce labels of various sizes, generally one to five across on a page. In addition, adhesive file folder labels, labels for shelves, name tags, and dozens of other practical tags can be produced by accessing data stored in a database.

Access provides *Label Wizard* for you to use to create standard Avery mailing labels or custom labels. In the following steps you will use Label Wizard to create mailing labels three across a page that print in order of zip code.

Tip If you do not want to print a label for each record in a table, you can set up selection criteria in a query and then base the label design on the query instead of the table.

To create standard mailing labels for all customers:

1 If necessary, load Access and open the Designer Tees database.

2 Select the Reports tab, and then select New.

3 Select Label Wizard, and then select the Customers table, as shown in Figure 6.36.

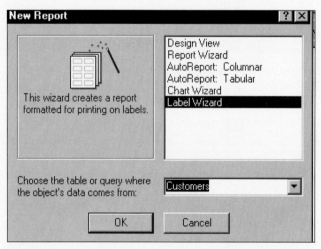

Figure 6.36

4 Select OK.
Access asks what label size you would like.

5 Select the specifications shown in Figure 6.37.

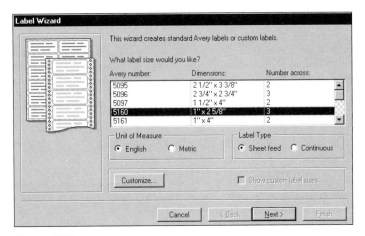

Figure 6.37

6 Select Next>.

Access asks what font and color you would like for the text.

7 Select Next> to accept the default font and color settings.

Access asks what you would like on your mailing label.

8 Follow directions in the dialog box to construct the prototype label shown in Figure 6.38.

> ***Tips*** Press (ENTER) to move to the next row in the label. Enter spaces and punctuation from the keyboard as necessary, such as entering a comma and space between the City and State fields.

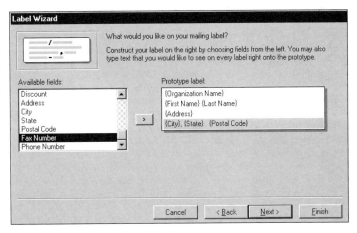

Figure 6.38

9 Select Next>.

Access asks which fields you would like to sort by.

10 Select Postal Code, as shown in Figure 6.39, and then select Next.

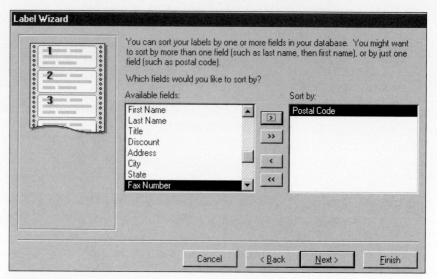

Figure 6.39

11 Type **Customer Labels** as the name of the report, specify that you would like to see the labels as they will look printed, and then select Finish.

12 Select a 75 percent zoom factor.
The labels appear in order of zip code three across a page as shown in Figure 6.40.

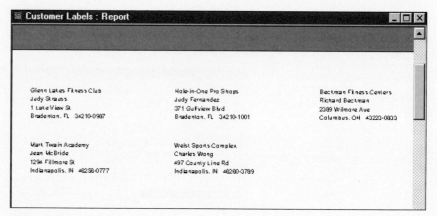

Figure 6.40

13 Close the report preview, and then close the report.
Two reports named Customer Labels and Sales Summary by Customer appear in the Database window.

14 Close the database.

THE NEXT STEP

In this project you learned how bands control the sections of a report, and then you worked in report design view to revise a report created with Report Wizard. You also used Label Wizard to create mailing labels of a predefined size.

As a next step, you might open the Northwind database provided by Access and view your choice of several reports, switching between preview mode and report design view. By doing so you will have a better understanding of how bound, unbound, and calculated controls defined in bands determine the content and layout of a report. You can also read extensive on-screen Help on creating reports and labels. Finally you will gain confidence through additional practice. Let Report or Label Wizard do most of the work for you, and then make minor changes as necessary.

This concludes Project 6. You can either exit Access or go on to work the Study Questions, Review Exercises, and Assignments.

SUMMARY AND EXERCISES

Summary

- An Access report contains at least five sections, or bands: Report Header, Page Header, Detail, Page Footer, and Report Footer. If records are grouped within a report, you can also have Group Header and Group Footer bands.
- Each section is defined by the controls you set up in the associated band in report design view. A control is an object such as a label, text box, check box, image, or line that you place on a form or report to display data or enhance appearance.
- The Report Header band lets you define objects that appear once at the beginning of the report, such as a report title and company logo. The Report Footer band lets you define text or calculations that appear once at the bottom of the last page in a report.
- Page Header and Footer bands allow you to define text that appears at the beginning and end of each page in a multipage report.
- You will use the Detail band to specify the fields you want to see in the report. Controls in this band pull data from fields in tables or queries.
- Group bands allow you to display information pertaining to a group of records, such as identifying the group in the Group Header band and displaying summary data in the Group Footer band.
- Controls can be bound, unbound, and calculated. A bound control pulls data from a table or query, and the most common type is a text box.
- An unbound control does not have a data source, and the most common type of unbound control is a label. A calculated control uses an expression as its source of data.
- You can use the toolbox to select a predefined control, such as a label and a text box.

- You can edit, size, move, add, and align controls. You can also apply font changes and special effects.
- The report capabilities in Access include making labels. Using Label Wizard you can create standard Avery labels and custom labels.

Key Terms and Operations

Key Terms	Operations
band	View on-screen Help about report sections and bands
bound control	
calculated control	Create a report based on a query using Report Wizard
control	
Detail band	Create a backup copy of an original report
Group Header band	
label control	Edit a label control
Label Wizard	Move a line control
Page Footer band	Add an unbound control
Page Header band	Center and right-align controls
Report Footer band	Use Grouping and Sorting to specify a sort
Report Header band	
text box control	Apply a number format
toolbox	Move a control from one band to another
unbound control	
	Change font size
	Add a vertical line control
	Apply a special effect
	Preview and print a report
	Create labels

Study Questions

Multiple Choice

1. Specifying a label control in the Report Header band allows you to print a heading
   a. at the top of each page.
   b. once at the top of the first page.
   c. at the top and bottom of each page.
   d. None of the above.

2. The control to calculate a subtotal for a group of records would appear in which band?
   a. Page Footer
   b. Report Footer
   c. Group Footer
   d. Control Footer

3. In a Detail band you can enter
   a. an unbound object such as a picture.
   b. a calculated field.
   c. Both a and b.
   d. Neither a nor b.

4. Which is not an example of a control?
   a. label
   b. group header
   c. text box
   d. check box

5. Which is a characteristic of the report design work surface?
   a. band name
   b. vertical ruler
   c. horizontal ruler
   d. All of the above.

6. Which report design control displays text that is not stored in the database?
   a. label control
   b. text box control
   c. documentation box control
   d. None of the above.

7. Which type of control does not have a data source?
   a. bound control
   b. unbound control
   c. calculated control
   d. Both b and c.

8. To avoid having Report Wizard move a field to be sorted to the left side of the report, you should
   a. not sort the field.
   b. sort the field in report design view.
   c. specify grouping for the field.
   d. All of the above.

9. You cannot change the format of a number field
   a. in table design view.
   b. in query design view.
   c. in report design view.
   d. in report preview mode.

10. Which is not a true statement about a calculated control?
    a. A calculated control uses an expression as its source of data.
    b. A text box is the most common type of control for displaying a calculated value.
    c. You must type the expression because Expression Builder is not active in report design view.
    d. The contents of a calculated control can be aligned.

Short Answer

1. Each section of a report is controlled by a(n) _____ .

2. You will specify a _____ control in the Detail band to display data from a field in a table.

3. Access provides _____ Wizard to help you create mailing labels.

4. In which band would you specify a control for printing page numbers in a report?

5. What should you do first before making major changes to a report's design?

6. What can you do to see more of the report design view?

7. While working in report design view, you can select predefined controls from the _____ .

8. Report Wizard creates reports based on _____ and _____ .

9. When report design is the current view, Access displays _____ and rulers to assist in creating and changing the report design.

10. To move a control, click within the control and _____ it to its new location.

For Discussion

1. Name the five basic bands in a report, and discuss the role that each plays in creating a report (do not include group bands).

2. Explain the differences between bound, unbound, and calculated controls.

3. What is the toolbox? Describe the purpose of your choice of three tools in the toolbox.

4. What kind of information can you display in the group bands of a report?

5. Describe the process to create a label using a wizard.

Review Exercises

Most of Project 6 involved working in report design view to modify a report created by Report Wizard. In these review exercises you will apply what you have learned to a similar situation. First you will create the report shown in Figure 6.41. You will then make the changes annotated on the figure.

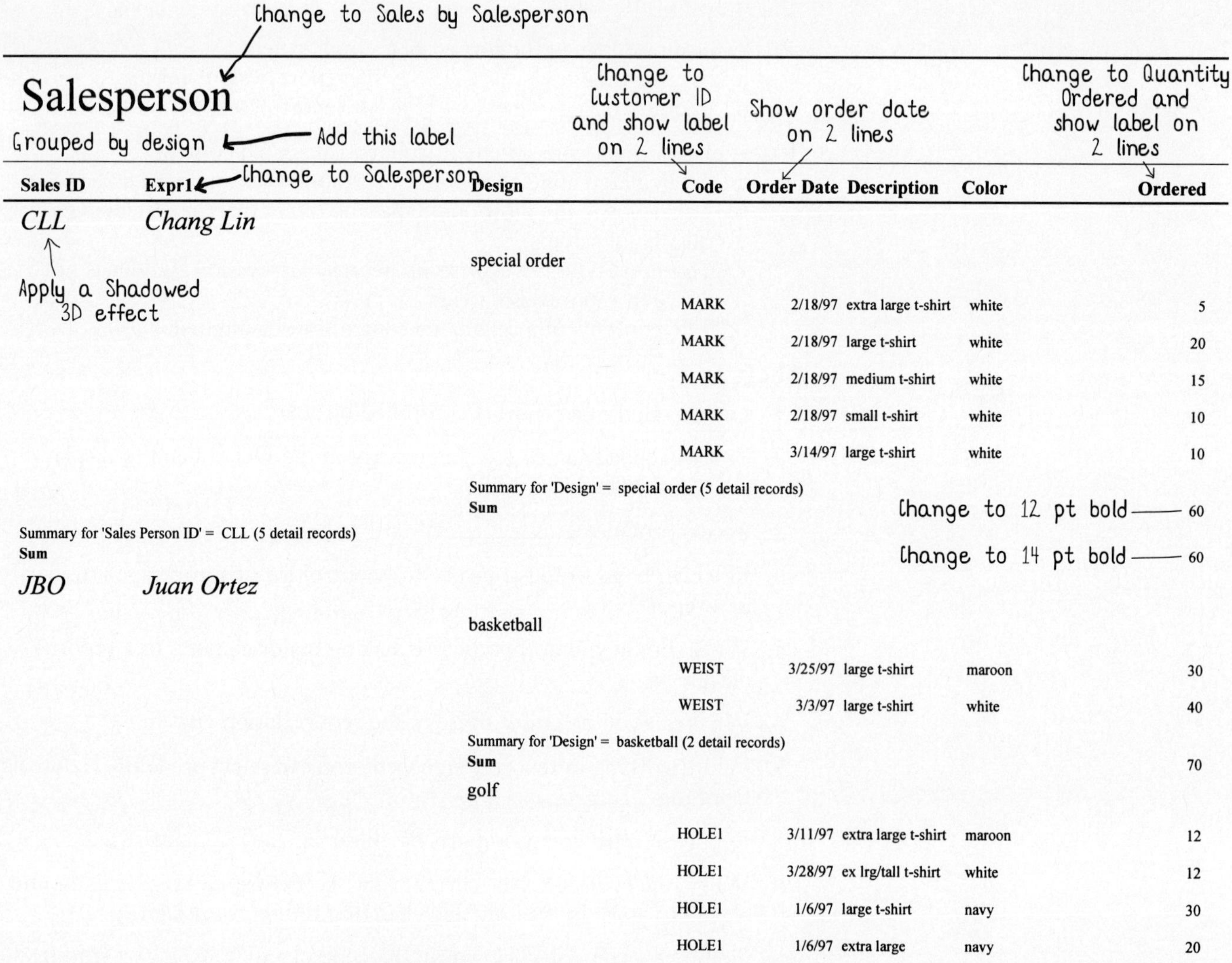

Figure 6.41

As you make your changes, compare each result to the revised report shown in Figure 6.42.

Sales by Salesperson

Grouped by Design

Sales ID	Salesperson	Design	Customer ID	Order Date	Description	Color	Quantity Ordered
CLL	Chang Lin						
		special order					
			MARK	2/18/97	extra large t-shirt	white	5
			MARK	2/18/97	large t-shirt	white	20
			MARK	2/18/97	medium t-shirt	white	15
			MARK	2/18/97	small t-shirt	white	10
			MARK	3/14/97	large t-shirt	white	10
		Summary for 'Design' = special order (5 detail records)					
		Sum					**60**
Summary for 'Sales Person ID' = CLL (5 detail records)							
Sum							**60**
JBO	Juan Ortez						
		basketball					
			WEIST	3/25/97	large t-shirt	maroon	30
			WEIST	3/3/97	large t-shirt	white	40
		Summary for 'Design' = basketball (2 detail records)					
		Sum					**70**
		golf					
			HOLE1	3/11/97	extra large t-shirt	maroon	12
			HOLE1	3/28/97	ex lrg/tall t-shirt	white	12

Figure 6.42

Modifying an Existing Query

1. Start Access, open the Designer Tees database, and open the Order details query in design view.

2. Choose Save As/Export from the File menu, and then save the query within the current database using the name *Sales by Salesperson*.

3. Select Show Table in the toolbar and add the Salesperson table.

4. Drag the Sales Person ID field from the Salesperson table to the Field row in the first blank column within the query design grid.

5. In the Field row of the next blank column, use Expression Builder to create a calculated field for the salesperson's full name (do not name the calculated field yet).

6. Run the query and verify the addition of two fields that show the salesperson's ID and full name for each order.

7. Close the query, saving your changes.

Creating a Report with Report Wizard

1. Create a report using Report Wizard, and select the following fields in the order given from the Sales by Salesperson query: Sales Person ID,

Expr1, Design, Customer ID, Order Date, Description, Color, and Quantity Ordered.

2. Respond to Report Wizard prompts and tell Access that you want to view the data by Salesperson, add grouping by Design, and sum data by Quantity Ordered.

3. Specify Stepped layout and Landscape orientation.

4. Select Formal style, and then select Finish.

5. Check in preview mode that your report includes the content and layout shown in Figure 6.41, and then close report preview.

Making Changes in Report Design View

Reminder   After each step below, check your results against the revised report shown in Figure 6.42.

1. If necessary, open the Salesperson report in design view, and then change *Salesperson* to *Sales by Salesperson* in the Report Header band.

2. Add the additional heading Grouped by Design and center it below Sales by Salesperson in the Report Header band. Apply a slightly smaller font size to the new label than the one assigned to Sales by Salesperson.

3. Change *Expr1* to *Salesperson* in the Page Header band.

4. Change *Code* to the 2-line centered *Customer ID* in the Page Header band.

5. Change Order Date to the 2-line centered *Order Date* in the Page Header band.

6. Change *Ordered* to the 2-line centered *Quantity Ordered* in the Page Header band.

7. Change the font size for the sum control in the Design Footer band to 12pt and turn on bold print. Also change the font size for the sum control in the Sales Person ID Footer band to 14pt and turn on bold print.

8. Apply a Shadowed 3D effect to the Sales Person ID control in the Sales Person ID Header band.

9. Preview your report, compare it to the report shown in Figure 6.42, and make changes in design view as necessary.

10. Choose Save As/Export from the File menu, and then save the report within the current database using the name *Sales by Salesperson*.

11. Print your report (optional), and then close the report.

12. Select the Salesperson report on the Reports tab, press ⟨DEL⟩ and then select Yes to delete the earlier version of the report.

Assignments

Changing Report Format

Display on-screen Help about improving a report's appearance, and then read how to change the style of the entire report. Apply your new knowledge by changing the report format from Formal to Corporate in your Sales Summary by Customer report.

Revising a Fund-Raiser Report in Report Design View

Open the fund-raising database you created in prior assignments, and then use Report Wizard to create a report that includes grouping. Preview the report and note where you might make changes to enhance the appearance of the report. Working in report design view, make the suggested changes. Preview, print, and save your results.

Creating Fund-Raiser Mailing Labels

Use Label Wizard to create donor mailing labels. Select a standard Avery label 1 inch by 4 inches that prints two across a page.

Objectives

After completing this project, you should be able to:

- ▶ Edit records using an update query
- ▶ Archive records using make table and append queries
- ▶ Work with subforms within forms
- ▶ Merge data with a word-processed document
- ▶ Create a switchboard

CASE STUDY: TRACKING SALES III

Up to this point your focus in using the Designer Tees database has been on creating queries and reports. Now that your most urgent information needs are met, you want to work with Access features that make it easy to maintain data. You also want to merge existing data into word-processed letters to customers and set up a menu structure so that your assistants can run a form or report with the click of a button.

Designing the Solution

Routine data maintenance tasks include editing field contents, adding new records, and deleting records you no longer need. For one or more of these tasks, you may be able to use an *action query*, which performs a database management operation on a group of specified records. For example, if the phone company assigns a new area code or a customer changes the name of his or her organization, one action query can update all records. You can also create a form within a form to facilitate adding and editing data.

For those times you want to send a common word-processed letter to customers, you can create a mail merge document in Word that links to Microsoft Access data. The link allows you to avoid typing names, addresses, and other data in word-processed documents if that data already exist in a table or query.

If you set up a system of menus called a *switchboard*, your assistants can run a query or report with the click of a button. You can build a switchboard for a database you created yourself by using Switchboard Manager.

Let's begin with action queries and forms and then generate personalized form letters to customers whose orders were not shipped within 14 days.

The final touch will involve creating menus and submenus that make it easy to navigate between the forms and reports in your database.

USING ACTION QUERIES TO MAINTAIN DATA

There are four types of action queries: *make table*, *update*, *append*, and *delete*. You will select one using the Query Type pull-down list shown in Figure 7.1. A solid dot appears to the left of the current selection in the pull-down list. An exclamation point indicates an action query.

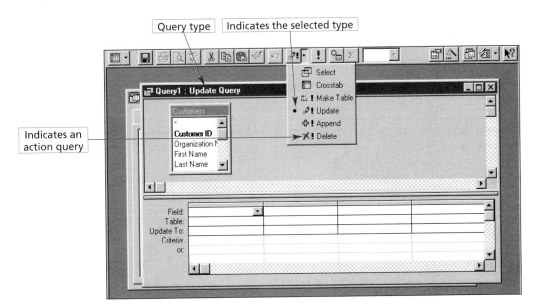

Figure 7.1

A *delete query* removes a group of records from one or more tables. For example, you could remove customers that had not made a purchase in more than a year or products that you want to discontinue. Because the Designer Tees company has only been in business a few months, there is no need to delete a group of records. You will, however, create and run each of the other action queries in the following sections.

Editing Records with an Update Query

An *update query* allows you to make global changes to a group of records in one or more tables. After selecting Update, as shown in Figure 7.1, you will drag the fields you want to change to the query design grid. Next you will specify the records you want to change in the Criteria row, type a value or expression in the Update To row, and run the query.

> **Tip** If you proceed with an update query, Access provides a warning that you cannot select Undo to reverse the changes. It's a good idea to view the records you want to change before you set up and run an update query.

Suppose that the Designer Tees customer identified as BECKF took on a partner and changed the organization's name to Omega Health Clubs. You could update both the Customer ID and Organization Name fields using one update operation. Figure 7.2 shows the update query settings.

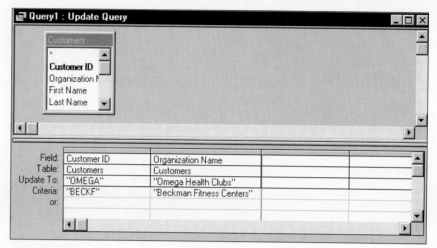

Figure 7.2

Because there is a one-to-many relationship between the Customers and Orders tables, and the referential integrity setting Cascade Update Related Fields is active, running the query shown in Figure 7.2 will update one record in the Customers table and all records in the Orders table for which BECKF is the Customer ID. You will create this query in the following steps.

To view records you want to change:

1 Start Access and open the Designer Tees database.

2 Open the Customers table in datasheet view.
Five records appear, one of which is Beckman Fitness Centers, with the code BECKF.

3 Close the Customers table, and then open the Orders table in datasheet view.

4 Select any occurrence of BECKF, and then select Filter By Selection in the toolbar.
Four records appear showing that Beckman Fitness Centers placed orders 970002, 970006, 970007, and 970008.

5 Close the table without saving your changes.

To set up criteria for selection and verify results:

1 Select the Queries tab, and then select New.

2 Select Design View, and then select OK.

3 Add the Customers table, and then close the Show Table dialog box.

4 Drag Customer ID to the Field row in column one.

5 Drag Organization Name to the Field row in column two.

6 Type **BECKF** in the Criteria row of column one.

7 Type **Beckman Fitness Centers** in the Criteria row of column two.

8 Click outside the criteria cell, and then widen the Organization Name field to display the entire criteria.
Your settings should match those shown in Figure 7.3.

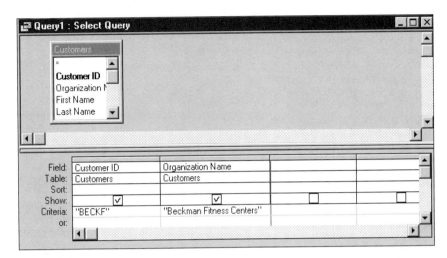

Figure 7.3

9 Run the query.
Only the record for Beckman Fitness Centers appears.

To convert the select query to an update query:

1 Switch to design view, and then select Update from the Query Type pull-down list.
Access inserts an Update To row above the Criteria row in the query design grid.

2 Type **OMEGA** in the Update To row in column one.

3 Type **Omega Health Clubs** in the Update To row in column two.
Your specifications should match those shown in Figure 7.2.

4 Select Run in the toolbar.
Access asks if you are sure you want to update one row.

5 Select Yes.

To check results of an update operation:

1 Close the query.
Access asks if you would like to save the query.

2 Select No.

3 Open the Customers table in datasheet view.
Data for BECKF and Beckman Fitness Centers has been replaced with OMEGA and Omega Health Clubs.

4 Close the Customers table, and then open the Orders table in datasheet view.
Orders 970002, 970006, 970007, and 970008 display the code OMEGA for Omega Health Clubs instead of BECKF for Beckman Fitness Centers.

5 Close the Orders table.

Archiving Records with a Make Table Query

A *make table query* creates a new table from all or part of the data in one or more tables. You can use this query to make a backup copy of a subset of records in a table or to archive old records, such as those for customers who had not placed an order for more than one year. You can also use this query to create a history table that holds data for a specific period of time, such as orders in the first quarter. You can then easily make comparisons to other quarters.

To create a make table query, you will first create a select query or open an existing one that contains the records you want to put in the new table. After entering or editing criteria as needed, you will select Make Table from the Query Type pull-down list and specify a table name, as shown in Figure 7.4.

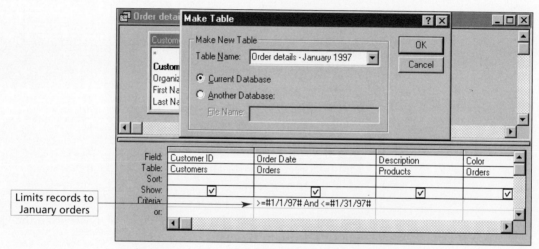

Figure 7.4

In the following steps you will open an existing query and create a make table query to archive records for January orders in the Designer Tees database.

To create a make table query:

1 Select the Queries tab, and then open the Order details query in design view.

2 Type `>=01/01/97 AND <=01/31/97` in the Criteria row of the Order Date field, and then click outside the expression.

3 Widen the Order Date column to display the entire expression. The criteria specification should match that shown in Figure 7.4.

> ***Tip*** Access automatically suppresses zeros and inserts the # symbols that indicate the starting and ending points of a date condition.

4 Select Make Table from the Query Type pull-down list. The Make Table dialog box appears.

5 Type `Order details – January 1997` in the Table Name box.
The specifications in the Make Table dialog box should match those shown in Figure 7.4.

6 Select OK to close the Make Table dialog box, and then select Run in the toolbar.
Access tells you that you are about to paste eight rows into a new table.

7 Select Yes.

To check results of a make table operation:

1 Close the query without saving your changes.

2 Select the Tables tab in the Database window.
The new table, Order details – January 1997, appears in the list of tables.

3 Open the new table in datasheet view.
Eight records with January order dates appear as shown in Figure 7.5.

Customer ID	Order Date	Description	Color	Design	Quanti
OMEGA	1/10/97	ex lrg/tall t-shirt	white	workout	
OMEGA	1/22/97	ex lrg/tall t-shirt	navy	workout	
OMEGA	1/25/97	small t-shirt	navy	workout	
HOLE1	1/6/97	large t-shirt	navy	golf	
HOLE1	1/6/97	extra large t-shi	navy	golf	
HOLE1	1/13/97	large t-shirt	white	golf	
HOLE1	1/14/97	ex lrg/tall t-shirt	maroon	golf	
GLENL	1/13/97	small t-shirt	maroon	workout	

Order details - January 1997 : Table

Figure 7.5

4 Close the table.

Adding Records with an Append Query

An *append query* adds a group of records from one or more tables to the end of one or more tables. You can even append records when some of the fields in one table don't exist in the other table. The append query will add the data in matching fields and ignore the others.

> **Tip** When you create an append query, you can specify that the records be added to a database developed in another software program such as Microsoft FoxPro, Paradox, or dBASE.

To create an append query, you will first create a select query or open an existing one that contains the records you want to append. From design view you will then select Append from the Query Type pull-down list and specify a table name in the Append dialog box, as shown in Figure 7.6.

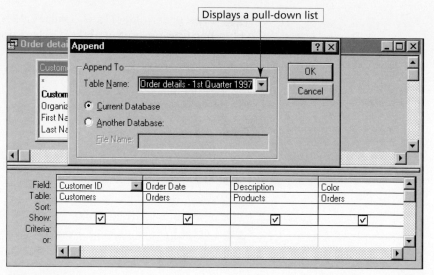

Figure 7.6

Access will insert an Append To row in the query design grid and automatically fill in the field names if the fields in the query match those in the table you selected. You can then enter selection criteria, if any, such as selecting only records with February 1997 order dates, as shown in Figure 7.7.

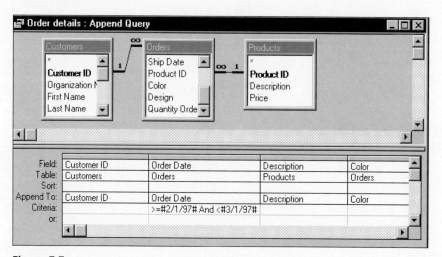

Figure 7.7

To work with appending records, you will rename the Order details–January 1997 table to one that indicates you'll be accumulating order details for the first quarter of the year. You will then append records for February.

To rename a table:

1 Select Order details–January 1997 in the Tables tab of the Designer Tees database.

2 Choose Rename from the Edit menu.

3 Change the time framework in the name to 1st Quarter 1997 instead of January 1997, and then click outside the name to deselect it.

To create and run an append query:

1 Select the Queries tab, and then open the Order details query in design view.

2 Select Append from the Query Type pull-down list.
The Append dialog box appears.

3 Display the table name pull-down list and select Order details – 1st Quarter 1997, as shown in Figure 7.6.

4 Check that Current Database is selected, and then select OK to close the Append dialog box.
Access inserts an Append To row above the Criteria row in the design grid.

5 Type `>=02/01/97 AND <03/01/97` in the Criteria row in the Order Date field, and then click outside the expression.

6 Widen the Order Date column to display the entire expression.
Your criteria specification should match that shown in Figure 7.7.

7 Switch to datasheet view to verify that only the ten records with February order dates are selected.

8 Switch to design view, and then select Run in the toolbar.
Access tells you that you are about to append ten rows.

9 Select Yes, and then close the query without saving your changes.

10 Select the Tables tab, and then open the Order details – 1st Quarter 1997 table in datasheet view.
Ten records with February order dates appear in addition to the eight records with January order dates.

11 Close the table.

 If necessary, you can close this database now. You can then exit Access and continue this project later.

ENTERING DATA IN A SUBFORM

A *subform* is a form within a form. A form/subform combination is sometimes referred to as a master/detail form, and it can be very useful when you want to view or edit data from tables or queries with a one-to-many relationship. In the Designer Tees database, for example, there is a one-to-many relationship between the Customers and Orders table. If you create an Orders subform within a Customers form, as shown in Figure 7.8, you can quickly view any record and field within either table.

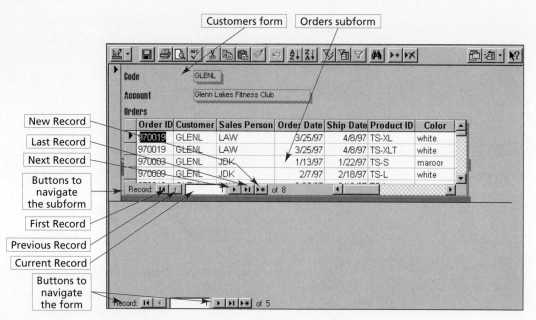

Customers form   Orders subform

New Record
Last Record
Next Record
Buttons to navigate the subform
First Record
Previous Record
Current Record
Buttons to navigate the form

Figure 7.8

Unless you specify otherwise, a subform displays data in the foreground in datasheet layout, with fields in columns and records in rows. You can use the navigation buttons at the bottom of the subform and the horizontal and vertical scroll bars to view other data in the subform.

The main form occupies the rest of the screen and has its own set of navigation buttons at the bottom. In Figure 7.8, the main form displays GLENL as the code for the first of five customer records. Access automatically included the eight GLENL records in the Orders subform. Selecting the Next button at the bottom of the screen will display the code HOLE1 and the account name Hole-in-One Pro Shops in the form. The subform will automatically change to display the six records with a matching customer code.

In the following steps you will use Form Wizard to create the subform within a form shown in Figure 7.8. You will then add a record using the new form.

To create a form within a form:

1 If necessary, load Access and open the Designer Tees database.

2 Select the Forms tab, and then select New.
The New Form dialog box appears.

3 Select Form Wizard, select Customers from the Tables/Queries pull-down list, and then select OK.

4 Transfer Customer ID and Organization Name from the Available Fields box to the Selected Fields box.

5 Display the Tables/Queries pull-down list, and then select the Orders table.

6 Transfer all fields in the Orders table to the Selected Fields box.
The selected fields should be displayed as shown in Figure 7.9.

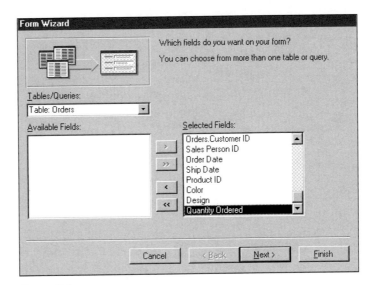

Figure 7.9

7 Select Next>.

Access asks how you want to view your data and offers a choice of Form with subform(s) or Linked forms, as shown in Figure 7.10.

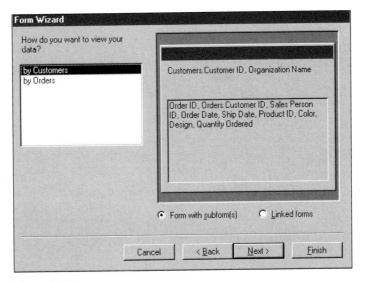

Figure 7.10

8 Check that your specifications match those shown in Figure 7.10, and then select Finish.

Form Wizard creates the form within a form shown in Figure 7.8.

> ***Tip*** Some of the column widths in your form may not match those shown in Figure 7.8. Recall that you can change the display width of a field by dragging the right edge of its column heading. You can also double-click the right edge and Access will automatically adjust the width to that of the field name or data, whichever is larger.

To view records in both forms:

1 Select the Next Record button at the bottom of the main form. The code HOLE1 and its associated organization name appear at the top of the screen, and six HOLE1 records are available for viewing in the subform, as shown in Figure 7.11.

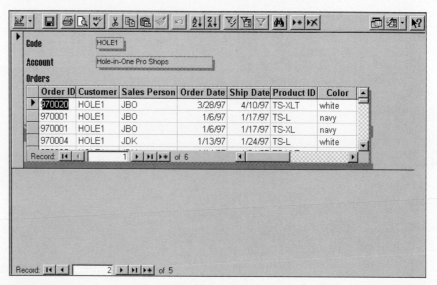

Figure 7.11

2 Select the Next Record button at the bottom of the main form. The code MARKT and its associated organization name appear at the top of the screen, and five MARKT records are available for viewing in the subform.

3 Select the First Record button at the bottom of the main form. The GLENL data reappears in both forms.

4 Select the Last Record button at the bottom of the subform. The initial fields in record 8 of 8 GLENL records appear in the last row of the subform.

5 Move the horizontal scroll bar to view all fields within the subform.

To add a record using a subform:

1 Select the New Record button at the bottom of the Orders subform. Access inserts a blank row in the subform.

2 Type **0021** in the Order ID column, and then press ⟨**TAB**⟩ twice.

3 Enter the following data in the appropriate columns:

Sales Person ID	LAW
Order Date	040297
Product ID	TS-M
Color	navy
Design	workout
Quantity Ordered	6

4 Close the form.

Two forms named Customers and Orders Subform appear in the Forms tab.

5 Open the Orders table in datasheet view, and check that order number 970021 appears in the table.

6 Close the Orders table.

CREATING FORM LETTERS

Being successful at running a small business means staying in contact with your customers. A customized letter that refers to each customer by name has proven to be far more effective than an impersonal letter that begins "Dear Valued Customer."

If you are using Microsoft Word version 6.0 or later, you can use its *Mail Merge Wizard* to create documents that pull data from your Access databases. You can use this feature to produce a *form letter*, which primarily contains text, punctuation, and spacing that does not change. With minor revisions at specified places in the form letter, such as the name, address, and order date, you can send the same document to many people.

Text that will change in each letter is called *variable data*. You can set up a placeholder for variable data pulled from a database by defining a *merge code*, which includes a field name surrounded by double angle brackets. In Figure 7.12, for example, there are 12 merge codes. The rest of the text in the document will not change from letter to letter.

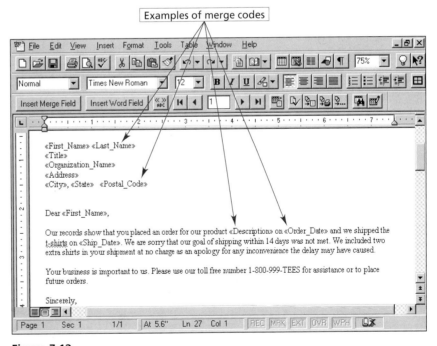

Figure 7.12

Tip Word has an optional function that will automatically alert you when you enter words that are not in its dictionary. This is why the word t-shirts in Figure 7.12 has a wavy underline beneath it.

A Word merge begins by replacing the merge codes with the corresponding data from the first record in an Access table or query. The result is a customized letter, such as the one shown in Figure 7.13. The process continues until a custom document has been produced for each record in the table or query.

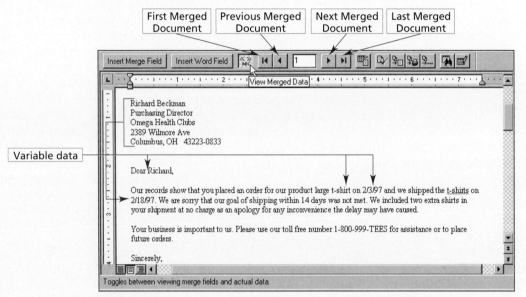

Figure 7.13

Tip You can save a form letter and run merge again if variable data change. However, be careful not to move the Word merge document and its associated Access table or query from their original locations or the merge will not work. To keep track of which files are involved in a merge, you might use the same name and location for both objects.

You can print merge results in two ways. Selecting the Print button in the Standard toolbar will print only the letter currently in view. You will use this method if you want to modify some aspect of each letter before printing, such as entering a different date. You can also select the Merge to Print button in the Merge toolbar to print all custom letters without modification in a single operation.

In the following sections you will create the merge document shown in Figure 7.12 and then run a merge operation to create personalized letters to each customer in the Designer Tees database whose order was not shipped in 14 days.

To make a copy of an existing query:

1 Select the Queries tab and select Orders exceeding 2-week shipment.

2 Select Copy in the toolbar.

3 Select Paste in the toolbar.
The Paste As dialog box opens.

4 Type `Late delivery form letter` in the Query Name box, as shown in Figure 7.14.

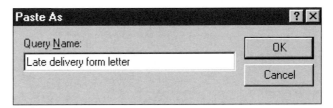

Figure 7.14

5 Select OK.

To modify the new query:

1 Open the Late delivery form letter query in design view.
The design grid shows four fields from one table, one of which has criteria specified, as shown in Figure 7.15.

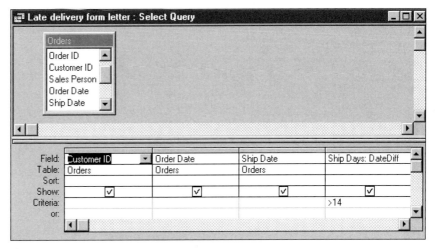

Figure 7.15

2 Select Show Table in the toolbar.
The Show Table dialog box opens.

3 Add the Customers and Products tables to the query, and then close the Show Table dialog box.

4 Hold down (CTRL) and highlight Organization Name, First Name, Last Name, Title, Address, City, State, and Postal Code fields in the Customers table.

5 Drag the group of selected field names from the Customers table to the Field row in the first column of the design grid.
The original four fields shift to the right, and each incoming field name occupies a column in the order you selected the fields.

6 Drag the Description field name from the Products table to the Field row in the first column of the design grid.

7 Drag the Order ID field name from the Orders table to the Field row in the first column of the design grid.

8 Select Run in the toolbar to view the results.

Two records meeting the selection criteria should appear as shown in Figure 7.16. The query should also contain 14 fields.

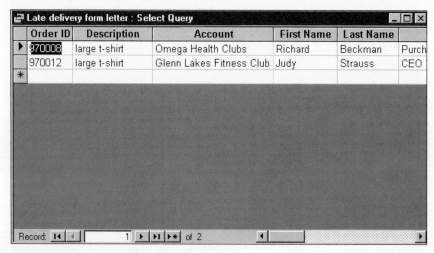

Figure 7.16

9 Close the query, saving your changes.

To link Access and Word using Microsoft Word Mail Merge Wizard:

1 Check that Late delivery form letter is selected on the Queries Tab.

2 Display the OfficeLinks pull-down menu, as shown in Figure 7.17.

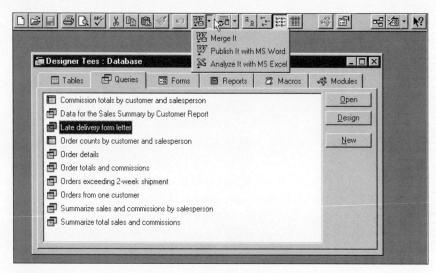

Figure 7.17

3 Select Merge It.
The Microsoft Word Mail Merge Wizard dialog box appears.

4 Select Create a new document and then link the data to it, as shown in Figure 7.18, and then select OK.

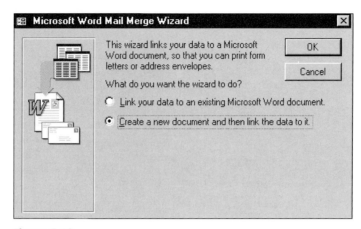

Figure 7.18

5 Wait until Microsoft Word opens, and then maximize the window and set zoom to 75%.
A blank Word document appears with a merge toolbar, as shown in Figure 7.19. Toolbars, margins, and other settings may vary depending on how Word is configured on your system.

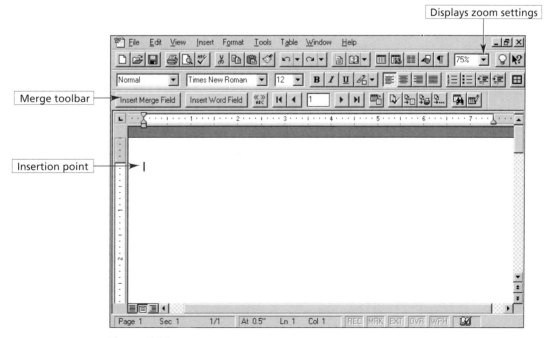

Figure 7.19

To create a document with merge codes:

1 Type **ENTER DATE HERE** and press (ENTER) three times for spacing.

2 Select Insert Merge Field in the Merge toolbar.
A pull-down list of field names from the Late delivery form letter query appears as shown in Figure 7.20.

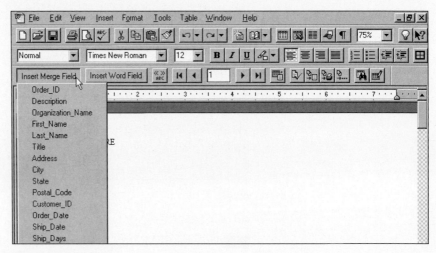

Figure 7.20

3 Select First_Name, and then press (SPACE)
Word inserts the merge code shown in Figure 7.21.

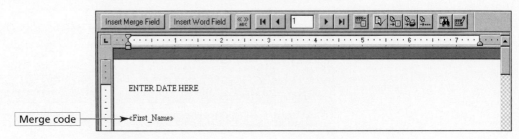

Figure 7.21

4 Select Insert Merge Field, select Last_Name, and then press (ENTER)
Word inserts a second merge code, as shown in Figure 7.22.

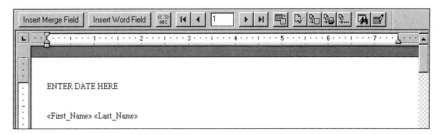

Figure 7.22

5 Enter the text, punctuation, spacing, and merge codes shown in Figure 7.23.

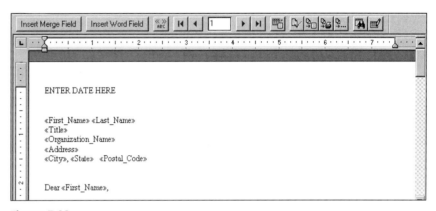

Figure 7.23

Tip If necessary, you can delete a merge code by selecting it and then pressing DEL

6 Enter the text, punctuation, spacing, and merge codes for the body of the letter shown in Figure 7.24, substituting your first and last names in place of *your name*.

Additional merge codes

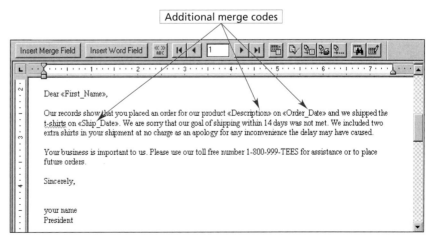

Figure 7.24

To view results of a merge, save the merge document, and close Word:

1 Select View Merged Data in the Merge toolbar.

Data from the first record in the Late delivery form letter query replaces the merge codes in the Word document, as shown in Figure 7.13.

2 Use a navigation button in the toolbar to view the next form letter shown in Figure 7.25.

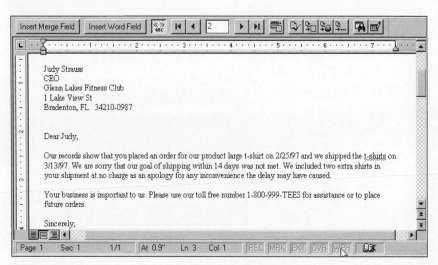

Figure 7.25

3 Select View Merged Data again to restore display of the merge codes.

4 Select Save in the toolbar.

The Save As dialog box appears.

5 Select the folder containing the Designer Tees database.

6 Type **Late delivery form letter** in the File name box, as shown in Figure 7.26.

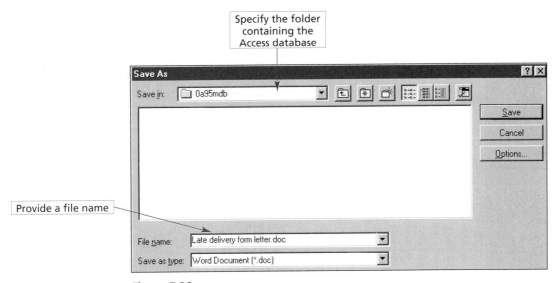

Figure 7.26

7 Select Save, and then close Word.
The Access database window appears.

EXIT If necessary, you can close this database now. You can then exit Access and continue this project later.

VIEWING OBJECTS WITH A SWITCHBOARD

A *switchboard* is a system of menus and submenus you can use to move among the forms and reports in your database. When you use Database Wizard to create a database, the wizard creates a switchboard for you. For example, if you use Database Wizard to create a Music Collection database, the wizard creates several submenus, including Forms Switchboard and Reports Switchboard, in addition to the Main Switchboard shown in Figure 7.27.

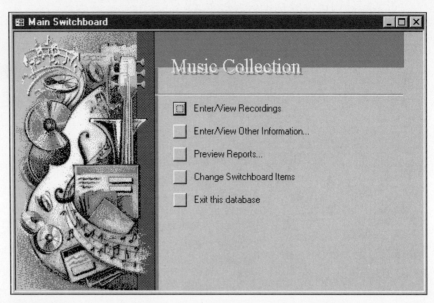

Figure 7.27

Access provides an add-in feature called ***Switchboard Manager*** if you want to build a system of menus and submenus yourself. You will build one menu or submenu at a time by specifying its name in the Edit Switchboard Page dialog box shown in Figure 7.28 and then adding items to the switchboard.

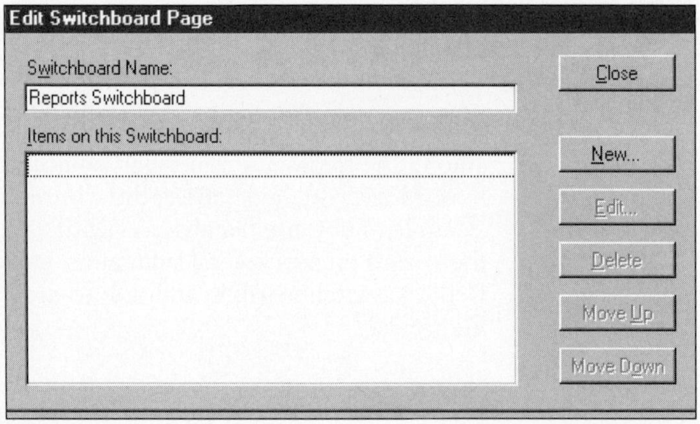

Figure 7.28

For each menu item, you will specify the text to appear on the switchboard and the command to be executed by Access when you select the item on the switchboard. If the item involves viewing a form or report, you will also specify its name. For example, Figure 7.29 shows the specifications for adding a report to a Reports switchboard.

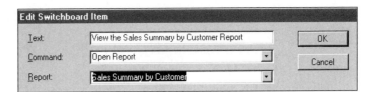

Figure 7.29

Tip When you use Switchboard Manager, Access automatically creates a Switchboard form to activate the menu system and a Switchboard Items table that describes the buttons on a menu and what action each button performs.

In the following steps you will create a Reports Switchboard submenu and a Main Switchboard for the Designer Tees database. Later you can work a review exercise to create a Forms Switchboard submenu.

To access Switchboard Manager:

1 If necessary, load Access and open the Designer Tees database.

2 Choose Add-ins from the Tools menu, and then select Switchboard Manager.
Access indicates it cannot find a valid switchboard and prompts you to create one.

3 Select Yes.
After a slight delay while Access creates the Switchboard Items table, the Switchboard Manager dialog box appears as shown in Figure 7.30.

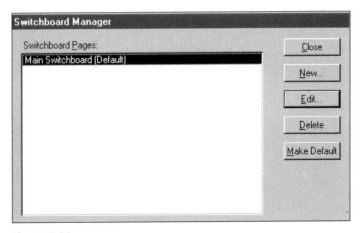

Figure 7.30

To add a new switchboard page:

1 Select New in the Switchboard Manager dialog box.
The Create New dialog box appears.

2 Type **Reports Switchboard** in the Switchboard Page Name box, and then select OK.
Access adds a switchboard page, as shown in Figure 7.31.

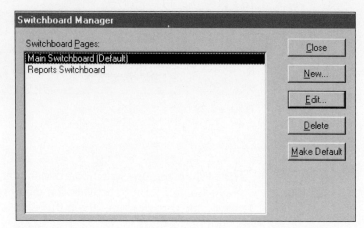

Figure 7.31

To add items to a switchboard:

1 Select Reports Switchboard in the Switchboard Pages list, and then select Edit.
The Edit Switchboard Page dialog box opens as shown in Figure 7.28.

2 Select New.
The Edit Switchboard Item dialog box opens as shown in Figure 7.32.

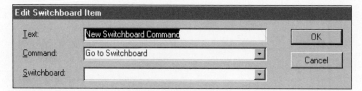

Figure 7.32

3 Type `View the Sales Summary by Customer Report` in the Text box.

4 Select the Command pull-down list, as shown in Figure 7.33.

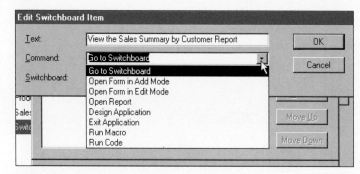

Figure 7.33

5 Select Open Report.
The last of three choices in the Edit Switchboard Item dialog box changes from Switchboard to Report.

6 Display the Report pull-down list, and then select Sales Summary by Customer.
The specifications in the Edit Switchboard Item dialog box should match those shown in Figure 7.29.

7 Select OK.

To add a second item to a switchboard:

1 Select New in the Edit Switchboard Page dialog box.

2 Type `View the Customer Labels Report` in the Text box.

3 Select Open Report from the Command pull-down list.

4 Select Customer Labels from the Report pull-down list.

5 Check that the specifications match those shown in Figure 7.34.

Figure 7.34

6 Select OK.
Two items are now defined on the Reports Switchboard, as shown in Figure 7.35.

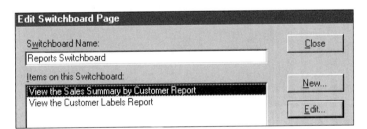

Figure 7.35

7 Select Close.
The Switchboard Manager dialog box shown in Figure 7.31 reappears.

To change the title of a switchboard:

1 Select Main Switchboard (Default) in the Switchboard Pages list, and then select Edit.

2 Type `Designer Tees Main Menu` in the Switchboard Name box, as shown in Figure 7.36.

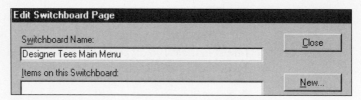

Figure 7.36

3 Select Close.

The new name of the default switchboard appears in the Switchboard Pages list.

 To define an item on a submenu switchboard that returns the user to the main switchboard:

1 Select Reports Switchboard, and then select Edit.

2 Select New in the Edit Switchboard Page dialog box.

3 Type **Return to the Designer Tees Main Menu** in the Text box.

4 Select Designer Tees Main Menu from the Switchboard pull-down list.

5 Check that the specifications match those shown in Figure 7.37.

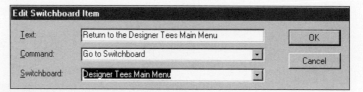

Figure 7.37

6 Select OK.

Access adds a third item to the Reports Switchboard, as shown in Figure 7.38.

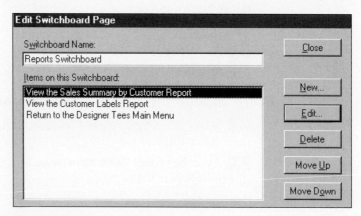

Figure 7.38

7 Select Close to view the list of switchboard pages.

To attach the Reports Switchboard to the Designer Tees main menu:

1 Select Designer Tees Main Menu (Default), and then select Edit.

2 Select New in the Edit Switchboard Page dialog box.

3 Type **View Reports** in the Text box.

4 Select Reports Switchboard from the Switchboard pull-down list.
The specifications should match those shown in Figure 7.39.

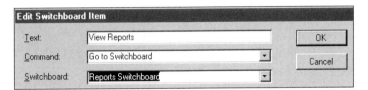

Figure 7.39

5 Select OK.

6 Select Close to exit the Edit Switchboard Page dialog box.

7 Select Close to exit the Switchboard Manager dialog box.
You see the Tables tab in the Database window. The list of tables includes the new Switchboard Items table.

To view a report using a switchboard:

1 Select the Forms tab, and then open the new Switchboard form.
The Designer Tees main menu appears as shown in Figure 7.40.

Figure 7.40

2 Select View Reports.
The Reports Switchboard shown in Figure 7.41 appears.

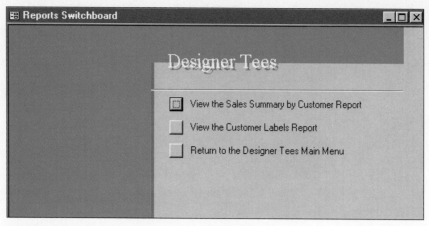

Figure 7.41

3 Select View the Sales Summary by Customer Report.

4 Close the report preview.

5 Select View the Customer Labels Report.

6 Close the report preview.

7 Select Return to the Designer Tees Main Menu.

8 Close the Designer Tees main menu.

9 Close the database.

THE NEXT STEP

In this project you learned a variety of ways to make maintaining an Access database easy. You used action queries to add and update records, created a subform to view or edit records, generated custom letters that pulled existing data from your database, and set up your own menu system to select reports. In this module you worked extensively with four of the six tabs in the Database window: Tables, Queries, Forms, and Reports.

Access provides many other features in addition to the ones you worked with in the module. As a next step, you might use on-screen Help to learn about Find Duplicates Query Wizard and Find Unmatched Query Wizard. You worked in report design view to modify a report created by Report Wizard. You can also work in form design view to make similar changes to a form created by Form Wizard. Your forms and reports can include graphs based on data from tables or queries. If this feature is available on your system, use on-screen Help to learn about graphs and then create some. For a challenge, work with the Macros and Modules tabs in the Database window.

This concludes Project 7 and the module. You can either exit Access or go on to work the Study Questions, Review Exercises, and Assignments.

SUMMARY AND EXERCISES

Summary

- Action queries perform a database management operation on a group of specified records. There are four types of action queries: make table, update, append, and delete.
- A delete query removes a group of records from one or more tables.
- An update query allows you to make global changes to a group of records in one or more tables.
- A make table query creates a new table from all or part of the data in one or more tables.
- An append query adds a group of records from one or more tables to the end of one or more tables.
- A subform is a form within a form. This type of form can be very useful when you want to view, add, or edit data from tables or queries with a one-to-many relationship.
- If you are using Microsoft Word version 6.0 or later, you can use its Mail Merge Wizard to create documents containing merge codes that pull data from your Access database.
- A switchboard is a system of menus and submenus you can use to move among the forms and reports in your database. Access provides an add-in feature called Switchboard Manager if you want to build a system of menus and submenus yourself.

Key Terms and Operations

Key Terms	**Operations**
action query	Edit records with an update query
append query	Create a table with a make table query
delete query	
form letter	Add records with an append query
Mail Merge Wizard	Create a form within a form
make table query	Add a record using a subform
merge code	Use Mail Merge Wizard to create a custom form
subform	
switchboard	Generate word-processed letters pulling data from a query
Switchboard Manager	Create a switchboard
update query	
variable data	

Study Questions

Multiple Choice

1. Routine data maintenance does not include which operation?
   a. merging data from Access into Word documents
   b. adding new records to the database
   c. changing existing records
   d. deleting records from the database

2. The four types of action queries are
   a. mail merge, update, append, and delete.
   b. make table, update, select, and delete.
   c. make table, update, append, and delete.
   d. None of the above.

3. A delete query serves what function?
   a. deletes one or more records from a single table only
   b. deletes the contents from one or more fields in a record
   c. deletes tables from the database
   d. deletes a group of records from one or more tables

4. What type of query allows you to make global changes to a group of records in one or more tables?
   a. add query   c. update query
   b. global query   d. search and replace query

5. A subform
   a. is a form within a report.
   b. is sometimes referred to as a detail/detail form.
   c. can be very useful when you want to view or edit data from tables or queries with a one-to-many relationship.
   d. Both a and c.

6. If a column in a query or table is too narrow to display the entire contents of a field, what action can you take to widen the column?
   a. Drag the left edge of the column heading.
   b. Double-click the right edge of the column heading.
   c. Both a and b.
   d. None of the above.

7. You can save a form letter and run merge again if variable data changes, but you should not
   a. move the Word merge document from its original location.
   b. move the Access table or query from its original location.
   c. run the merge unless a minimum of five Access records change.
   d. Both a and b.

8. Which of the following could be a merge code in a Word document that pulls data from the State field in an Access query?
   a. <<state>>   c. {state}
   b. <state>   d. None of the above.

9. Which of the following is true if you use Switchboard Manager to create a menu system?
   a. Access creates a Switchboard Items table.
   b. Access creates a Switchboard form.
   c. Both a and b.
   d. None of the above.

10. Using an append query, you can
    a. add records when some of the fields in one table don't exist in the other table.
    b. add records to a database developed in another software program such as Paradox or dBASE.
    c. Both a and b.
    d. None of the above.

Short Answer

1. What symbol appears to the left of the current query type in the Query Type pull-down menu?

2. Name the Word Wizard that you can use to create documents that pull data from an Access database.

3. What term applies to text that will change in each merge letter?

4. What is the name of the Access add-in feature that helps you create a system of menus and submenus yourself?

5. What term applies to a placeholder in a Word document for data pulled from an Access database?

6. Describe the navigation keys available in a subform.

7. Which button on Word's merge toolbar would you use to insert a merge code?

8. You can select Merge It from a pull-down menu to begin a merge operation from within Access. What action would you take to display that pull-down menu?

9. You must specify three settings to set up an item on a switchboard. Entering text to describe the menu item is the first one. What is the second specification?

10. Before you can proceed with executing an action query, what warning does Access provide?

For Discussion

1. How does an action query differ from a select query?

2. Assume that you manage a database for a university that tracks all information about students. Give an example of how you might use each of the four action queries available in Access?

3. Describe how Mail Merge works. Draw a diagram showing the flow of data. Use appropriate terminology.

4. Under what circumstances is a form/subform useful? Provide an example of a useful form/subform for a database other than Designer Tees.

5. What is a switchboard as it applies to an Access database? Explain what support Access provides for creating a switchboard.

Review Exercises

In Project 7 you worked with a variety of features to help you maintain a database. In these review exercises you will apply what you have learned by making additional changes to the Designer Tees database.

Appending Records

1. Open the Order details query in design view, and then select Append from the Query Type pull-down list.

2. Select the Order details – 1st Quarter 1997 table from the pull-down list in the Append dialog box, specify that you want to append records in the current database, and then select OK.

3. Specify criteria to select only records with a March order date, check that the proper records appear in datasheet view, and then select Run in the toolbar.

4. Close the query, open the Order details – 1st Quarter 1997 table, check that 30 records appear, including those for March orders, and then close the table, saving your changes.

Creating a Forms Switchboard

1. Choose Add-ins from the Tools menu, and then select Switchboard Manager.

2. Select New, type **Forms Switchboard**, and then select OK.

3. Select Forms Switchboard from the list of Switchboard Pages, and then select Edit.

4. Select New in the Edit Switchboard Page dialog box, specify the settings shown in Figure 7.42, and then select OK.

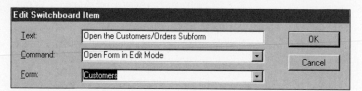

Figure 7.42

5. Select New in the Edit Switchboard Page dialog box, specify the settings shown in Figure 7.43, and then select OK.

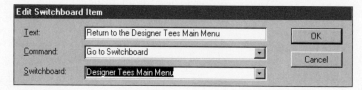

Figure 7.43

6. Close the Edit Switchboard Page dialog box.

7. Select Designer Tees Main Menu (Default) from the Switchboard Pages list, and then select Edit.

8. Select New, specify the settings shown in Figure 7.44, and then select OK.

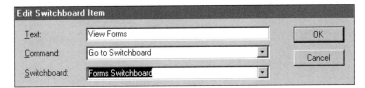

Figure 7.44

9. Close the Edit Switchboard Page dialog box, and then close the Switchboard Manager.

10. From the Forms tab, open the Switchboard form.
Access displays the revised Designer Tees Main Menu shown in Figure 7.45.

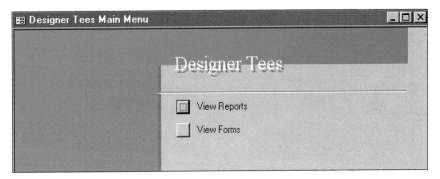

Figure 7.45

11. Select View Forms, and then select Open the Customers/Orders Subform.

12. Close the form, select Return to the Designer Tees Main Menu, and then close the switchboard.

Changing a Sales Commission with an Update Query

1. Create a select query containing all the fields in the Salesperson table but with records restricted to those in which the commission rate is 5 percent.

2. Convert the select query to an update query that will change the commission in all selected records to 10 percent.

3. Run the query to verify the increase in percentage from 5 to 10 percent, close the query, and save it using the name Rate Increase.

4. Open the Salesperson table in datasheet view, check that all records now display a sales commission percentage of 10 percent, and close the table.

Creating a Merge Application

1. Highlight the Salesperson table and then select Merge It from the OfficeLinks pull-down list.

2. Enter the initial lines of a memo to salespersons.
   To: (enter merge codes for salesperson first and last names)
   From: (enter your name)
   Date: (enter the current date)

3. Insert several blank lines for spacing, and then enter a message that praises the salesperson for work performed and invites him/her to a picnic in two weeks. Include a merge code to enter the person's name somewhere in the text.

4. View the merged records, and then save the custom memo using the name Picnic Memo.

5. Close Word, restore display of the Database window, and then close the database.

Assignments

Learning about Delete Queries

Once you delete records using a delete query, you can't undo the operation. Use Answer Wizard to view a Help screen on *Important considerations when using a query that deletes records,* and explain the five points presented.

Applying Skills to the Fund-Raising Database

Set up action queries to add and edit data in your fund-raising database. Create a subform within a form to view and edit tables involved in a one-to-many relationships. Look for an opportunity to merge data into a word-processed document, create the appropriate query and form letter, and then run the merge. Create a switchboard to display your forms and reports quickly.

Learning about Macros

Look for challenges! Use Answer Wizard to find out what macros are and how they work. Write a brief paragraph summarizing your findings.

Appendix A

Order ID	Customer	Sales	Order date	Ship date	Product	Color	Design	Ordered
970001	HOLE1	JBO	1/6/97	1/17/97	TS-L	navy	golf	30
970001	HOLE1	JBO	1/6/97	1/17/97	TS-XL	navy	golf	20
970002	BECKF	LAW	1/10/97	1/22/97	TS-XLT	white	workout	10
970003	GLENL	JDK	1/13/97	1/22/97	TS-S	maroon	workout	8
970004	HOLE1	JDK	1/13/97	1/24/97	TS-L	white	golf	20
970005	HOLE1	JDK	1/14/97	1/24/97	TS-XLT	maroon	golf	15
970006	BECKF	JBO	1/22/97	2/1/97	TS-XLT	navy	workout	4
970007	BECKF	JBO	1/25/97	2/1/97	TS-S	navy	workout	4
970008	BECKF	JDK	2/3/97	2/18/97	TS-L	maroon	workout	8
970009	GLENL	JDK	2/7/97	2/18/97	TS-L	white	workout	12
970010	WEIST	LAW	2/10/97	2/20/97	TS-M	navy	special order	25
970010	WEIST	LAW	2/10/97	2/20/97	TS-L	navy	special order	40
970010	WEIST	LAW	2/10/97	2/20/97	TS-XL	navy	special order	25
970011	MARKT	CLL	2/18/97	3/3/97	TS-S	white	special order	10
970011	MARKT	CLL	2/18/97	3/3/97	TS-M	white	special order	15
970011	MARKT	CLL	2/18/97	3/3/97	TS-L	white	special order	20
970011	MARKT	CLL	2/18/97	3/3/97	TS-XL	white	special order	5
970012	GLENL	LAW	2/25/97	3/13/97	TS-L	navy	workout	12
970013	WEIST	JBO	3/3/97	3/14/97	TS-L	white	basketball	40
970013	WEIST	JBO	3/3/97	3/14/97	TS-L	white	tennis	25
970014	GLENL	LAW	3/10/97	3/22/97	TS-M	navy	workout	6
970014	GLENL	LAW	3/10/97	3/22/97	TS-XL	navy	workout	6
970015	HOLE1	JBO	3/11/97	3/24/97	TS-XL	maroon	golf	12
970016	MARKT	CLL	3/14/97	3/24/97	TS-L	white	special order	10
970017	GLENL	LAW	3/20/97	4/1/97	TS-XLT	navy	workout	3
970018	WEIST	JBO	3/25/97	4/7/97	TS-L	maroon	basketball	30
970018	WEIST	JBO	3/25/97	4/7/97	TS-L	maroon	tennis	25
970019	GLENL	LAW	3/25/97	4/8/97	TS-XL	white	workout	6
970019	GLENL	LAW	3/25/97	4/8/97	TS-XLT	white	workout	2
970020	HOLE1	JBO	3/28/97	4/10/97	TS-XLT	white	golf	12

Orders

Customers

Code	Account	First Name	Last Name	Title	Discount	Address	City	State	Zip Code	Fax Number	Phone Number
BECKF	Beckman Fitness Centers	Richard	Beckman	Purchasing Director	20.00%	2389 Wilmore Ave	Columbus	OH	43223-0833	(614)382-7894	(614)382-7894
GLENL	Glenn Lakes Fitness Club	Judy	Strauss	CEO	20.00%	1 Lake View St	Bradenton	FL	34210-0987	(941)756-1234	(941)756-1234
HOLE1	Hole-in-One Pro Shops	Judy	Fernandez	Owner	25.00%	371 Gulfview Blvd.	Bradenton	FL	34210-1001	(941)795-1827	(941)795-1736
MARKT	Mark Twain Academy	Jean	McBride	Purchasing Agent	20.00%	1294 Filmore St	Indianapolis	IN	46256-0777	(317)594-9803	(317)594-9800
WEIST	Weist Sports Complex	Charles	Wong	Purchasing Agent	25.00%	497 County Line Rd	Indianapolis	IN	46260-3789	(317)257-1579	(317)257-3210

Salesperson

Sales ID	First Name	Last Name	Commission
CLL	Chang	Lin	5.00%
JBO	Juan	Ortez	10.00%
JDK	Jeffrey	Keller	10.00%
LAW	Linda	Weist	5.00%

Products

Product ID	Description	Price
TS-L	large t-shirt	$30.00
TS-M	medium t-shirt	$30.00
TS-S	small t-shirt	$30.00
TS-XL	extra large t-shirt	$35.00
TS-XLT	ex lrg/tall t-shirt	$35.00

Operations Reference

The following are the most commonly used commands in Access

FILE

Button	Operation	Keystroke	Description
	New Database	CTRL + **N**	Creates a new database.
	Open Database	CTRL + **O**	Opens an existing database.
	Get External Data		Creates a table or object from an external source; creates a link to a table in an external source.
	Close	CTRL + **W**	Closes the current database.
	Save	CTRL + **S**	Saves the current action or object.
	Save As/Export		Saves the current action or object under a new name or export to another file.
	Database Properties		Views database properties.
	Page Setup		Sets page properties and/or selects or changes printer settings.
	Print Preview		Displays a table, query, form, or report on-screen as it will look when printed.
	Print	CTRL + **P**	Prints the current object.
	Send		Sends output from the current object to electronic mail.
	Exit		Exits to Windows 95.

EDIT

Button	Operation	Keystrokes	Description
	Undo	CTRL + Z	Undoes the last operation.
	Cut	CTRL + X	Cuts marked text.
	Copy	CTRL + C	Copies marked text.
	Paste	CTRL + V	Pastes a cut or copied block.
	Create Shortcut		Places a shortcut to the selected object on the Windows 95 desktop.
	Delete	DEL	Deletes the selected table, query, form, or report.
	Rename		Renames the selected table, query, form, or report.
	Format Painter		Copies formatting such as colors, line styles, and font settings.

VIEW

Button	Command	Keystroke	Description
	Database Objects		Selects the tables, queries, forms, reports, macros, or modules folder.
	Large Icons		Displays database objects as large icons.
	Small Icons		Displays database objects as small icons.
	List		Displays database object names in columns.
	Details		Displays database objects with detailed information.
	Arrange Icons		Arranges database objects by name, type, date created, or date modified.
	Line up Icons		Arranges icons in columns.
	Properties		Views database object properties.
	Code		Views the underlying code that supports a database object.
	Toolbars		Displays and hides toolbars and changes toolbar attributes.

INSERT

Button	Command	Keystroke	Description
New Table	Table		Inserts a new table in the current database.
New Query	Query		Inserts a new query in the current database.
New Form	Form		Inserts a new form in the current database.
New Report	Report		Inserts a new report in the current database.
New Macro	Macro		Inserts a new macro in the current database.
New Module	Module		Inserts a new module in the current database.
AutoForm	AutoForm		Inserts a new form in the current database.
AutoReport	AutoReport		Inserts a new report in the current database.

TOOLS

Button	Command	Keystroke	Description
	Spelling	F7	Checks the spelling of data in the current view mode.
	AutoCorrect		Corrects common spelling errors while typing.
	OfficeLinks		Exports data to other office applications.
	Relationships		Sets up or modifies relationships between tables.
	Analyze		Analyzes table structure and performance, and displays documentation about a table.
	Security		Sets and changes passwords and levels of access permission for the current database.
	Replication		Replicates the current database at a designated location.
	Startup		Controls and customizes various database startup properties and actions.
	Macro		Runs a macro.
	Custom Controls		Registers and unregisters custom controls in the Windows registration database.
	Add-ins		Installs and uninstalls add-ins such as Switchboard Manager, Database Splitter, and Menu Builder.
	Options		Customizes characteristics of the Microsoft Access environment.

WINDOW

Button	Command	Keystroke	Description
	Tile Horizontally		Arranges windows as nonoverlapping horizontal panes.
	Tile Vertically		Arranges windows as nonoverlapping vertical panes.
	Cascade		Arranges windows in an overlapping pattern with only the title bar showing.
	Arrange Icons		Arranges the icons of all minimized database objects in rows.
	Hide		Hides the active window.
	Unhide		Unhides the active window.

HELP

Button	Command	Keystroke	Description
	Microsoft Access Help Topics		Provides several entry points to Help.
	Answer Wizard		Provides help topics based on written questions.
	The Microsoft Network		Provides help about The Microsoft Network.
	About Microsoft Access		Provides information about Access for Windows 95 and the operating system installed on your computer.
			Gets help by clicking on an area of the screen.

Glossary

action query   Performs a database management operation on a group of specified records.

And criteria   Multiple criteria in which all conditions must be met for a record to be selected.

Answer Wizard   Provides a list of on-screen Help topics related to a search you define in your own words.

append query   Adds a group of records from one or more tables to the end of one or more tables.

band   Used to position data and descriptive text within specific portions of a report.

bound control   Pulls data from a table or query.

calculated control   Uses an expression as its source of data.

calculated field   Creates new data or presents existing data in a different way.

check box   Indicates an option in a dialog box that can be on or off. A checkmark in the box indicates the feature is active. The absence of a checkmark indicates the feature is not active.

combo box   Displays a list of allowable entries in a field.

command button   A button in a dialog box that you can select to execute the named operation.

comparison operator   Specifies the scope of a search, such as finding data that are equal to ($=$), greater than ($>$), less than ($<$), not equal to ($\neq$), or like stated criteria (also known as a relational operator).

context-sensitive Help   On-screen information about the operation in progress.

control   An object such as a label, text box, check box, image or line that you can place on a form or report to display data from a field or enhance the appearance of the form or report.

crosstab query   Displays summary data in spreadsheet form, with row and column headings based on fields in a table or query.

Crosstab Query Wizard   Used to create queries that display summary data in spreadsheet form, with row and column headings based on fields in a table or query.

data   Raw facts or assumptions stored in a database.

data dictionary   A worksheet that defines the tables and field specifications in a database.

database   A collection of related data.

database management software   A tool you can use to manage data electronically.

database management system (DBMS)   A system that stores data in a database and permits retrieval of selected information.

database objective statement   A design document that states the goal of the complete system in a brief paragraph.

Database Wizard   Builds a complete application, including tables, forms, and reports. You can choose from 22 personal and business applications, including asset tracking, donations, event management, inventory, membership, and a music collection.

datasheet view   A view of a table in which data appear in rows (records) and columns (data fields).

default value   A value that appears automatically in a field when you add a new record.

delete query   Removes a group of records from one or more tables.

design view   A view in which you can create or modify the structure of a table, form, or report.

Detail band   Used to specify fields you want to see in a report.

dialog box   A box that appears on-screen, prompting the user to enter additional information.

expression   A combination of symbols and values used in a filter or query to create a search condition. ? is an example of an expression that would select a record if the value in the specified field was greater than or equal to 8.

field   A category of data in a table, such as last name or zip code.

field size   The maximum number of characters you can enter in a field.

filter   Restricts display of records to those meeting specified criteria.

form letter   A document that contains text, punctuation, and spacing that does not change.

format   The field property that determines how a value displays but not how it is stored in a table.

function   A program that returns a single value.

Group Footer band   Used to enter text or an object that will appear at the end of each group of data in a report.

Group Header band   Used to enter text or an object that will appear at the beginning of each group of data in a report.

icon   An on-screen symbol that represents a program file, data file, or some other function.

information Data presented in a usable form.

input mask A pattern, usually applied to text and date/time fields, that controls data entry.

Input Mask Wizard Allows you to select a predefined pattern such as one that controls entry of social security numbers or phone numbers.

label control Used to display literal text on a form or report.

label Describes its associated text box or some other portion of a form or report.

Label Wizard Used to create standard Avery mailing labels or custom labels.

logical operator Specifies a logical relationship of inclu$sion or exclusion.

Lookup Wizard Creates a lookup column which allows you to enter data by choosing a value from a list of values.

Mail Merge Wizard Used to create documents that pull data from your Access databases.

make table query Creates a new table from all or part of the data in one or more tables.

mathematical operator Performs a calculation such as addition ($+$), subtraction ($-$), multiplication ($*$), or division ($/$).

menu bar A horizontal listing of commands located near the top of the screen. Choosing an option on a menu bar displays its associated pull-down menu.

merge code A place holder for variable data pulled from a database.

normalization The process of eliminating unnecessary duplication of data by separating related data into tables.

one-to-many relationship A relationship between two tables that share a common field. Data restricted to one entry in one table can be entered many times in its related table.

Or criteria Multiple criteria in which a record will be selected if any search condition is met.

Page Footer band Used to enter text or an object that will appear at the bottom of each page.

Page Header band Used to enter text or an object that will appear at the top of each page.

primary key A single field or a combination of fields that makes each record unique.

pull-down list A list of related items that appears after selecting a down arrow at the right end of a box.

pull-down menu A list of options that appears after choosing an item on the menu bar.

query A tool you can use to ask questions and receive information about data stored in one or more tables.

radio button Allows you to select only one choice from a set of options.

record A collection of related fields.

redundant data Data that has been unnecessarily duplicated within one or more tables.

referential integrity A set of rules that makes sure relationships between records in related tables are valid.

relational database management system (RDBMS) A system that stores data by subject and retrieves information based on predefined relationships among subjects.

report An effective way to print professional-looking output based on a table or query.

Report Footer band Used to enter text or an object that will appear once on the last page of the report.

Report Header band Used to enter text or an object that will appear once on the first page of the report.

required field A field property that prevents saving a new record if data are missing from the field.

select query Displays data from specified fields in one or more tables based if field contents match search criteria.

shortcut key Keystroke or a combination of keystrokes that let you bypass several menu selections to execute a command.

Simple Query Wizard Guides the creation of a select query based on your answers to a series of questions.

source document A standard paper form with spaces to enter details that vary from one record to the next.

string operator Performs a calculation on alphanumeric characters, such as connecting two text fields.

subform A form within a form.

switchboard A system of menus and submenus you can use to move among the forms and reports in your database.

Switchboard Manager An add-in feature you can use to build a system of menus and submenus.

syntax Refers to required form and content.

table A collection of data about a specific topic.

Table Wizard Builds a table based on your answers to a series of questions.

text box In a form or report, displays data pulled directly from a table or data resulting from a calculation involving the contents of one or more fields.

text box control Displays data pulled from a table or calculated field.

toolbar A set of buttons representing commands. You can execute a command clicking the appropriate button.

toolbox Used to add controls to a report.

unbound control A control that has no data source.

update query Used to make global changes to a group of records in one or more tables.

validation rule A field property that determines whether attempted data entry should be rejected.

validation text A message that appears on-screen if attempted data entry violates a validation rule.

variable data Text that will change in each form letter.

wizard A series of windows and dialog boxes that ask you questions. Access creates a database, table, query, form, or report based on your answers.

Index

Access. *See also specific component or operation*
  exiting, 15
  loading, 6
  opening screen for, 6
  overview, 2–4
  starting, 7
Action queries, 224, 225
Add-ins, 243
Aligning controls, 205–206, 212
ALT, 7
Ampersand (&), as Concatenate button, 167, 168
And criteria, 120
Answer Wizard, 181
Append queries, 229–231
Archiving records, 228–229
Arithmetic operators, 163–167
Asterisk (*)
  in mathematical expressions, 163, 165
  as wildcard character, 115
AutoForms, 94–97
AutoReports, 137

Bands, for reports, 198–199. *See also* Designing reports
Bitmap files, 27
Bound controls, 204

Calculated controls, 205
Calculated fields
  with arithmetic operators, 163–167
  functions in. *See* Functions, in queries
  overview, 162
  with string operators, 167–172
Calculations, predefined, in queries, 177–181
Cascade Delete Related Records, 86, 88
Cascade Update Related Fields, 86, 88
Case, in field names, 43
Centering controls, 205
Check boxes, 8, 9
Chiseled effect, 211
Closing
  databases, 15
  previews, 34, 35
  reports, 140
  report switchboards, 34, 36
Color bars (Help), 12
Columnar forms, 94–97
Columns
  as database component, 2
  hiding, 131

lookup columns, 61–63
  moving, 116–117
  width, 130–131
Combo boxes, 31–32
Command buttons, 8
Comments, 47
Comparison operators, 163
Contents (Help), 9–11
Context-sensitive Help, 9
Controls, in report design. *See* Designing reports, controls
Copying
  field names, 51
  queries, 236–237
  reports, 199
Criteria, selection. *See* Selecting
Crosstab queries
  creating, 182–183
  Help for, 181–182
  overview, 154, 181
  saving, 183
  symbol for, 184
  using, 183
CTRL, 8
Currency format, 208, 209

Database management software. *See also* Access
  non-Access, adding records to, 229
  overview, 1–2
Databases
  closing, 15
  columns. *See* Columns
  creating
    from predefined databases. *See* Database Wizard
    from scratch, 19, 20. *See also* Table Wizard
  data entry
    via datasheet view, 90–92
    via forms. *See* Forms
  datasheet view. *See* Datasheet view
  design, 41–45, 59, 78
  fields. *See* Fields
  filters for. *See* Filters
  graphics in, 27–29
  matches in, finding, 114–117
  naming, 21
  navigating, via switchboards. *See* Switchboards
  normalization, 43
  objective statement for, 42
  overview, 1
  predefined. *See* Database Wizard
  records. *See* Records

rows, 2
  saving, 21, 22–23
  sorting. *See* Sorting
  tables. *See* Tables
Database Wizard
  display styles, 25
  fields, adding, 23–24
  graphics, 27–29
  overview, 18–20
  print styles, 26
  selecting predefined databases, 20–22
  titles, 27–29
Data dictionaries, 43–47
Datasheet form layout, 94
Datasheet view
  column manipulation, 130–131
  data entry and editing, 90–92
  overview, 59, 78, 90
  switching between Design view and, 78
Data types, in databases, 46–47, 78–79
DBMS. *See* Database management software
Default values, in fields, 83–84
Delete queries, 225
Deleting
  fields, 48, 59, 95
  filters, 120
  lines, from reports, 211
  merge codes, 241
  records, 86, 88, 225
  search criteria, 121
  table relationships, 89
Designing reports
  controls
    adding, 205
    aligning, 205–206, 212
    bound controls, 204
    calculated controls, 205
    editing, 201, 202–203
    moving, 201, 203, 210
    overview and types, 198, 199, 200, 204–205
    sizing, 201
    special effects in, 212–213
    unbound controls, 204, 205
  fonts in, 210–211
  lines in, 211–212
  number formats, 208–209
  overview, 198–199
  special effects in, 211, 212–213
  tools for, 199–201
Design view, 59, 78

Detail Band, in reports, 199, 209–210
Dialog boxes, 6, 8–9
Dictionary, data, 43–47
Display style, 25
Duplicating queries, 180

Effects, in reports, 211, 212–213
Ellipsis (...), in menus, 7
ENTER
  moving between fields with, 90
  moving between label rows with, 215
  selecting options with, 8
Etched effect, 211
Exiting Access, 15
Expression Builder, 163–164
Expressions
  with calculated fields. *See* Calculated fields
  filtering with, 120–121, 123

Field properties
  default values, 83–84
  editing, 80–83
  formats, 78–79
  input masks, 79–81
  required fields, designating, 77–78
  setting, Help for, 74–77
  validation settings, 84–85
  viewing, 82
Fields. *See also* Databases
  adding, 23–24, 59–60, 95
  calculated fields. *See* Calculated fields
  copying, 51
  customizing, 72–74. *See also* Field properties
  deleting, 48, 59, 95
  editing, 51–53
  formats for, 78–79, 208–209
  as keys, 46
  matches for, finding, 115–117
  naming, 43, 52
  number formats for, 208–209
  overview, 2–3
  properties. *See* Field properties
  in reports. *See* Reports
  selecting via queries. *See* Queries
  size, 47, 80
  sorting on. *See* Sorting
  updating, related tables and, 86, 88
Files. *See* Databases

Filters
    deleting, 120
    Help for, 118
    overview, 113, 117–118
    printing results of, 134–136
    using one or more search
        condition (by form), 120–
        125
    using one search condition
        (by selection), 118–120
Finding
    field matches, 114–117
    fields. See Queries
    Help information, 12–13
    records. See Selecting, records
Fonts, 209–211
Footer band, for reports, 198
Formats, for fields, 78–79, 208–
    209
Form letters
    linking applications for, 238
        239
    merge codes in, 235, 240–
        241
    merging, 243–244
    overview, 235–236
    preparing files for, 236–238,
        240–241
    printing, 236
Forms
    adding records via, 29–31,
        97–98
    creating, 93–97
    editing records via, 31–32
    layouts for, 94
    modifying, 98–100
    overview, 3
    predefined, 20 30
    saving, 103
    subforms. See Subforms
Form Wizard, 93–96
Functions, in queries
    inserting, 174
    modifying, 174–176
    overview, 172–174
    using, 176–177

Graphics, 27–29. See also Lines,
    in reports
Greater than (>)
    as comparison operator, 163
    in functions, 174
    in mail merge, 235, 240
Group Header band, in reports,
    198, 199

Header band, for reports, 198
Help. See also specific operation
        via Answer Wizard, 13–
        14
    button for, 14–15
    via Contents tab, 9–11
    overview, 9
    printing Help
        information, 13
    searching for Help
        information, 11–13
Hiding columns, 130–131
How Do I, 14

Index (Help), 11–12
Input masks, 79–81
Insert Row, 59–60

Keys, database, 46, 53–55
Label controls, 200, 205
Labels, mailing, 214–216
Less than (<)
    as comparison operator, 163
    in functions, 174
    in mail merge, 235, 240
Lines, in reports, 202–203, 211,
    212
Linking
    applications, for form letters,
        238–239
    tables, 46
List, of predefined databases, 21
Logical operators, 163
Lookup columns, 61–63

Mailing labels, 214–216
Mail merge. See Form letters
Make table queries, 228–229
Maximize, 30
Menus
    menu bar, 6, 7
    pull–down menus, 6, 7
    switchboards. See
        Switchboards
    Merging documents. See
        Form letters
    Microsoft
        Access. See Access
        Word, mail merge feature of.
            See Form letters
Minimize, 30
Moving
    columns, 116–117
    controls, 201, 203, 210

Naming
    databases, 21
    expressions, 166
    fields, 52
    tables, 53
New Database, 49
Normalization, 43
Numbers, formats for, 208–209
Number sign (#), as wildcard
    character, 115

One-to-many relationships, 73,
    85. See also Relationships
        between tables
Operators
    arithmetic, 163–167
    comparison (relational), 163
    logical, 163
    string, 163, 167–172
Or criteria
    in filters, 124
    overview, 120, 121
    in queries, 160

Page Header and Page Footer
    bands, in reports, 198
Parentheses
    in functions, 173
    in overriding order of
        precedence, 163
Preview box, 25
Previewing reports, 34, 35
Primary keys, 46
Printing
    form letters, 236
    Help information, 13
    reports, 26, 36, 34, 35

results of find, filter, and
    query operations, 134–
    136
Properties, field. See Field
    properties
Pull-down lists, 8, 9

Queries
    action queries, 224, 225
    append queries, 229–231
    calculated fields in. See
        Calculated fields
    converting, 227
    copying, 236–237
    creating, with Simple Query
        Wizard, 128–129
    crosstab queries. See Crosstab
        queries
    duplicating, 180
    functions in. See Functions,
        in queries
    Help for, 125–126
    make table queries, 228–229
    modifying, 237–238
    from multiple tables, 156–
        159
    overview, 113, 125–128
    predefined calculations in,
        177–181
    printing results of, 134–136
    reports from, 196–198
    saving, 159
    sorting in, 131–134, 157
    summary data from. See
        Crosstab queries
    switching views of, 127
    update queries, 225–227
Question mark (?), as wildcard
    character, 115
Quotation marks ("), designating
    default values, 83–84

Radio buttons, 8
Raised effect, 211
Records. See also Databases
    adding, 29–31, 91–92, 229–
        231
    archiving, 228–229
    deleting, 86, 88
    editing, 31–32, 225–227
    entering in forms, 97–98
    overview, 2–3
    selecting. See Selecting,
        records
Redundant data, 45
Referential integrity, in table
    relationships, 74, 86, 104
Relational database management
    systems, 2
Relational operators, 163
Relationships between tables
    deleting, 89
    overview, 73, 85–86
    selecting tables for, 87–88
    setting, 88–90
    status of, viewing, 132
Reports
    adding to switchboards, 246–
        247
    closing, 140
    copying, 199
    databases vs., 33–34
    deleting, 213

designing. See Designing
    reports
    Help for, 136–137, 192–194
    lists, 138–140
    from multiple tables, 141–
        147
    overview and components, 4,
        34, 113
    predefined, 20
    previewing, 34, 35
    printing, 26, 36
    from queries, 196–198
    saving, 213
    subgroups in, 144–147
    summaries of information,
        140–144
    tool for (Report Wizard),
        137, 194
    viewing, via switchboards,
        249–250
Required fields, 77–78
Rows, 2
Rulers, in report design, 198

Saving
    databases, 21, 22–23
    forms, 103
    queries, 159, 183
    reports, 213
Searching. See Finding
Selecting
    fields, via queries. See Queries
    records
        with filters. See Filters
        in forms, 32
Select queries. See Queries
Separator lines, in reports, 202–
    203
Shadowed effect, 211
Shortcut keys, 7, 8
Simple Query Wizard, 127–129
Sizing
    columns, 130–131
    controls, 201
    forms, 30
    text boxes, 99–100
Sorting
    on multiple fields, 133–134
    on one field, 132–133
    overview, 113, 131–132
    in reports, 138–139, 206–208
Source documents, 90
Special effects, in reports, 211,
    212–213
Starting Access, 7
String operators, 163, 167–172
Subforms
    creating, 232–233
    overview, 231–232
    using, 234–235
Subgroups, in reports, 144–147
Sunken effect, 211
Switchboards
    adding to, 245–247, 248
    attaching to menus, 249
    overview, 28, 224, 243–245
    titles for, 247–248
    tool for (Switchboard
        Manager), accessing, 245
    using, 34, 249–250
Syntax, in functions, 173

TAB , 90, 91–92

Tables
  comments, adding to, 47
  in database design, 44
  data types in, 46–47
  field size, 47
  keys in, 46
  links between, 46
  multiple, reports from, 141–147
  organizing data in, 45–46
  overview, 2
  referential integrity in, 74, 86, 104
  relationships between. *See* Relationships between tables

  predefined, using. *See* Table Wizard
Table Wizard
  creating tables, 49–51
  fields in
    adding, 59–61
    editing, 51–53
    selecting sample, 56
  keys, 53–55
  naming tables, 53
  overview, 48–49
Tabular form layout, 94
Tell Me About, 14

Text
  in databases. *See* Databases
  as data type, 46–47
  in reports. *See* Reports
Text boxes, 30–31, 99–100, 200
Titles
  database, 27–29
  switchboard, 247–248
Toolbars, 6, 7. *See also specific toolbar or operation*
Toolbox, for report design, 199–201

Unbound controls, 204, 205
Undo, limitations of, 130, 225

Unhide Columns, 131
Update queries, 225–227
Uppercase, in field names, 43

Validation settings, for fields, 84–85
Variable data, 235, 236

Wildcard characters, in searches, 115
Word, mail merge feature of. *See* Form letters

Zoom, 34